Childhood Cognitive Development

Essential Readings in Developmental Psychology

Series Editors: Darwin Muir and Alan Slater

Queen's University, Kingston, Ontario and the *University of Exeter*

In this brand new series of nine books, Darwin Muir and Alan Slater, together with a team of expert editors, bring together selections of readings illustrating important methodological, empirical and theoretical issues in the area of developmental psychology. Volumes in the series and their editors are listed below:

Infant Development	Darwin Muir and Alan Slater
Childhood Social Development	Wendy Craig
Childhood Cognitive Development	Kang Lee
Adolescent Development	Gerald Adams
The Psychology of Aging	William Gekoski
The Nature/Nurture Issue	Steven Ceci and Wendy Williams
Educational Attainment	Charles Desforges
Language Development	Elizabeth Bates and Michael Tomasello
Developmental Disorders	Darwin Muir, Alan Slater, Wendy Williams and Steven Ceci

Each of the books is introduced by the volume editor with a rationale behind the chosen papers. Each reading is then introduced and contextualized within the individual subject debate as well as within the wider context of developmental psychology. A selection of further reading is also assigned, making each volume an ideal teaching resource for both classroom and individual study settings.

Childhood Cognitive Development
The Essential Readings

Edited by Kang Lee

BLACKWELL
Publishers

Copyright © Blackwell Publishers Ltd 2000
Editorial matter and organization copyright © Kang Lee,
Darwin Muir and Alan Slater 2000

First published 2000

2 4 6 8 10 9 7 5 3 1

Blackwell Publishers Inc.
350 Main Street
Malden, Massachusetts 02148
USA

Blackwell Publishers Ltd
108 Cowley Road
Oxford OX4 1JF
UK

Library of Congress Cataloging-in-Publication Data has been applied for.

ISBN 0-631-21655-3 (hbk.)
ISBN 0-631-21656-1 (pbk.)

British Library Cataloguing-in-Publication Data

A CIP catalogue record for this book is available from the British Library.

Typeset in $10\frac{1}{2}$ on 13 pt Photina
by Best-set Typesetter Ltd., Hong Kong
Printed in Great Britain by MPG Books, Bodmin, Cornwall

This book is printed on acid-free paper

Contents

Preface   viii
Acknowledgments   x

Introduction: What Is Cognitive Development Research and
What Is It For?   1
Kang Lee

**1 The History and Future of Cognitive Development
   Research**   7
   Cognitive Development: Past, Present, and Future   8
   J. H. Flavell

2 Piaget's Theory of Cognitive Development   31
   Piaget's Theory   33
   J. Piaget

3 Developmental Research: Microgenetic Method   49
   Cognitive Variability: A Key to Understanding Cognitive
   Development   51
   R. S. Siegler

4 Information Processing and Connectionism   63
   Development in a Connectionist Framework: Rethinking
   the Nature–Nurture Debate   65
   K. Plunkett

5 Motor Learning and Development   91
Three-Month-Old Infants Can Learn Task-Specific Patterns
of Interlimb Coordination   93
E. Thelen

6 Attention   107
Facilitation of Saccades Toward a Covertly Attended
Location in Early Infancy   108
M. H. Johnson, M. I. Posner, and M. K. Rothbart

7 Perceptual Development   119
Young Infants' Perception of Object Unity: Implications for
Development of Attentional and Cognitive Skills   120
S. P. Johnson

8 Early Numerical Knowledge   135
Infants Possess a System of Numerical Knowledge   137
K. Wynn

9 Intentionality and Imitation   149
Understanding the Intentions of Others: Re-Enactment
of Intended Acts by 18-Month-Old Children   151
A. N. Meltzoff

10 Theory of Mind   175
Children's Understanding of Representational Change and
Its Relation to the Understanding of False Belief and
the Appearance–Reality Distinction   177
A. Gopnik and J. W. Astington

11 Memory and Suggestibility   201
The Suggestibility of Young Children   202
M. Bruck and S. J. Ceci

12 Language   213
Why Do Children Say "Breaked"?   215
G. F. Marcus

13 Symbolic Development   227
Rapid Change in the Symbolic Functioning of Very Young
Children   229
J. S. DeLoache

14 Spatial Knowledge and Gender Differences 237
The Water-Level Task: An Intriguing Puzzle 238
R. Vasta and L. S. Liben

15 Mathematical Knowledge 253
Preschool Origins of Cross-National Differences in
Mathematical Competence: The Role of Number-Naming
Systems 254
K. F. Miller, C. M. Smith, J. Zhu, and H. Zhang

16 Scientific Reasoning 265
Young Children's Psychological, Physical, and Biological
Explanations 267
H. M. Wellman, A. K. Hickling, and C. A. Schult

17 Physical Knowledge 289
The Development of Beliefs about Falling Objects 290
M. K. Kaiser, D. R. Proffitt, and M. McCloskey

18 Moral Understanding 307
Lying and Truthfulness: Children's Definitions, Standards,
and Evaluative Reactions 309
K. Bussey

19 Cognitive Developmental Pathology 323
Cognitive Explanations of Autism 324
U. Frith

Index 338

Preface

Cognitive development research as a field of developmental science has existed for almost a century. Over this period of time, particularly in the last 50 years, tremendous advancements have been made in our understanding of how the child's mind works. Numerous theoretical and empirical papers have been published to describe and explain how children's cognitive capacities develop and why cognitive development occurs. In the past, there were many erroneous commonsense views about the cognitive capacity of children in various domains of cognitive functioning (e.g., perception, memory, language, thinking). For example, one of those erroneous views was that children are essentially blind and deaf at birth; another one was that children had to learn language by rote memory. Empirical research in the past 50 years has dispelled these and other erroneous commonsense views, and helped developmental psychologists to rethink and reexamine earlier cognitive development theories and empirical work. As a result, new theories have been proposed, new methodologies have been invented, and new understandings of children's minds have been achieved. Like any other field of scientific inquiry, cognitive development research is dynamic and constantly undergoes exciting developments itself. *Childhood Cognitive Development* is an attempt to introduce students to this exciting and ever-evolving field of research.

This book is intended for readers who are newcomers to the field of cognitive development research and who are interested in reading current and original articles by developmental theorists and researchers on various aspects of cognitive development. It is also designed as a supplementary text to undergraduate and graduate courses in cognitive sciences (e.g., cognitive development, cognitive psychology). Several criteria have been used for the selection of articles. First, to offer readers a sense of the *current state* of cognitive development research, we selected articles that have been published recently (all but three articles were published in the 1990s). Second, we chose articles that are *representative* of current theoretical and methodological approaches to the study of cognitive development. We did not intend to compile an exhaustive anthology of papers that have made significant contributions to cognitive development research. Rather, we provide a selection of theoretical and research papers to showcase the current theoretical debates in the field and to illustrate how empirical research is done in several major areas of cognitive development. Third, we also considered the *accessibility* of articles. We are targeting an audience of newcomers to the field who may not be experienced with the highly specialized technical terminology in the field. For those readers who are interested in pursuing a topic further, additional references can be found in our introductions to the articles and the articles themselves. Given the increasingly large number of excellent papers advancing our understanding of cognitive development and space limitations, it was very difficult to select only a small sample of papers for this reader! Fourth, because this book is one in a series of readers, we have tried to avoid repeating the same article in different readers to maximize the coverage of articles by the series as a whole. Hence, some excellent articles that were very suitable for the present book were not selected because they are in the other readers.

I would like to thank Alan Slater and Darwin Muir for their excellent editorial work and their encouragement. I also thank four anonymous reviewers for their constructive comments and suggestions. Last but not least, I am grateful for the assistance of editors from Blackwell Publishers.

Kang Lee

Acknowledgments

Bruck, M., & Ceci, S. J. "The suggestibility of young children," *Current Directions in Psychological Science* 6, 1997 (Cambridge University Press, 1997).

Bussey, K. "Lying and truthfulness: Children's definitions, standards, and evaluative reactions," *Child Development* 63, 1992. © Society for Research in Child Development, Inc., University of Michigan.

DeLoache, J. S. "Rapid change in the symbolic functioning of very young children," *Science* 238, 1987. Reprinted with permission from *Science*, 238, 1987. Copyright 1987 American Association for the Advancement of Science.

Flavell, J. H. "Cognitive development: Past, present, and future," *Developmental Psychology* 28, 1992. Copyright © 1992 by the American Psychological Association. Reprinted with permission.

Frith, U. "Cognitive explanations of autism," *Acta Paediatrics Supplement* 416, 1996.

Gopnik, A., & Astington, J. W. "Children's understanding of representational change and its relation to the understanding of false belief and the appearance–reality distinction," *Child Development*

59, 1988. © Society for Research in Child Development Inc., University of Michigan.

Johnson, M. H., Posner, M. I., & Rothbart, M. K. "Facilitation of saccades toward a covertly attended location in early infancy," *Psychological Science* 5, 1994 (Cambridge University Press, 1994).

Johnson, S. P. "Young infants' perception of object unity: Implications for development of attentional and cognitive skills," *Current Directions in Psychological Science* 6(5) 1997 (Cambridge University Press, 1997).

Kaiser, M. K., Profitt, D. R., & McCloskey, M. "The development of beliefs about falling objects," *Perception and Psychophysics* 38, 1985.

Marcus, G. F. "Why do children say 'breaked'?," *Current Directions in Psychological Science* 5, 1996 (Cambridge University Press, 1996).

Meltzoff, A. N. "Understanding of the intentions of others: Re-enactment of intended acts by 18-month-old children," *Developmental Psychology* 31, 1995. Copyright © 1995 by the American Psychological Assocation. Reprinted with permission.

Miller, K. F., Smith, C. M., Zhu, J., & Zhang, H. "Preschool origins of cross-national differences in mathematical competence: The role of number-naming systems," *Psychological Science* 6, 1995 (Cambridge University Press, 1995).

Piaget, J. "Piaget's theory," from (ed. P. H. Mussen) *Carmichael's Manual of Child Psychology* (3rd edn) (Copyright © 1970 Reprinted by permission of John Wiley & Sons, Inc. New York).

Plunkett, K. "Development in a connectionist framework: Rethinking the nature–nurture debate," original article.

Siegler, R. S. "Cognitive variability: A key to understanding cognitive development," *New Directions in Psychological Science* 3, 1994.

Thelen, E. "Three-month-old infants can learn task-specific patterns of interlimb coordination," *Psychological Science* 5(5) 1994 (Cambridge University Press, 1994).

Vasta, R., & Liben, L. S. "The water-level task: An intriguing puzzle," *Current Directions in Psychological Science* 5, 1996 (Cambridge University Press, 1996).

Wellman, H. M., Hickling, A. K., & Schult, C. A. "Young children's psychological, physical, and biological explanations," *New Directions for Child Development* 75, 1997.

Wynn, K. "Infants possess a system of numerical knowledge," *New Directions in Psychological Science* 4, 1995.

Introduction
What Is Cognitive Development
Research and What Is It For?

Kang Lee

What Is Cognitive Development Research?

Cognitive development research is a major area of developmental psychology that investigates the acquisition of knowledge in children. It describes and explains systematic changes in children's knowledge about physical and social worlds. Three interrelated issues are the major foci of cognitive development research.

First, cognitive developmentalists are interested in the *structure* of children's knowledge, which concerns the question of how knowledge is represented by children and how the representation of knowledge changes systematically over time. There has been much debate about whether the way in which knowledge is represented changes systematically with age, as well as how changes in knowledge structure, if any, take place. For example, Piaget, one of the founding fathers of cognitive development research, not only believed that children's knowledge structure changes systematically over time but also theorized that such changes are stagelike and global (see chapter 2). That is, at each stage of cognitive development, children's entire knowledge structure differs qualitatively from the previous and future stages. Within a stage, knowledge structure remains the dominant format in which all knowledge is represented. Eventually this structure is reorganized due to the need to adapt to new experiences, and then a qualitatively new knowledge structure is formed.

Many theorists disagree with Piaget. Some (who are often referred to as symbolic-information-processing theorists) believe that cognitive development is more about systematic changes in children's *capacity* to represent knowledge than about the structure in which knowledge is represented (see Klahr, 1992). Others, such as the domain-specificity theorists (see Ceci, 1989), argue that while children's knowledge structure may undergo systematic changes, the changes may not be global. Some domains of knowledge (e.g., linguistic knowledge) may be more developmentally advanced than other domains (e.g., mathematical knowledge). Furthermore, knowledge structures may be altogether different for different domains (see Karmiloff-Smith, 1992). By contrast, those subscribing to a dynamic systems theory suggest that cognitive structural changes can be chaotic and nonlinear; knowledge structures may change unexpectedly rather than in a series of hierarchical stages prescribed by Piaget (see chapter 5). Currently, debate continues. Several articles in this reader touch upon this controversy. Students who intend to do more in-depth reading about cognitive development theories are referred to the *Handbook of child psychology*, Volume 1 (Lerner, 1998).

Second, cognitive developmentalists also study the *processes* by which knowledge is acquired. The questions addressed include how children obtain knowledge from environmental inputs, how they store, organize, and reorganize knowledge, and how they use existing knowledge to generate new knowledge and to regulate their actions. As knowledge acquisition is a multifaceted and complex process, cognitive developmentalists tend to focus their research on specific cognitive processes and their respective developmental courses. These processes include sensation, perception, attention, memory, concept formation, language, symbolic functioning, and thinking. The majority of research on cognitive development has been devoted to understanding how these cognitive processes change with age. For example, in the area of sensation and perception, researchers have been investigating how children's perceptual systems develop (e.g., see chapter 7); in the area of language development, researchers have studied how children acquire the grammatical rules (e.g., see chapter 12); in the area of thinking, investigators study how children solve mathematical problems (e.g., see chapter 8). In addition, much research has been conducted into the relationships between the development of these cognitive processes (e.g., relations between language and thought: chapter 15), between children's cognitive processes and actions (e.g., memory and motor behavior: chapter 5), and between cognitive development and brain maturation (e.g., attention and frontal lobe growth: chapter 6; neural plasticity and cognitive development: Nelson & Bloom, 1997).

Third, cognitive developmentalists research the acquisition of the *content* of a specific knowledge domain. While the second issue mentioned above deals with the developmental course of *knowing*, this present issue deals with what is *known* by children about the physical and social world around them. Of course, anything that children know is part of their world knowledge; it ranges from knowing something as simple as the colors of a rainbow to knowing something as complex as Newton's laws of physics. Developmentalists are selective in their choice of research topics when it comes to studying the question of what children know about the physical and social world. With regard to knowledge about the physical world, researchers, for example, have studied extensively how children come to grips with the notions of time and space (chapter 14), how they develop an understanding of number and mathematics (chapter 8), and how they learn about basic principles of physics (chapter 17). With regard to knowledge about the social world, much research has been devoted to children's understanding of self, gender role, and morality (chapter 18). In the last two decades, extensive research has also been devoted to investigating how children acquire theory-like knowledge about people's mental activities (e.g., intentions, desires, beliefs, emotions etc.: chapter 10), as well as their theory-like biological knowledge (e.g., life, death, reproduction: chapter 16).

What Is Cognitive Development Research For?

Developmentalists study cognitive development for both theoretical and practical reasons. There are several major theoretical reasons.

First, cognitive development research can be used to answer some of the fundamental philosophical questions about epistemology (i.e., the origin of knowledge). While philosophers tend to debate such questions with the use of logical reasoning and armchair thought experiments, cognitive developmentalists attempt to answer them with the use of scientific methods. For this reason, Piaget (1970) suggests that cognitive development research is in a sense experimental epistemology, and cognitive developmentalists are experimental philosophers.

Second, cognitive development research is also believed to hold one of the keys to reveal how human cognition evolves. Human cognitive evolution can be studied from a number of perspectives. Archeologists study cultural artifacts that may help reveal the state of mind of ancient people who produced these artifacts. Anthropologists speculate about how primitive cultures operate, which may reflect the workings of ancient minds. Cognitive development research, Piaget believed, may provide additional information about how the human mind evolved, because modern children's cognitive processes, though undoubtedly influenced by their current environments, may still have characteristics that are shared by their ancestors.

Third, cognitive development research may enrich our understanding of adult cognition. Cognitive processes of adults have been the main focus of research in cognitive psychology. Many theories about human cognition have been based on empirical evidence obtained from adults, but a theory about the human mind is incomplete without explaining the origins of adult cognition. This is not only because children's cognition is part and parcel of human cognition (children are humans after all!) but also because adult cognition does not suddenly appear from thin air; it is the outcome of several decades of development, beginning in the womb. In addition, the adult's cognitive capacity is not static; it undergoes development as well. Therefore, in the absence of a developmental account, any theory about adult cognition is incomplete.

Cognitive development research also has tremendous practical value for individuals working with children, such as parents, educators, medical practitioners, and legal professionals. For example, a universal concern shared by parents is whether their children will have a healthy development, and how they can facilitate their children's mental growth. Some cognitive development research addresses this concern by discovering parenting and home factors that may impede or enhance children's intellectual development (e.g., television watching or early exposure to reading materials on children's later reading-skill acquisition). Cognitive development research also provides empirical evidence to address issues important to the construction of educational curricula. For example, research findings may help teachers design instructional programs of mathematics and physics that optimally tap into children's existing mathematical and physical knowledge (chapter 17). Another example is the research on children's understanding of moral issues (e.g., lying: chapter 18), which may be useful for designing a moral education program.

Also, research on cognitive development has contributed to medical diagnosis and treatment of children with various disorders. One of the prime examples of this is our increased understanding of autism. In the last several decades, research on autistic children's cognitive abilities has revealed that autism is not the outcome of poor parenting as was suggested in the past. Rather, it is a cognitive disorder which is probably genetically caused (chapter 19), involving attentional deficits and lack of knowledge about other people's mental activities. Last, but not least, cognitive development research can play an important role in legal practices. In the last two decades, there has been an increase in the number of children who have testified in court. The youngest age at which children's testimony is deemed admissible has been lowered or abandoned outright. To meet legal needs, recent studies have addressed questions of whether children are reliable eyewitnesses for police lineups, whether they can remember events that are traumatic to them, and whether their memory can be compromised by misleading questions (chapter 11).

In summary, cognitive development research is a scientific study of knowledge acquisition in children with a focus on the development of knowledge structure, knowledge content, and the processes of knowing. This work is theoretically important because it helps us understand the human mind. It also has practical applications in parenting, education, medicine, and law. In the last century, much has been learned about how children acquire knowledge. Given the rapid advancement in knowledge from recent research, there is no doubt that this area will experience an even greater growth in the new millennium. New theory, methodology, and technology will allow us to answer the century-old question: How do children's minds work?

References

Ceci, S. J. (1989). On domain specificity ... more or less: General and specific constraints on cognitive development. *Merrill-Palmer Quarterly*, *35*, 131–42.

Karmiloff-Smith, A. (1992). *Beyond modularity: A developmental perspective on cognitive science*. Cambridge, MA: MIT Press.

Klahr, D. (1992). Information-processing approaches to cognitive development.
   In M. H. Bornstein & M. E. Lamb (eds), *Developmental psychology: An advanced
   textbook*, 3rd edn (pp. 273–335). Hillsdale, NJ: Lawrence Erlbaum.
Lerner, Richard M., ed. (1998). *Handbook of child psychology: Vol. 1. Theoretical
   models of human development*, 5th edn. New York: J. Wiley.
Nelson, C. A., & Bloom, F. E. (1997). Child development and neuroscience. *Child
   Development, 68*, 970–87.
Piaget, J. (1970). *Genetic epistemology.* New York: Columbia University Press.

ONE

The History and Future of Cognitive Development Research

Introduction

This article was written to celebrate the centennial of developmental psychology. The author, John Flavell, is one of the most prominent and influential cognitive researchers in the world and one of the first to translate Piaget's theory into English. His research on memory development, especially in the areas of memory strategy and metamemory (i.e., children's knowledge about and monitoring of memory processes), has made a lasting impact on the current thinking and research on children's memory development. He and his colleagues also have used ingenious methods to reveal children's understanding of perspective-taking (i.e., understanding that others may have a different view of the world) and appearance–reality distinction (i.e., the understanding that the appearance of an object or a person may differ from what they truly are). Flavell's studies on these issues set the stage for an upsurge of research on children's understanding of mental activities, or their "theory of mind" (see chapter 10), producing one of the most significant advancements in our understanding of cognitive development in the last two decades. Given Flavell's background, he is the ideal person to write an article reviewing the research in cognitive development and speculating about its future.

Further reading

Mandler, J. M. (1994). The death of developmental psychology. In R. L. Solso & D. W. Massaro (eds), *The science of the mind: 2001 and beyond*. Oxford: Oxford University Press.

Cognitive Development: Past, Present, and Future

John H. Flavell

This article has two objectives. The first and most important one is to summarize where we developmental psychologists currently are in our understanding and conceptualization of human cognitive development. That is, what do we know about it, and how do we think about it? What are and have been the field's different images of what cognitive development is like? The focus is thus on our past and, especially, our present ideas about it. The second objective is to speculate briefly about the future of the field – some possible directions in which it could or should go. Space limitations preclude consideration of two important topics one might expect to see included in an overview of cognitive development: namely, language acquisition and cognitive changes during adulthood.

The Past and Present

What have developmentalists come to believe about human cognitive development after over a century of study? First, some obvious things: Children do undergo extensive and varied cognitive growth between birth and adulthood. That is, there is most definitely a phenomenon called *cognitive development*, and it is an extremely rich, complex, and multifaceted process. Moreover, it has proved amenable to productive scientific inquiry. Cognitive development has become a large and thriving scientific field, a fact that would have surprised some of our forebears: "Titchener, like his mentor Wundt, thought an experimental psychology of children impossible" (Kessen, 1983, p. viii). Studies have yielded a large number and variety of interesting facts about cognitive development, many of them quite surprising. Some are surprising because they show that children of a certain age have not yet acquired something we would have expected them to have acquired by that age, if indeed it needed acquiring at all. The Piagetian conservations are everyone's favorite examples. Others surprise us for the opposite reason. The remarkable infant competencies revealed by recent research are cases in point, for example, the young infant's capacities for speech perception and intermodal matching. Actually most of what developmentalists have discovered about cognitive development is surprising at least in the sense of being unexpected, and perhaps virtually nonexpectable, without a scientific background in the field. For example, what newcomer to the field could anticipate the possible existence of such "developables" as Piagetian concrete-operational skills or a naive "desire psychology" (Wellman, 1990)?

The child as constructive thinker

Another thing developmentalists have come to believe about children is that they are very active, constructive thinkers and learners. Children are clearly not blank slates that passively and unselectively copy whatever the environment presents to them. Rather, the cognitive structures and processing strategies available to them at that point in their development lead them to select from the input what is meaningful to them and to represent and transform what is selected in accordance with their cognitive structures. As Piaget correctly taught us, children's cognitive structures dictate both what they accommodate to (notice) in the environment and how what is accommodated to is assimilated (interpreted). The active nature of their intellectual commerce with the environment makes them to a large degree the manufacturers of their own development:

> One major impetus to cognitive development is the child himself. Much of cognitive development is *self-motivated*. Children are knowledge seekers, they develop their own theories about the world around them, and continually subject their theories to tests, even in the absence of external

feedback. They perform thought and action experiments on their own, continually, and without external pressure. Children as well as adults "play" with their developing knowledge. . . . They engage in knowledge-extending and knowledge-refining activities spontaneously, arguing with themselves via an internal dialogue. They question the veracity or range of applicability of their theories, they perform *thought experiments*, question their own basic assumptions, provide counterexamples to their own rules, and reason on the basis of whatever knowledge they have, even though it may be incomplete, or their logic may be faulty. . . . This metaphor of the child as *little scientist* is compelling and central to many theories of development. *(Brown, 1983, pp. 31–32)*

New methods

Acquiring all these facts and beliefs about the cognition of infants, children, adolescents, and adults required the invention of new research methods. Historically, there seems to have been at least a rough and irregular trend from an almost exclusive reliance on observational methods and highly verbal, talky testing procedures to the addition of mixed verbal-nonverbal and wholly nonverbal experimental methods. To illustrate the early emphasis on verbal methods, in the 1880s G. Stanley Hall used the newly invented questionnaire in his pioneering study of the "contents of children's minds" (Cairns, 1983). Likewise, most of Piaget's early research made use of the interview method, in which both the questions and problems posed by the experimenter and the responses given by the child subject were entirely verbal (Flavell, 1963).

There is now a variety of different methods at the developmentalist's disposal, most of them not wholly verbal in nature. Recent innovations intended mainly for use with older, postinfancy subjects include procedures involving modeling and imitation (Watson & Fischer, 1980), double imitation (Smith, 1984), information integration (Anderson & Cuneo, 1978), rule assessment (Siegler, 1981), double assessment (Wilkinson, 1982), surprise (Gelman, 1972), and deception (Chandler, Fritz, & Hala, 1989). For example, what children can and cannot successfully imitate gives us some indication of what they do and do not understand.

However, it is in cognitive research with infants that the historical movement toward nonverbal measures is most clearly seen. The nonverbal methods devised for use with infants have been ingenious and their scientific payoff enormous. Before their invention, developmentalists knew very little about the young infant's cognitive capabilities, Piaget's astute observations notwithstanding – "infancy was like the dark side of the moon," as Bower put it (1977, p. 5). The key to studying infant cognition proved to be the exploitation by experimenters of nonverbal response patterns, patterns that provide information about the infant's perceptual–cognitive states and activities. The main patterns exploited in this way have been sucking, heart-rate changes, head turning, reaching, and – most useful of all – looking. It seems that infants will look longer at one object or event than another for much the same reasons that adults would: because they like it better, because it takes longer to process completely, and because it violates their expectations. If we find that infants seem surprised – as indexed by prolonged looking time – at a display that violates some physical law (e.g., a display suggesting that two solid objects are occupying the same space at the same time), it seems reasonable to credit them with some sort of tacit knowledge of that law. Recent studies of infants' knowledge about objects by Baillargeon (in press) and Spelke (1988) illustrate this research strategy. Technological advances have also played an important role in research with both infants and older subjects, for example, eye-movement cameras, videorecorders, and computers.

The diagnosis problem

Despite the impressive array of different methods now at their disposal, present day developmentalists are still often unable to characterize a given child's knowledge or abilities with precision and confidence. The diagnosis problem in cognitive development has proved to be a formidable one (e.g., Brown, 1983; Flavell, 1985; Greeno, Riley, & Gelman, 1984). It turns out that a child is likely to "have" a target competency in different degrees, ways, and forms at different ages, and precisely how best to characterize each child's "has," both in itself and in relation to its preceding and succeeding "haves," is a difficult problem. Some common ways that competencies change with age are the following:

A competency may be improved in the course of development by becoming more reliably invoked and used on any one task, more generalized and differentiated in its use across tasks, more dominant over competing, inappropriate approaches, more integrated with other competencies, more accessible to conscious reflection and verbal expression, and more consolidated and solidified. *(Flavell, 1985, pp. 116–117)*

A good example of a current developmental diagnosis problem is to be found in the area of theory-of-mind development: Despite a great deal of recent research using a variety of methods, researchers in this area are still not sure exactly what the average three-year-old does and does not understand about the mental state of belief (Perner, 1991; Wellman, 1990).

Revised estimates of competence

Recent research with these new methods has led to a somewhat different estimate of subjects' cognitive abilities than that suggested by Piagetian and other earlier work. Infants and young children now seem more competent, and adults less competent, than developmentalists used to think (Brown, 1983; Flavell, 1985; Gelman & Brown, 1986; Siegler, 1991). For example, recent research suggests that infants can perceptually discriminate most of the speech sounds used in human language, discriminate between small numerosities (e.g., sets of two vs. three objects), distinguish causal from noncausal event sequences, understand a number of basic properties of objects including object permanence, distinguish between animate agents and inanimate objects, detect intermodal correspondences, imitate facial gestures, form concepts and categories, and recall past events. As precocious infant abilities continue to be discovered, the difference between infant and postinfant competencies, although still substantial, seems less and less discontinuous and qualitative. Similarly, young children also turn out to be not as incompetent – not as "pre" this and "pre" that (precausal, preoperational, and so on) – as we once thought. To mention but two of many examples, their understanding of numbers and mental states, although still elementary, is more advanced than previously believed. For instance, even two-year-olds are nonegocentric in the sense that they realize that another person will not see an object they see if the person is blindfolded or is looking in a different direction (Lempers, Flavell, & Flavell, 1977). Finally, adult cognition is less developmentally advanced than we had assumed:

At the other end of the age spectrum, adults' reasoning has turned out to be not as rational as was once thought. Without training, event high school and college students rarely solve Piagetian formal operations tasks. . . . These difficulties are not limited to Piaget's tasks or scientific reasoning. Shaklee (1979) reviewed a host of irrational aspects of adult's thinking. *(Siegler, 1991, p. 350)*

In summary,

The recent trend in the field has been to highlight the cognitive competencies of young children. . . . the cognitive shortcomings of adults, and the cognitive inconsistencies of both, effectively pushing from both ends of childhood towards the middle and blurring the difference between the two groups. *(Flavell, 1985, p. 84)*

The question of general stages

A longstanding controversial issue in the field has been whether the mind develops in a more general, unified fashion or in a more specific, fractionated manner (e.g., Case, 1992; Demetriou & Efklides, in press; Fischer & Silvern, 1985; Flavell, 1982, 1985). Development would be very general and unified if it proceeded through a fixed sequence of broad, across-tasks-and-domains structures of the whole, such as the sensory-motor, concrete-operational, and formal-operational stages described by Piaget. If development were very general in this sense, the child's mind would be uniformly and homogeneously stage-x-like (e.g., concrete operational-like) in its approaches to all cognitive tasks while the child was in that stage. That is, the child would have a characteristic mental structure at that stage and would apply it to all content areas. In contrast, development would be very specific and fractionated if each developmental acquisition proceeded at its own rate and in its own manner, independent of all the others. If this were true there would be nothing homogeneous or unified about the child's mind at any age. Rather, it would be as if the child's mind were a collection of different and unrelated "mindlets," each developing independently of the others according to its own timetable.

Virtually all contemporary developmentalists agree that cognitive development is not as general stagelike or grand stagelike as Piaget and most of the rest of the field once thought. They disagree, however, as to just how general or specific it is. Neo-Piagetian theorists recognize that development is specific in many respects but also believe that it contains important general properties (Case, 1987, 1992; Demetriou & Efklides, in press; Fischer & Farrar, 1987; Halford, in press; Pascual-Leone, 1987; see also Sternberg, 1987). They assume that there is a regular, probably maturation-based increase with age in some aspect of the child's information-processing capacity, such as the child's processing speed or processing efficiency. As the child's information-processing capacity increases with increasing age, it makes possible new and more complex forms of cognition in all content domains, because the child can now hold in mind and think about more things at once. Conversely, capacity limitations at any given age constrain and limit the possible forms of cognition the child can enact. Thus, capacity limitations and their progressive reduction with age act as governors and enablers of cognitive growth, making for important across-domain similarities in the child's cognitive functioning at each point in development. In support of this view, neo-Piagetians have obtained empirical evidence suggesting that cognitive development does have some general stagelike as well as specific properties. Indeed, for it not to have any general-stage properties at all would seem counterintuitive: an extreme "unrelated mindlets" view does not seem to me any more likely to be right than Piaget's "grand stage" view.

Effects of expertise

Most contemporary developmentalists seem either to ignore or to doubt the existence of such general, transdomain developmental similarities and synchronisms, focusing instead on more specific developments within a single content area or knowledge domain. Some emphasize the surprisingly powerful effects of well-organized content knowledge or expertise on the child's cognitive level within that specific content area (e.g., Chi & Glaser, 1980). They argue that a child may function at a higher developmental level or stage in one content area than in another if he or she has acquired expertise in that area through extensive practice and experience. The result is that the child may operate less consistently and uniformly across domains at a single general stage of development than general-stage theorists would predict. One way that domain-specific knowledge and experience benefits children's thinking is that it permits them "to solve many problems more by memory processes than by complex reasoning processes – that is, by recognizing familiar problem patterns and responding to them with overlearned solution procedures" (Flavell, 1985, p. 115).

Natural domains and constraints

Other developmentalists stress the importance of cognitive acquisitions in special, biologically natural rather than arbitrary knowledge domains (Carey & Gelman, 1991; Wellman & Gelman, 1992; see also Gardner, 1983). Unlike Piagetians, neo-Piagetians, or advocates of the expertise approach, these developmentalists emphasize the fact that, as members of a biological species, humans have evolved to find some things much easier and more natural to acquire than others. Humans are born with, or develop early on through maturation, specific predispositions and potentials for achieving these "privileged acquisitions" (Gallistel, Brown, Carey, Gelman, & Keil, 1991, p. 5). We are equipped with specific, possibly modular or encapsulated processing biases or constraints that give us a crucial leg up in developing these biologically natural competencies (Leslie, 1991). The most obvious and long-recognized of these natural domains is language. Chomsky and his followers have convinced virtually everyone that human beings have evolved very powerful mechanisms dedicated to extracting grammatical knowledge about a language from fairly impoverished linguistic input (Cook, 1988). The young infant's innately given ability to discriminate subtle differences in speech sounds mentioned previously suggests that phonological learning is also a natural domain for humans. Children may also be endowed with additional constraints (e.g., mutual exclusivity) that facilitate lexical and perhaps other nonlinguistic acquisitions (Markman, 1992).

Cognitive development as theory development

For some domains, the knowledge that children acquire may be such as to warrant being called an informal, naive, nonscientific "theory" (e.g., Carey, 1985; Keil, 1989; Wellman, 1990). Wellman and Gelman (1992) argued that children can be said to possess a "framework" or "foundational" theory in a domain if: (*a*) they honor the core ontological distinctions made in that domain, (*b*) they use domain-specific causal principles in reasoning about phenomena in the domain, and (*c*) their causal beliefs cohere to form an interconnected theoretical framework.

Wellman and Gelman reviewed evidence suggesting that children acquire naive foundational theories in at least three areas: physics, psychology, and biology. Children's naive physics includes their understanding of the physical properties and behavior of inanimate objects and their physical–causal interactions. Children's naive psychology consists of their knowledge of mental states and how these states interact in a psychological–causal way with one another, with environmental input, and with behavioral output. Their naive biology comprises an ontology of biological kinds and beliefs about specifically biological–causal mechanisms that affect these kinds. This view of cognitive development as domain-specific theory development is new and exciting and poses numerous important questions for the field. One that Wellman and Gelman rightly cited as being particularly critical is that of how one would "test and therefore potentially disconfirm the hypothesis that early understandings develop within distinct domains of thought" (p. 365; see also Gallistel et al., 1991).

Synchronisms, sequences, and qualitative changes

A large number of cognitive–developmental entities (concepts, skills, etc.) enter a person's cognitive repertoire during childhood. Developmentalists have long been interested in determining whether or how these entities might be related to one another psychologically (Flavell, 1985). Research suggests that many of them are indeed interrelated. Some may enter the child's repertoire at the same time, be substantially positively intercorrelated within children of the same age, and appear to be psychologically related within some theory. This suggests that they are different manifestations of the same underlying ability or conceptual structure and thus comprise an emerging psychological unit. Whether there are some units of this sort that are very general and transdomain, such as Piaget's concrete-operational structures, is of course the general-stage issue that was previously noted as being controversial. However, developmentalists of both domain-general and domain-specific persuasion sometimes find more modest-sized units within individual domains as well. Here is an example from the domain of naive psychology: Children's understanding of so-called Level 2 visual-perspective differences (e.g., recognizing that something may look upside down from one person's side but right side up from another's), of the appearance-reality distinction, and of false beliefs all emerge at about the same time in early childhood, are substantially correlated within three-year-olds, and can be plausibly interpreted as being different expressions of an emerging representational theory of mind (Flavell, Green, & Flavell, 1990).

Other cognitive entities within a domain may develop in a fixed sequence rather than synchronously – another kind of orderliness and connectedness in development. The entities comprising such sequences may be linked by one or more of at least five major types of sequential relationships: addition, substitution, modification, inclusion, and mediation (Flavell, 1985). As an example of an addition sequence. Wellman (1990) cites evidence suggesting that earlier in their development of knowledge about the mind children acquire some understanding of people's desires (a *desire psychology*); later, they add to it some understanding of beliefs (a *belief–desire psychology*). As is well known, the Piagetians have also described a prodigious number of varied and interesting cognitive–development sequences over the years.

A perennial question about developmental sequences has been whether at least some of them represent big, qualitative-looking changes in the child's thinking about whatever the sequences concern. The answer is that many changes do look quite qualitative at face value, even though they are probably produced by a succession of underlying changes of a more quantitative and continuous nature. Again, Piagetian psychology has shown us many qualitative-looking changes. For a striking example, Carey (1991) proposed that the child's intuitive theory of physical objects is not just qualitatively different from the adult's intuitive theory of material entities but is actually incommensurable with it, that is, so different that the concepts contained in one theory cannot be defined or expressed by the concepts contained in the other.

Mechanisms of development

It is not easy to describe cognitive development, but it is even harder to explain it:

> Serious theorizing about basic mechanisms of cognitive growth has actually never been a popular pastime, now or in the past. It is rare indeed to encounter a substantive treatment of the problem in the annual flood of articles, chapters and books on cognitive development. The reason is not hard to find: good theorizing about mechanisms is very, very hard to do. *(Flavell, 1984, p. 189)*

Understanding mechanisms is important because they can help explain the various developments that are described. The question of mechanisms is similar to that of stages in that one can distinguish domain-specific and domain-general approaches. The main developmental mechanisms of any putatively natural, privileged acquisition such as language development would presumably be some specialized, perhaps modular neural system dedicated to engendering that development and controlling its timing and form (Gallistel et al., 1991). Psychologists who study development in specific, natural domains may also consider the possibility of general, domain-neutral mechanisms (true for many developmental psycholinguists, for example), but domain-specific ones will understandably be of particular interest to them (Gallistel et al., 1991, pp. 32–33).

Other developmentalists have been more concerned with describing general mechanisms, ones potentially capable of engendering cognitive growth in any domain. The best-known general mechanism is the process of equilibration that Piaget (1985) spent much of his professional life elaborating; the clearest and most readable exegesis of this abstractly described and difficult-to-understand change process is probably that of Chapman (1988). For a current and very interesting attempt to work with the concept experimentally, see Acredelo and O'Connor (1991).

Another undoubtedly important general mechanism already mentioned is the increase with age in some aspect of information-processing capacity that neo-Piagetians regard as the main engine of development. Recent work by Kail (1991) makes it seem increasingly likely that this capacity increase is the result of some hard-wired maturational change in the brain rather than just the result of age-associated accumulations of specific or nonspecific cognitive experience (although experience can also lead to capacitylike increases). Developmentalists have long searched for a maturational process that could serve as a kind of universal regulator and pacesetter for cognitive growth, thereby making for similarities among all of the cognitive–development courses. This might be one such process. Another might be maturational changes in the brain that make it possible for the child to delay or inhibit responding (e.g., Llamas & Diamond, 1991).

Finally, the quest for general mechanisms has been reinvigorated by some of Siegler's work (1989; Siegler & Crowley, 1991). Siegler defined a mechanism of cognitive development broadly as "any mental process that improves children's ability to process information" (1989, p. 354) and described recent research on five classes of such mechanisms: (*a*) *neural mechanisms*, including synaptogenesis, segregation of neuronal input, and experience-expectant and experience-dependent processes; (*b*) *associative competition*, especially connectionist models; (*c*) *encoding*, including his scale-balance research and others' work on transitive inference; (*d*) *analogy*, particularly the work of Brown and Gentner; and (*e*) *strategy choice*, featuring Siegler's own theory and research. He concluded by arguing that most mechanisms involve the creation and subsequent resolution of *competition* between neurological or psychological entities, a position that he notes to be similar to Piaget's. In a subsequent article Siegler and Crowley (1991) described a microgenetic method for obtaining information about mechanisms and presented two interesting conclusions about the typical course of cognitive growth that the use of such methods have suggested: (*a*) Even after children discover a new competency they may continue for some time to use previous, less adequate approaches; and (*b*) contrary to what might be predicted from Piaget's equilibration model, cognitive change often follows successes rather than failures in the use of current approaches (see also Karmiloff-Smith, 1984).

Sociocultural influences

Not all mechanisms of cognitive development are situated wholly within the child. Although not usually classified as "mechanisms of development," activities and environmental settings involving other people clearly play a critical role in children's cognitive development. The crucial importance of the sociocultural environment in this development has been particularly emphasized by Vygotsky (1978) and other theorists (e.g., Bronfenbrenner, 1979; Bruner, 1990; Cole, 1985; Laboratory of Comparative Human Cognition, 1983; Rogoff, 1990; Wertsch, 1985). Rogoff's (1990) ideas will serve to illustrate this sociocultural or contextualistic approach. She views cognitive development as an apprenticeship in which children acquire knowledge and skills by participating in societally structured activities together with their parents, other adults, and children. Children learn in specific contexts through a process of guided participation in which others provide various kinds of help tailored to the children's current level of knowledge and skill (within their "zone of proximal development," in

Vygotsky's words). Rogoff (1990) differs from many theorists of both domain-general and domain-specific orientation on at least two points. First, she expects to see multiple, highly specific, and variable developments as a function of individual children's specific and variable cultural experiences, rather than universal, specieswide developmental outcomes (1990, p. 30). Second, unlike most developmentalists, she does not view the child as a separate entity interacting with another separate entity, namely, an environment that can be differentiated from the child. Rather, "the child and the social world are mutually involved to an extent that precludes regarding them as independently definable" (Rogoff, 1990, p. 28). It is clear that her image of the developing child is most decidedly not that of the solitary little scientist constructing naive theories about the world through his or her own unaided effects.

Individual differences

One can distinguish between developmentalists who focus more on similarities among children and specieswide, universal developmental outcomes (either transdomain or domain-specific outcomes) and those who focus more on individual differences among children and their developmental outcomes. As Maccoby (1984) has pointed out, the former focus has been dominant in cognitive development since the ascendance of Piagetian psychology, whereas the latter has been dominant in social–emotional and personality development. Nevertheless, there have always been developmentalists with strong interests in individual variation in children's cognitive behavior and development (Wohlwill, 1973).

For example, since Binet, a number of developmentalists have been interested in individual differences in tested intelligence. Others have examined individual variation in cognitive traits such as cognitive style and creativity (Kogan, 1983). Some have studied genetic and environmental contributions to individual differences using the powerful tools of behavior genetics (e.g., Loehlin, Willerman, & Horn, 1988; Plomin & Rende, 1991) – another example of how new methods lead to new knowledge. Developmental behavior geneticists have not only documented the power of genetic differences to produce cognitive differences between children, but more surprisingly, they have also shown how the different nonshared environments that individual children experience even within the same family can increase these individual differences (Plomin & Rende, 1991). Other developmentalists have recently succeeded in doing something that the field had long given up on as being impossible: predict individual differences in cognition in later childhood from individual differences in cognition during infancy (Bornstein & Sigman, 1986; Thompson, Fagan, & Fulker, 1991). For example, it turns out that infants who show greater preference for visual novelty tend in later childhood to perform better on intelligence measures.

Practical applications

Finally, another very important thing developmentalists have learned about cognitive development is that what has been learned can be applied to the solution of real-world problems involving children. That is, scientific information about children's cognitive growth has been very useful to parents, educators, child-care givers, mental health professionals, jurists, and others concerned with promoting the welfare and optimal development of children. Palincsar and Brown's (1984) reciprocal teaching method for fostering comprehension-monitoring activity during reading is but one of many examples that could be cited here. Of this accomplishment the field can be justly proud.

The development of the child

A quick way to suggest what developmentalists think cognitive development is like is simply to list the main things that seem to develop. Here are two such lists (see also Sternberg & Powell, 1983). Siegler (1991) follows Brown and DeLoache (1978) in proposing that the main things that develop are (*a*) basic processes, (*b*) strategies, (*c*) metacognition, and (*d*) content knowledge. I (Flavell, 1985) have suggested that there are seven cognitive–developmental trends during middle childhood and adolescence: (*a*) increases in information-processing capacity, (*b*) increases in domain-specific knowledge, (*c*) concrete and formal operations, (*d*) the ability to engage in quantitative thinking, (*e*) the acquisition of "a sense of the game" of thinking, (*f*) the acquisition of metacognitive knowledge and experiences, and (*g*) improvement of the cognitive competencies the child already possesses.

The development of the field[1]

Another way to convey what developmentalists think cognitive development is like is to summarize the history of that thinking. Although the following is obviously a much oversimplified account of that history, it may provide a useful additional perspective. A century ago we knew virtually nothing about children's cognitive growth and were not even sure it could be studied scientifically. In subsequent years a large number of facts were accumulated about what children know and can do at different ages, but there was no general theory that could integrate them. Piaget provided such a theory and also added vastly to the store of facts. Since Piaget the field has made progress in at least three ways. First, the invention of new methods (e.g., infant looking measures) allowed developmentalists to challenge both Piagetian and common-sense assumptions about the competencies of infants and young children. New data were also gathered to support or refute key aspects of Piagetian theory (e.g., concerning general stages). Second, new "developables" (e.g., memory strategies) were identified, making it possible to learn about acquisitions not previously envisioned by Piaget or others. Finally, new ways of thinking about cognitive development (e.g., as theory change or as the growth of information-processing capacity) have emerged to supplement or compete with Piagetian approaches.

The Future

Attempts to predict the future of the field have been few in number (e.g., Siegler, 1983). One has only to try to make such predictions to understand why. On the one hand, the most accurate-seeming ones are also the most obvious-seeming and, therefore, less revealing to reader and forecaster alike. Thus, although likely to be right, these predictions are also likely to be unsurprising and uninteresting. On the other hand, lines of research that may seem novel and nonobvious to the forecaster may have already been tried and quietly abandoned as unpromising by others. After all, many child researchers have tried to study many things in many ways during the past century. Still, the temptation to do a little crystal ball gazing is hard to resist.

Probably the most obvious prediction one could make is that currently productive lines of work will continue to be active, at least for a while. A number of such lines were described in the previous section. Among these, the biological-constraints and cognitive-development-as-theory-development approaches strike me as being particularly promising. I am somewhat less optimistic about the future of general-stage theories and contextualistic approaches. Almost as obvious is the prediction that some newly emerging approaches in related fields will invigorate future research in this one. Possible candidates here are connectionism and neuropsychology (Llamas & Diamond, 1991; McClelland, 1991), dynamic systems theory (Thelen & Ulrich, 1991), comparative developmental psychology (Parker, 1990; Povinelli & deBlois, 1991; Whiten, 1991), evolutionary psychology (Cosmides, 1989), and perhaps "gains–losses" and other conceptualizations of adult cognitive changes (Baltes, 1987).

A less obvious prediction emerges from consideration of what developmentalists have and have not learned about children's mental lives. Quite a lot has been learned about their knowledge and abilities at different ages: the tasks they can and cannot solve, the concepts they have and have not acquired, and so forth. Developmentalists have even learned something about how what children have acquired cognitively affects their everyday social and nonsocial behavior, for example, the character of their play and peer relationships, as well as their response to curricula in school. These are the things developmentalists have been studying all these years. However, we have seldom examined the implications of the knowledge and skills children have and have not developed for the nature of their inner lives. That is, we have seldom tried to infer what it is like to be them and what the world seems like to them, given what they have and have not achieved cognitively. When knowledge and abilities are subtracted from the totality of what could legitimately be called "cognitive," an important remainder is surely the person's subjective experience: how self and world seem and feel to that person, given that knowledge and those abilities. This gap between what developmentalists have and have not learned is clearest in the case of infants. We have learned at least a fair amount about what infants know and can do. However, one rarely sees detailed accounts of what it might be *like* to be an infant of this or that age, based on what infants know and can do. The only good account of this kind that I have found is presented in a book by Stern (1990).

Some might object that such an effort could not be scientific, because there is no way to obtain objective, scientific data about the phenomenological experience of a nonverbal subject. Although this objection certainly has some force, it still seems possible that developmental psychologists, working together with highly skilled writers, film makers, and the like, could effectively convey a rich, evidence-based, and convincing picture of an infant's or child's inner world. This picture might be regarded more as an applied-science or engineering feat than a basic science one, but this would not make it any the less valuable a contribution to our understanding of children. To be convinced of this, just ask yourself if you would like to see an age-graded series of such portraits and if you would want students, teachers, and parents to see them. Moreover, well-done portraits of this kind, based on basic-scientific thinking and research, might in turn lead to new thinking and new research. For example, it is possible that cognitive development would appear more compellingly saltatory or stagelike (that is, showing large, qualitative-looking differences between children of different ages) if portraits rather than task performance were considered.

Whether cognitive developmentalists will actually pursue this line of inquiry in the future is of course hard to predict. They might not try it, or they might try it but find it unprofitable. The argument for at least trying it seems strong, however: If we are going to study the development of the mind, we should study the development of all of it.

Note

1   I am indebted to Robbie Case for most of the content of this paragraph.

References

Acredelo, C., & O'Connor, J. (1991). On the difficulty of detecting cognitive uncertainty. *Human Development, 34*, 204–223.

Anderson, N. H., & Cuneo, D. O. (1978). The height–width rule in children's judgments of quantity. *Journal of Experimental Psychology: General, 107*, 335–378.

Baillargeon, R. (in press). The object concept revisited: New directions. In C. E. Granrud (Ed.), *Visual perception and cognition in infancy. Carnegie-Mellon Symposia on Cognition, Vol. 23*. Hillsdale, NJ: Erlbaum.

Baltes, P. B. (1987). Theoretical propositions of life-span developmental psychology: On the dynamics between growth and decline. *Developmental Psychology, 23*, 611–626.

Bornstein, M. H., & Sigman, M. D. (1986). Continuity in mental development from infancy. *Child Development, 57*, 251–274.

Bower, T. G. R. (1977). *A primer of infant development.* New York: Freeman.

Bronfenbrenner, U. (1979). *The ecology of human development.* Cambridge, MA: Harvard University Press.

Brown, A. L. (1983). Cognitive development. Unpublished manuscript, National Institute of Child Health and Human Development, Bethesda, MD.

Brown, A. L., & DeLoache, J. S. (1978). Skills, plans, and self-regulation. In R. S. Siegler (Ed.), *Children's thinking: What develops?* (pp. 3–33). Hillsdale, NJ: Erlbaum.

Bruner, J. S. (1990). *Acts of meaning.* Cambridge, MA: Harvard University Press.

Cairns, R. B. (1983). The emergence of developmental psychology. In P. H. Mussen (Series Ed.) & W. Kessen (Vol. Ed.), *Handbook of child psychology: Vol. 1. History, theory, and methods* (4th ed., pp. 41–102). New York: Wiley.

Carey, S. (1985). *Conceptual change in childhood.* Cambridge, MA: MIT Press.

Carey, S. (1991). Knowledge acquisition: Enrichment or conceptual change? In S. Carey & R. Gelman (Eds.), *The epigenesis of mind: Essays on biology and cognition* (pp. 257–291). Hillsdale, NJ: Erlbaum.

Carey, S., & Gelman, R. (Eds.). (1991). *The epigenesis of mind: Essays on biology and cognition.* Hillsdale, NJ: Erlbaum.

Case, R. (1987). Neo-Piagetian theory: Retrospect and prospect. *International Journal of Psychology, 22*, 773–791.

Case, R. (Ed.) (1992). *The mind's staircase: Exploring the conceptual underpinnings of children's thought and knowledge.* Hillsdale, NJ: Erlbaum.

Chandler, M., Fritz, A. S., & Hala, S. (1989). Small scale deceit: Deception as a marker of 2-, 3-, and 4-year-olds' early theories of mind. *Child Development, 60*, 1263–1277.

Chapman, M. (1988). *Constructive evolution: Origins and development of Piaget's thought.* Cambridge, UK: Cambridge University Press.

Chi, M. T. H., & Glaser, R. (1980). The measurement of expertise: Analysis of the development of knowledge and skill as a basis for assessing achievement. In E. L. Baker & E. S. Quellmalz (Eds.), *Educational testing and evaluation: Design, analysis and policy* (pp. 37–47). Beverly Hills, CA: Sage.

Cole, M. (1985). The zone of proximal development: Where culture and cognition create each other. In J. V. Wertsch (Ed.), *Culture, Communication, and cognition: Vygotskian perspectives.* Cambridge, UK: Cambridge University Press.

Cook, V. J. (1988). *Chomsky's universal grammar: An introduction.* Oxford, UK: Basil Blackwell.

Cosmides, L. (1989). The logic of social exchange: Has natural selection shaped how humans reason? Studies with the Wason selection task. *Cognition, 31*, 187–276.

Demetriou, A., & Efklides, A. (in press). Experiential structuralism: A frame for unifying cognitive developmental theories. *Monographs of the Society for Research in Child Development.*

Fischer, K. W., & Farrar, M. J. (1987). Generalizations about generalization: How a theory of skill development explains both generality and specificity. *International Journal of Psychology, 22,* 643–677.

Fischer, K. W., & Silvern, L. (1985). Stages and individual differences in cognitive development. *Annual Review of Psychology, 36,* 613–648.

Flavell, J. H. (1963). *The developmental psychology of Jean Piaget.* Princeton, NJ: Van Nostrand.

Flavell, J. H. (1982). On cognitive development. *Child Development, 53,* 1–10.

Flavell, J. H. (1984). Discussion. In R. J. Sternberg (Ed.), *Mechanisms of cognitive development* (pp. 187–209). New York: Freeman.

Flavell, J. H. (1985). *Cognitive development* (2nd ed.). Englewood Cliffs, NJ: Prentice-Hall.

Flavell, J. H., Green, F. L., & Flavell, E. R. (1990). Developmental changes in young children's knowledge about the mind. *Cognitive Development, 5,* 1–27.

Gallistel, C. R., Brown, A. L., Carey, S., Gelman, R., & Keil, F. C. (1991). Lessons from animal learning for the study of cognitive development. In S. Carey & R. Gelman (Eds.), *The epigenesis of mind: Essays on biology and cognition* (pp. 3–36). Hillsdale, NJ: Erlbaum.

Gardner, H. (1983). *Frames of mind: The theory of multiple intelligences.* New York: Basic Books.

Gelman, R. (1972). Logical capacity of very young children: Number invariance rules. *Child Development, 43,* 75–90.

Gelman, R., & Brown, A. L. (1986). Changing views of cognitive competence in the young. In N. J. Smelser & D. R. Gerstein (Eds.), *Behavioral and social sciences: Fifty years of discovery* (pp. 175–207). Washington, DC: National Academy Press.

Greeno, J. G., Riley, M. S., & Gelman, R. (1984). Conceptual competence and children's counting. *Cognitive Psychology, 16,* 94–143.

Halford, G. S. (in press). *Children's understanding: The development of mental models.* Hillsdale, NJ: Erlbaum.

Kail, R. (1991). Development of processing speed in childhood and adolescence. *Advances in Child Development and Behavior, 23,* 151–185.

Karmiloff-Smith, A. (1984). Children's problem solving. In M. Lamb, A. L. Brown, & B. Rogoff (Eds.), *Advances in developmental psychology* (Vol. 3, pp. 39–90). Hillsdale, NJ: Erlbaum.

Keil, F. C. (1989). *Concepts, kinds, and cognitive development.* Cambridge, MA: Bradford Books/MIT Press.

Kessen, W. (Ed.). (1983). *Handbook of child psychology: Vol. 1. History, theory and methods* (4th ed., P. H. Mussen, Series Ed.). New York: Wiley.

Kogan, N. (1983). Stylistic variation in childhood and adolescence: Creativity, metaphor, and cognitive styles. In P. H. Mussen (Series Ed.), & J. H. Flavell & E. M. Markman (Vol. Eds.), *Handbook of child psychology: Vol. 3. Cognitive development* (4th ed., pp. 630–706). New York: Wiley.

Laboratory of Comparative Human Cognition. (1983). Culture and cognitive development. In P. H. Mussen (Series Ed.) & W. Kessen (Vol. Ed.). *Handbook of child psychology: Vol. 1. History, theory, and methods* (4th ed., pp. 295–356). New York: Wiley.

Lempers, J. D., Flavell, E. R., & Flavell, J. H. (1977). The development in very young children of tacit knowledge concerning visual perception. *Genetic Psychology Monographs, 95,* 3–53.

Leslie, A. (1991, April). *Information processing and conceptual development: The theory of ToMM.* Paper presented at the Biennial Meeting of the Society for Research in Child Development, Seattle, WA.

Llamas, C., & Diamond, A. (1991, April). *Development of frontal cortex abilities in children between 3–8 years of age.* Paper presented at the Biennial Meeting of the Society for Research in Child Development, Seattle, WA.

Loehlin, J. C., Willerman, L., & Horn, J. M. (1988). Human behavioral genetics. *Annual Review of Psychology, 39,* 101–133.

Maccoby, E. E. (1984). Socialization and developmental change. *Child Development, 55,* 317–328.

Markman, E. M. (1992). Constraints on word learning: Speculations about their nature, origins, and domain specificity. In M. R. Gunnar & M. P. Maratsos (Eds.), *Minnesota Symposia on Child Psychology* (*Vol. 25*). Hillsdale, NJ: Erlbaum.

McClelland, J. L. (1991, April). *Connectionist models of developmental change.* Paper presented at the Biennial Meeting of the Society for Research in Child Development, Seattle, WA.

Palincsar, A. S., & Brown, A. L. (1984). Reciprocal teaching of comprehension-monitoring activities. *Cognition and Instruction, 1,* 117–175.

Parker, S. T. (1990). The origins of comparative developmental evolutionary studies of primate mental abilities. In S. T. Parker & K. R. Gibson (Eds.), *"Language" and intelligence in monkeys and apes* (pp. 3–63). New York: Cambridge University Press.

Pascual-Leone, J. (1987). Organismic processes for neo-Piagetian theories: A dialectical causal account of cognitive development. *International Journal of Psychology, 22,* 531–570.

Perner, J. (1991). *Understanding the representational mind.* Cambridge, MA: Bradford Books/MIT Press.

Piaget, J. (1985). *The equilibration of cognitive structures: The central problem of intellectual development.* Chicago: University of Chicago Press.

Plomin, R., & Rende, R. (1991). Human behavioral genetics. *Annual Review of Psychology, 42,* 161–190.

Povinelli, D. J., & deBlois, S. (1991). Young children's (Homo sapiens) understanding of knowledge formation in themselves and others. Unpublished manuscript, Yale University.

Rogoff, B. (1990). *Apprenticeship in thinking: Cognitive development in social context*. New York: Oxford University Press.

Shaklee, H. (1979). Bounded rationality and cognitive development: Upper limits on growth? *Cognitive Psychology, 11*, 327–345.

Siegler, R. S. (1981). Developmental sequences within and between concepts. *Monographs of the Society for Research in Child Development, 46*(2, Serial No. 189).

Siegler, R. S. (1983). Information processing approaches to development. In P. H. Mussen (Series Ed.) & W. Kessen (Vol. Ed.), *Handbook of child psychology: Vol. 1. History, theory, and methods* (4th ed., pp. 129–211). New York: Wiley.

Siegler, R. S. (1989). Mechanisms of cognitive development. *Annual Review of Psychology, 40*, 353–379.

Siegler, R. S. (1991). *Children's thinking* (2nd ed.). Englewood Cliffs, NJ: Prentice-Hall.

Siegler, R. S., & Crowley, K. (1991). The microgenetic method: A direct means for studying cognitive development. *American Psychologist, 46*, 606–620.

Smith, L. B. (1984). Young children's understanding of attributes and dimensions: A comparison of conceptual and linguistic measures. *Child Development, 55*, 363–380.

Spelke, E. S. (1988). Where perceiving ends and thinking begins: The apprehension of objects in infancy. In A. Yonas (Ed.), *Perceptual development in infancy. Minnesota Symposia on Child Psychology* (Vol. 20, pp. 197–234). Hillsdale, NJ: Erlbaum.

Stern, D. N. (1990). *Diary of a baby*. New York: Basic Books.

Sternberg, R. J. (1987). A day at Developmental Downs: Sportscast for race #2 – neo-Piagetian theories of cognitive development. *International Journal of Psychology, 22*, 507–529.

Sternberg, R. J., & Powell, J. S. (1983). The development of intelligence. In P. H. Mussen (Series Ed.), & J. H. Flavell & E. M. Markman (Vol. Eds.), *Handbook of child psychology: Vol. 3. Cognitive development* (4th ed., pp. 341–419). New York: Wiley.

Thelen, E., & Ulrich, B. D. (1991). Hidden skills. *Monographs of the Society for Research in Child Development, 56*(1, Serial No. 223).

Thompson, L. A., Fagan, J. F., & Fulker, D. W. (1991). Longitudinal prediction of specific cognitive abilities from infant novelty preferences. *Child Development, 62*, 530–538.

Vygotsky, L. S. (1978). *Mind in society: The development of higher psychological processes*. Cambridge, MA: Harvard University Press.

Watson, M. W., & Fischer, K. W. (1980). Development of social roles in elicited and spontaneous behavior during the preschool years. *Developmental Psychology, 16*, 483–494.

Wellman, H. M. (1990). *The child's theory of mind.* Cambridge, MA: Bradford Books/MIT Press.

Wellman, H. M., & Gelman, S. A. (1992). Cognitive development: Foundational theories of core domains. *Annual Review of Psychology, 43*, 337–375.

Wertsch, J. V. (1985). *Vygotsky and the social formation of mind.* Cambridge, MA: Harvard University Press.

Whiten, A. (Ed.). (1991). *Natural theories of mind: Evolution, development and simulation.* Oxford, UK: Basil Blackwell.

Wilkinson, A. C. (1982). Partial knowledge and self-correction: Developmental studies of a quantitative concept. *Developmental Psychology, 18*, 876–893.

Wohlwill, J. F. (1973). *The study of behavioral development.* San Diego, CA: Academic Press.

TWO

Piaget's Theory of Cognitive Development

Introduction

A good theory of cognitive development must answer the following questions: (1) What develops? (2) How does development occur? and (3) Why does development occur? To answer the first question, the theory must identify milestones of cognitive functioning that children achieve at different points in the course of development. To address the second question, the theory must prescribe the trajectory of systematic changes of cognitive functioning along a developmental timeline (e.g.: Is cognitive development continuous or discontinuous? Is it stagelike or U-shaped?). For the third question, the theory must explain what drives children's cognitive system to change systematically.

A good, scientific theory of cognitive development not only must answer these three questions but also must be empirically verifiable. That is, the theory must be able to generate specific hypotheses about cognitive development that are logical outcomes of the theory. These hypotheses also must be empirically testable. Empirical tests of these hypotheses must lead to confirmation, modification, or rejection of the theory.

Piaget's theory of cognitive development is an ideal example of a good scientific theory. It not only addresses the three questions posed above but also generates testable hypotheses. Granted that many of Piaget's predictions have been proven wrong, his theory has spurred much of the empirical research on cognitive development since its inception and continues to have a significant impact on current research.

The lasting legacy of Piaget's work, I believe, lies in three testable tenets of his theory. First, Piaget posited that the schemas (i.e., knowledge structures) in which children represent knowledge are what develops. Children use sensorimotor schemas in infancy; in preschool years, symbolic schemas become part of their knowledge representation. Around seven years of age, children also use logical, operational schemas to represent knowledge. Second, Piaget proposed that cognitive development undergoes a stagelike change that affects all aspects of children's cognitive functioning. He also predicts that children all over the world go through the same four stages in an irreversible order: the *sensorimotor* stage (up to two years), the *preoperational* stage (two to seven years), the *concrete operational* stage (seven to eleven years), and the *formal operational* stage (11 years and up). Piaget proposed that important concepts such as object permanence and conservation are milestones that herald the onset of new stages of cognitive functioning. Third, he also theorized that adaptation mechanisms, namely accommodation, assimilation, and equilibrium, are the driving forces underlying children's cognitive growth. This last tenet of Piaget's theory is the focus of his article.

Further reading

Flavell, J. H. (1963). *The developmental psychology of Jean Piaget*. New York: Van Nostrand.

Halford, G. S. (1989). Reflections on 25 years of Piagetian cognitive developmental psychology: 1963–1988. *Human Development*, *32*, 325–57.

Siegler, R. S., & Ellis, R. (1996). Piaget on childhood. *Psychological Science*, *7*, 211–15.

Piaget's Theory

Jean Piaget

The following theory of development, which is particularly concerned with the development of cognitive functions, is impossible to understand if one does not begin by analyzing in detail the biologic presuppositions from which it stems and the espistemological consequences in which it ends. Indeed, the fundamental postulate that is the basis of the ideas summarized here is that the same problems and the same types of explanations can be found in the three following processes:

a The adaptation of an organism to its environment during its growth, together with the interactions and autoregulations which characterize the development of the "epigenetic system." (Epigenesis in its embryologic sense is always determined both internally and externally.)

b The adaptation of intelligence in the course of the construction of its own structures, which depends as much on progressive internal coordinations as on information acquired through experience.

c The establishment of cognitive or, more generally, epistemological relations, which consist neither of a simple copy of external objects nor of a mere unfolding of structures performed inside the subject, but rather involve a set of structures progressively constructed by continuous interaction between the subject and the external world.

We begin with the last point, on which our theory is furthest re-moved both from the ideas of the majority of psychologists and from "common sense."

The Relation Between Subject and Object

1   In the common view, the external world is entirely separate from the subject, although it encloses the subject's own body. Any objective knowledge, then, appears to be simply the result of a set of perceptive recordings, motor associations, verbal descriptions, and the like, which all participate in producing a sort of figurative copy or "functional copy" (in Hull's terminology) of objects and the connections between them. The only function of intelligence is systematically to file, correct, etc., these various sets of information; in this process, the more faithful the critical copies, the more consistent the final system will be. In such an empiricist prospect, the content of intelligence comes from outside, and the coordinations that organize it are only the consequences of language and symbolic instruments.

But this passive interpretation of the act of knowledge is in fact con-tradicted at all levels of development and, particularly, at the sensori-motor and prelinguistic levels of cognitive adaptation and intelligence. Actually, in order to know objects, the subject must act upon them, and therefore transform them: he must displace, connect, combine, take apart, and reassemble them.

From the most elementary sensorimotor actions (such as pushing and pulling) to the most sophisticated intellectual operations, which are interiorized actions carried out mentally (e.g., joining together, putting in order, putting into one-to-one correspondence), knowledge is constantly linked with actions or operations, that is, with *transformations.*

Hence the limit between subject and objects is in no way determined beforehand, and, what is more important, it is not stable. Indeed, in every action the subject and the objects are fused. The subject needs objective information to become aware of his own actions, of course, but he also needs many subjective components. Without long practice or the construction of refined instruments of analysis and coordination, it will be impossible for him to know what belongs to the object, what belongs to himself as an active subject, and what belongs to the action itself taken as the transformation of an initial state into a final one. Knowledge, then, at its origin, neither arises from objects nor from the subject, but from interactions – at first inextricable – between the subject and those objects.

Even these primitive interactions are so close-knit and inextricable that, as J. M. Baldwin noted, the mental attitudes of the infant are probably "adualistical." This means they lack any differentiation between an external world, which would be composed of objects independent of the subject, and an internal or subjective world.

Therefore the problem of knowledge, the so-called epistemological problem, cannot be considered separately from the problem of the development of intelligence. It reduces to analyzing how the subject becomes progressively able to know objects adequately, that is, how he becomes capable of objectivity. Indeed, objectivity is in no way an initial property, as the empiricists would have it, and its conquest involves a series of successive constructs which approximates it more and more closely.

2   This leads us to a second idea central to the theory, that of *construction*, which is the natural consequence of the interactions we have just mentioned. Since objective knowledge is not acquired by a mere recording of external information but has its origin in interactions between the subject and objects, it necessarily implies two types of activity – on the one hand, the coordination of actions themselves, and on the other, the introduction of interrelations between the objects. These two activities are interdependent because it is only through action that these relations originate. It follows that objective knowledge is always subordinate to certain structures of action. But those structures are the result of a *construction* and are not given in the objects, since they are dependent on action, nor in the subject, since the subject must learn how to coordinate his actions (which are not generally hereditarily programmed except in the case of reflexes or instincts).

An early example of these constructions (which begin as early as the first year) is the one that enables the nine- to twelve-month-old child to discover the permanence of objects, initially relying on their position in his perceptual field, and later independent of any actual perception. During the first months of existence, there are no permanent objects, but only perceptual pictures which appear, dissolve, and sometimes reappear. The "permanence" of an object begins with the action of looking for it when it has disappeared at a certain point A of the visual field (for instance, if a part of the object remains visible, or if its makes a bump under a cloth). But, when the object later disappears at *B*, it often happens that the child will look for it again at *A*. This very instructive behavior supplies evidence for the existence of the primitive interactions between the subject and the object which we mentioned (¶ 1). At this stage, the child still believes that objects depend on this action and that, where an action has succeeded a first time, it must succeed again. One real example is an 11-month-old child who was playing with a ball. He had previously retrieved it from under an armchair when it had rolled there before. A moment later, the ball went under a low sofa. He could not find it under this sofa, so he came back to the other part of the room and looked for it under the armchair, where this course of action had already been successful.

For the scheme[1] of a permanent object that does not depend on the subject's own actions to become established, a new structure has to be constructed. This is the structure of the "group of translations" in the geometric sense: (*a*) $AB + BC = AC$; (*b*) $AB + BA = O$; (*c*) $AB + O = AB$; (*d*) $AC + CD = AB + BD$. The psychologic equivalent of this group is the possibility of behaviors that involve returning to an initial position, or detouring around an obstacle (*a* and *d*). As soon as this organization is achieved – and it is not at all given at the beginning of development, but must be constructed by a succession of new coordinations – an objective structuration of the movements of the object and of those of the subject's own body becomes possible. The object becomes an independent entity, whose position can be traced as a function of its translations and successive positions. At this juncture the subject's body, instead of being considered the center of the world, becomes an object like any other, the translations and positions of which are correlative to those of the objects themselves.

The group of translations is an instance of the construction of a structure, attributable simultaneously to progressive coordination of the subject's actions and to information provided by physical experience, which finally constitutes a fundamental instrument for the organization of the external world. It is also a cognitive instrument so important that it contributes to the veritable "Copernican revolution" babies accomplish in 12 to 18 months. Whereas before he had evolved this new structure the child would consider himself (unconsciously) the motionless center of the universe, he becomes, because of this organization of permanent objects and space. (which entails moreover a parallel organization of temporal sequences and causality), only one particular member of the set of the other mobile objects which compose his universe.

3   We can now see that even in the study of the infant at sensorimotor levels it is not possible to follow a psychogenetic line of research without evolving an implicit epistemology, which is also genetic, but which raises all the main issues in the theory of knowledge. Thus the construction of the group of translations obviously involves physical experience and empirical information. But it also involves more, since it also depends on the coordinations of the subject's action. These coordinations are not a product of experience only, but are also controlled by factors such as maturation and voluntary exercise, and, what is more important, by continuous and active autoregulation. The main point in a theory of development is not to neglect the activities of the subject, in the epistemological sense of the term. This is even more essential in this latter sense because the epistemological sense has a deep biologic significance. The living organism itself is not a mere mirror image of the properties of its environment. It evolves a *structure* which is constructed step by step in the course of epigenesis, and which is not entirely preformed.

What is already true for the sensorimotor stage appears again in all stages of development and in scientific thought itself but at levels in which the primitive actions have been transformed into *operations*. These operations are interiorized actions (e.g., addition, which can be performed either physically or mentally) that are reversible (addition acquires an inverse in subtraction) and constitute set-theoretical structures (such as the logical additive "grouping" or algebraic groups).

A striking instance of these operational structurations dependent on the subject's activity, which often occurs even before an experimental method has been evolved, is *atomism* invented by the Greeks long before it could be justified experimentally. The same process can be observed in the child from four to five and 11 to 12 years of age in a situation where it is obvious that experience is not sufficient to explain the emergence of the structure and that its construction implies an additive composition dependent on the activities of the subject. The experiment involves the dissolution of lumps of sugar in a glass of water. The child can be questioned about the conservation of the matter dissolved and about the conservation of its weight and volume. Before age seven to eight the dissolved sugar is presumed destroyed and its taste vanished. Around this age sugar is considered as preserving its substance in the form of very small and invisible grains, but it has neither weight nor volume. At age nine to ten each grain keeps its weight and the sum of all these elementary weights is equivalent to the weight of the sugar itself before dissolution. At age 11 to 12 this applies to volume (the child predicts that after the sugar has melted, the level of the water in the container will remain at its same initial height).

We can now see that this spontaneous atomism, although it is suggested by the visible grains becoming gradually smaller during their dissolution, goes far beyond what can be seen by the subject and involves a step-by-step construction correlative to that of additive operations. We thus have a new instance of the origin of knowledge lying neither in the object alone nor in the subject, but rather in an inextricable interaction between both of them, such that what is given physically is integrated in a logicomathematical structure involving the coordination of the subject's actions. The decomposition of a whole into its parts (invisible here) and the recomposition of these parts into a whole are in fact the result of logical or logicomathematical constructions and not only of physical experiments. The whole considered here is not a perceptual "Gestalt" (whose character is precisely that of *non*additive composition, as Kohler rightly insisted) but a sum (additive), and as such it is produced by operations and not by observations.

4   There can be no theoretical discontinuity between thought as it appears in children and adult scientific thinking; this is the reason for our extension of developmental psychology to genetic epistemology. This is particularly clear in the field of logicomathematical structures considered in themselves and not (as in ¶ 2 and ¶ 3) as instruments for the structuration of physical data. These structures essentially involve relations of inclusion, order, and correspondence. Such relations are certainly of biologic origin, for they already exist in the genetic (DNA) programming of embryologic development as well as in the physiologic organization of the mature organism before they appear and are reconstructed at the different levels of behavior itself. They then become fundamental structures of behavior and of intelligence in its very early development before they appear in the field of spontaneous thought and later of reflection. They provide the foundations of these progressively more abstract axiomatizations we call logic and mathematics. Indeed, if logic and mathematics are so-called "abstract" sciences, the psychologist must ask: Abstracted from what? We have seen their origin is not in objects alone. It lies, in small part only, in language, but language itself is a construct of intelligence. Chomsky even ascribes it to innate intel-

lectual structures. Therefore the origin of these logicomathematical structures should be sought in the activities of the subject, that is, in the most general forms of coordinations of his actions, and, finally, in his organic structures themselves. This is the reason why there are fundamental relations among the biologic theory of adaptation by self-regulation, developmental psychology, and genetic epistemology. This relation is so fundamental that if it is overlooked, no general theory of the development of intelligence can be established.

Assimilation and Accommodation

5   The psychologic meaning of our previous points (¶ 1 to ¶ 4) is that the fundamental psychogenetic connections generated in the course of development cannot be considered as reducible to empirical "associations"; rather, they consist of *assimilations*, both in the biologic and intellectual sense.

From a biologic point of view, assimilation is the integration of external elements into evolving or completed structures of an organism. In its usual connotation, the assimilation of food consists of a chemical transformation that incorporates it into the substance of the organism. Chlorophyllian assimilation consists of the integration of radiation energy in the metabolic cycle of a plant. Waddington's "genetic assimilation" consists of a hereditary fixation by selection on phenotypes (phenotypic variations being regarded, in this case, as the genetic system's "answer" to stresses produced by the environment). Thus all the organism's reactions involve an assimilation process which can be represented in symbolic form as follows:

$$(T + I) \rightarrow AT + E \tag{1}$$

where T is a structure, I the integrated substances or energies, E the eliminated substances or energies, and A a coefficient >1 expressing the strengthening of this structure in the form of an increase of material or of efficiency in operation.[2] Put in this form it becomes obvious that the general concept of assimilation also applies to behavior and not only to organic life. Indeed, no behavior, even if it is new to the individual, constitutes an absolute beginning. It is always grafted onto previous schemes and therefore amounts to assimilating new elements to already constructed structures (innate, as reflexes are, or previously acquired).

Even Harlow's "stimulus hunger" cannot be reduced simply to subordination to the environment but must rather be interpreted as a search for "functional input" ("éléments fonctionnels") that can be assimilated to the schemes or structures actually providing the responses.

At this point it is appropriate to note how inadequate the well known "stimulus–response" theory appears in this context, as a general formulation of behavior. It is obvious that a stimulus can elicit a response only if the organism is first sensitized to this stimulus (or possesses the necessary reactive "competence" as Waddington characterizes genetic sensitization to specific inducers).

When we say an organism or a subject is sensitized to a stimulus and able to make a response to it, we imply it already possesses a scheme or a structure to which this stimulus is assimilated (in the sense of incorporated or integrated, as defined previously). This scheme consists precisely of a capacity to respond. Hence the original stimulus–response scheme should not have been written in the unilateral $S \rightarrow R$ form, but in the form:

$$S \rightleftharpoons R \quad \text{or} \quad S \rightarrow (AT) \rightarrow R \tag{2}$$

where AT is the assimilation of the stimulus S to the structure T.

We thus return to the equation $T + I \rightarrow AT + E$ where, in this case, T is the structure, I the stimulus, AT the result of the assimilation of I to T, that is, the response to the stimulus, and E is whatever in the stimulus situation is excluded in the structure.

6   If assimilation alone were involved in development, there would be no variations in the child's structures. Therefore he would not acquire new content and would not develop further. Assimilation is necessary in that it assures the continuity of structures and the integration of new elements to these structures. Without it an organism would be in a similar situation to that of chemical compounds, A, B, which, in interaction, give rise to new compounds C and D. (The equation would then be $A + B \rightarrow C + D$ and not $T \rightarrow AT$).

Biologic assimilation itself, however, is never present without its counterpart, accommodation. During its embryologic development, for instance, a phenotype assimilates the substances necessary to the conservation of its structures as specified by its genotype. But, depending on whether these substances are plentiful or rare or whether the usual substances are replaced by other slightly different ones, nonhereditary variations (often called "accommodates") such as changes in shape or height may occur. These variations are specific to some external conditions. Similarly, in the field of behavior we shall call accommodation any modification of an assimilatory scheme or structure by the elements it assimilates. For example, the infant who assimilates his thumb to the sucking schema will, when sucking his thumb, make different movements from those he uses in suckling his mother's breast. Similarly, an eight-year-old who is assimilating the dissolution of sugar in water to the notion that substance is conserved must make accommodations to invisible particles different from those he would make if they were still visible.

Hence cognitive adaptation, like its biologic counterpart, consists of an equilibrium between assimilation and accommodation. As has just been shown, there is no assimilation without accommodation. But we must strongly emphasize the fact that accommodation does not exist without simultaneous assimilation either. From a biologic point of view, this fact is verified by the existence of what modern geneticists call "reaction norms" – a genotype may offer a more or less broad range of possible accommodations, but all of them are within a certain statistically defined "norm." In the same way, cognitively speaking, the subject is capable of various accommodations, but only within certain limits imposed by the necessity of preserving the corresponding assimilatory structure. In equation 1 the term A in AT specifies precisely this limitation on accommodations.

The concept of "association," which the various forms of associationism from Hume to Pavlov and Hull have used and abused, has thus only been obtained by artificially isolating one part of the general process defined by the equilibrium between assimilation and accommodation. Pavlov's dog is said to associate a sound to food, which elicits its salivation reflex. If, however, the sound is never again followed by food, the conditioned response, or temporary link, will disappear; it has no intrinsic stability. The conditioning persists as a function of the need for food, that is, it persists only if it is part of an assimilatory scheme and its satisfaction, hence of a certain accommodation to the situation. In fact, an "association" is always accompanied by an assimilation to previous structures, and this is a first factor that must not be overlooked. On the other hand, insofar as the "association" incorporates some new information, this represents an active accommodation and not a mere passive recording. This accommodatory activity, which is dependent on the assimilation scheme, is a second necessary factor that must not be neglected.

7   If accommodation and assimilation are present in all activity, their ratio may vary, and only the more or less stable equilibrium which may exist between them (though it is always mobile) characterizes a complete act of intelligence.

When assimilation *outweighs* accommodation (i.e., when the characteristics of the object are not taken into account except insofar as they are consistent with the subject's momentary interests) thought evolves in an egocentric or even autistic direction. The most common form of this situation in the play of the child is the "symbolic games" or fiction games, in which objects at his command are used only to represent what is imagined.[3] This form of game, which is most frequent at the beginning of representation (between one and a half and three years of age), then evolves toward constructive games in which accommodation to objects becomes more and more precise until there is no longer any difference between play and spontaneous cognitive or instrumental activities.

Conversely, when accommodation prevails over assimilation to the point where it faithfully reproduces the forms and movements of the objects or persons which are its models at that time, representation (and the sensorimotor behaviors which are its precursors and which also give rise to exercise games that develop much earlier than symbolic games) evolves in the direction of imitation. Imitation through action, an accommodation to models that are present, gradually extends to deferred imitation and finally to interiorized imitation. In this last form it constitutes the origin of mental imagery and of the figurative as opposed to the operative aspects of thought.

But as long as assimilation and accommodation are in equilibrium (i.e., insofar as assimilation is still subordinate to the properties of the objects, or, in other words, subordinate to the situation with the accommodations it entails; and accommodation itself is subordinate to the already existing structures to which the situation must be assimilated) we can speak of cognitive behavior as opposed to play, imitation, or mental imagery, and we are back in the proper domain of intelligence. But this fundamental equilibrium between assimilation and accommodation is more or less difficult to attain and to maintain depending on the level of intellectual development and the new problems encountered. However, such an equilibrium exists at all levels, in the early development of intelligence in the child as well as in scientific thought.

It is obvious that any physical or biologic theory assimilates objective phenomena to a restricted number of models which are not drawn exclusively from these phenomena. These models involve in addition a certain number of logicomathematical coordinations that are the operational activities of the subject himself. It would be very superficial to reduce these coordinations to a mere "language" (though this is the position of logical positivism) because, properly speaking, they are an instrument for structuration. For example, Poincaré narrowly missed discovering relativity because he thought there was no difference between expressing (or translating) phenomena in the "language" of Euclidian or of Riemanian geometry. Einstein was able to construct his theory by using Riemanian space as an instrument of *structuration*, to "understand" the relations between space, speed, and time. If physics proceeds by assimilating reality to logicomathematical models, then it must unceasingly accommodate them to new experimental results. It cannot dispense with accommodation because its models would then remain subjective and arbitrary. However, every new accommodation is conditioned by existing assimilations. The significance of an experiment does not derive from a mere perceptive recording (the "Protokollsätze" of the first "logical empiricists"); it cannot be dissociated from an *interpretation*.

8   In the development of intelligence in the child, there are many types of equilibrium between assimilation and accommodation that vary with the levels of development and the problems to be solved. At sensorimotor levels (before one and a half to two years of age) these are only practical problems involving immediate space, and as early as the second year, sensorimotor intelligence reaches a remarkable state of equilibrium (e.g., instrumental behaviors, group of displacements; see ¶ 2). But this equilibrium is difficult to attain, because during the first months, the infant's universe is centered on his own body and actions, and because of distortions due to assimilation not yet balanced by adequate accommodations.

The beginning of thought creates multiple problems of representation (which must extend to distant space and can no longer be restricted to near space) as well as the problem of adaptation no longer measured by practical success alone; thus intelligence goes through a new phase of assimilatory distortion. This is because objects and events are assimilated to the subject's own action and viewpoint and possible accommodations still consist only of fixations on figural aspects of reality (hence on states as opposed to transformations). For these two reasons – egocentric assimilation and incomplete accommodation – equilibrium is not reached. On the other hand, from the age of seven to eight the emergence of reversible operations ensures a stable harmony between assimilation and accommodation since both can now act on transformations as well as on states.

Generally speaking, this progressive equilibrium between assimilation and accommodation is an instance of a fundamental process in cognitive development which can be expressed in terms of centration and decentration. The systematically distorting assimilations of sensorimotor or initial representative stages, which distort because they are not accompanied by adequate accommodations, mean that the subject remains centered on his own actions and his own viewpoint. On the other hand, the gradually emerging equilibrium between assimilation and accommodation is the result of successive decentrations, which make it possible for the subject to take the points of view of other subjects or objects themselves. We formerly described this process merely in terms of *ego*centrism and socialization. But it is far more general and more fundamental to knowledge in all its forms. For cognitive progress is not only assimilation of information; it entails a systematic decentration process which is a necessary condition of objectivity itself.

The Theory of Stages

9   We have seen that there exist structures which belong only to the subject (¶ 1), that they are built (¶ 2), and that this is a step-by-step process (¶ 7). We must therefore conclude there exist stages of development. Even authors who agree with this idea may use different criteria and interpretations of stage development. It therefore becomes a problem that requires discussion in its own right. The Freudian stages, for instance, are only distinct from each other in that they differ in one dominant character (oral, anal, etc.) but this character is also present in the previous – or following – stages, so that its "dominance" may well remain arbitrary. Gesell's stages are based on the hypothesis of the quasi-exclusive role of maturation, so that they guarantee a constant order of succession but may neglect the factor of progressive construction. To characterize the

stages of cognitive development we therefore need to integrate two necessary conditions without introducing any contradictions. These conditions for stages are (*a*) that they must be defined to guarantee a constant order of succession, and (*b*) that the definition allow for progressive construction without entailing total preformation. These two conditions are necessary because knowledge obviously involves learning by experience, which means an external contribution in addition to that involving internal structures, and the structures seem to evolve in a way that is not entirely predetermined.

The problem of stages in developmental psychology is analogous to that of stages in embryogenesis. The question that arises in this field is also that of making allowance for both genetic preformation and an eventual "epigenesis" in the sense of construction by interactions between the genome and the environment. It is for this reason that Waddington introduces the concept of "epigenetic system" and also a distinction between the genotype and the "epigenotype." The main characteristics of such an epigenetic development are not only the well-known and obvious ones of succession in sequential order and of progressive integration (segmentation followed by determination controlled by specific "competence" and finally "reintegration") but also some less obvious ones pointed out by Waddington. These are the existence of "creodes," or necessary developmental sequences, each with its own "time tally," or schedule, and the intervention of a sort of evolutionary regulation, or "homeorhesis." Homeorhesis acts in such a way that if an external influence causes the developing organism to deviate from one of its creodes, there ensures a homeorhetical reaction, which tends to channel it back to the normal sequence or, if this fails, switches it to a new creode as similar as possible to the original one.

Each of the preceding characteristics can be observed in cognitive development if we carefully differentiate the construction of the structures themselves and the acquisition of specific procedures through learning (e.g., learning to read at one age rather than another). The question will naturally be whether development can be reduced to an addition of procedures learned one by one or whether learning itself depends on developmental laws which are autonomous.

Notes

The present chapter is, in part, the expansion of an article on my conceptions of development published in *Journal International de Psychologie*, a summary of previous publications, but it also takes into account recent or still unpublished work by the author or his collaborators and colleagues. As a matter of fact, "Piaget's theory" is not completed at this date and the author of these pages has always considered himself one of the chief "revisionists of Piaget." (Author's note)

1   Throughout this chapter the term *scheme* (plural, *schemes*) is used to refer to *operational* activities, whereas *schema* (plural, *schemata*) refers to the figurative aspects of thought – attempts to represent reality without attempting to transform it (imagery, perception, and memory). Later in this chapter the author says, "images . . . , however schematic, are not schemes. We shall therefore use the term schemata to designate them. A schema is a simplified image (e.g., the map of a town), whereas a scheme represents what can be repeated and generalized in an action (for example, the scheme is what is common in the actions of 'pushing' an object with a stick or any other instrument)."

2   For example, take T to be an already established classification on a set of objects, O, which divides it into two distant subclasses. I is a set of new objects that are added to the original ones and to which the classification T must be extended. When this is done (I has been assimilated to T), it turns out that there are say two new subclasses (the whole structure is now AT) and some properties of the new objects I (e.g., the number of elements in I, or their shape, size or color) have been neglected in the process. We now have $T + I \rightarrow AT + E$, where T = the two original subclasses, I = the new elements. AT = the four subclasses, and E = the irrelevant properties of the new elements, that is, the properties which are not used as criteria for classifying in this specific instance.

3   The categories of play defined by Piaget are the following:
    a   *Exercise games.* These consist of any behavior without new structuration but with a new functional finality. For example, the repetition of an action such as swinging an object, if its aim is to understand or to prac-tice the movement, is *not* a game. But the same behavior, if its aim is functional pleasure, pleasure in the activity in itself, or the pleasure of "causing" some phenomenon, becomes a game. Examples of this are the vocalizations of infants and the games of adults with a new car, radio, etc.
    b   *Symbolic games.* These consist of behaviors with a new structuration, that of representing realities that are out of the present perceptual field. Examples are the fiction games where the child enacts a meal with pebbles standing for bread, grass for vegetables, etc. The symbols used here are individual and specific to each child.

c   *Rule games.* These are behaviors with a new structuration involving the intervention of more than one person. The rules of this new structure are defined by social interaction. This type of game ranges over the whole scale of activities, starting with simple sensorimotor games with set rules (the many varieties of marble games, for instance) and ending with abstract games like chess. The symbols here are stabilized by convention and can become purely arbitrary in the more abstract games. That is, they bear no more relation (analogy) with what they represent. (Translator's note)

THREE

Developmental Research: Microgenetic Method

Introduction

One of the goals of cognitive development research is to reveal how systematic cognitive change takes place. Cognitive developmentalists have at their disposal two main developmental methods to answer this question: cross-sectional and longitudinal. Cross-sectional designs assess a cognitive function of different age groups *at the same point in time*, and age differences obtained are used to suggest a developmental change in children between these ages. While this design can be efficient for collecting sufficient data in a short period of time, it has a major problem: it tends to gloss over both inter-individual and intra-individual variations and to present only a picture of what the cognitive developmental pattern of children as a group may look like, which does not necessarily reflect the developmental pattern of any individual child.

In longitudinal studies the same group of children are tested repeatedly over a period of time. Although it is more time-consuming than cross-sectional design, because each individual's cognitive functioning is tracked over time, both inter-individual and intra-individual variations can be examined. Traditionally, however, rather long time intervals are used in longitudinal studies (e.g., tests are given monthly or yearly), so that important developmental changes are often missed. For this reason, a number of researchers have proposed a new developmental research approach that is referred to as the microdevelopmental approach (Karmiloff-Smith, 1979) or the microgenetic method (Kuhn, 1995). Siegler's article introduces the microgenetic method that he helped pioneer. It basically is a longitudinal design with much smaller time intervals (sometimes as short as a few minutes) than the traditional longitudinal design (normally monthly or yearly). In addition, microgenetic method focuses on variabilities in children's cognitive functioning; by contrast, the traditional longitudinal design focuses on regularities in children's cognitive abilities and treats variabilities as measurement errors. In this article Siegler demonstrates that when we pay close attention to what children do, irregularities in their behavior can be very informative about regularities in cognitive development.

References

Karmiloff-Smith, A. (1979). Micro- and macro-developmental changes in language acquisition and other representational systems. *Cognitive Science, 3,* 91–118.

Kuhn, D. (1995). Microgenetic study of change: What has it told us? *Psychological Science, 6,* 133–9.

Further reading

Catan, L. (1986). The dynamic display of process: Historical development and contemporary uses of the microgenetic method. *Human Development, 29,* 252–63.

Cognitive Variability: A Key to Understanding Cognitive Development

Robert S. Siegler

Among the most remarkable characteristics of human beings is how much our thinking changes with age. When we compare the thinking of an infant, a toddler, an elementary school student, and an adolescent, the magnitude of the change is immediately apparent. Accounting for how these changes occur is perhaps the central goal of researchers who study cognitive development.

Alongside this agreement about the importance of the goal of determining how change occurs, however, is agreement that we traditionally have not done very well in meeting it. In most models of cognitive development, children are depicted as thinking or acting in a certain way for a prolonged period of time, then undergoing a brief, rather mysterious, transition, and then thinking or acting in a different way for another prolonged period. For example, on the classic conservation-of-liquid quantity problem, children are depicted as believing for several years that pouring water into a taller, thinner beaker changes the amount of water; then undergoing a short period of cognitive conflict, in which they are not sure about the effects of pouring the water; and then realizing that pouring does not affect the amount of liquid. How children get from the earlier to the later understanding is described only superficially.

Critiques of the inadequacy of such accounts have been leveled most often at stage models such as Piaget's. The problem, however, is far more pervasive. Regardless of whether the particular approach describes development in terms of stages, rules, strategies, or theories; regardless of whether the focus is on reasoning about the physical or the social world; regardless of the age group of central interest, most theories place static states at center stage and change processes either in the wings or offstage altogether. Thus, three-year-olds are said to have non-representational theories of mind and five-year-olds representational ones; five-year-olds to have absolute views about justice and ten-year-olds relativistic ones; ten-year-olds to be incapable and 15-year-olds capable of true scientific reasoning. The emphasis in almost all cognitive-developmental theories has been on identifying sequences of one-to-one correspondences between ages and ways of thinking or acting, rather than on specifying how the changes occur.

If developmentalists are so interested in change processes, why would the topic be given such cursory treatment in most contemporary theories? Part of the problem is that studying change is inherently difficult. It poses all the conceptual and methodological demands of studying performance at any one time, and imposes the added demands of determining what is changing and how the change is being accomplished.

An additional part of the difficulty, however, may be self-imposed. In our efforts to describe differences among age groups in as simple, dramatic, and memorable terms as possible, we may unwittingly have made understanding change more difficult than it needs to be. In particular, portraying children's thinking and knowledge as monolithic for several years at a time creates a need to explain the wide gulfs between the successive hypothesized understandings – even though such gulfs may not exist. The typical depictions make change a rare, almost exotic, event that demands an exceptional explanation. If children of a given age have for several years had a particular understanding, why would they suddenly form a different understanding, and why would they regularly form it at a particular age? The problem is exacerbated by the fact that for many of the competencies of interest, generally relevant experience is available at all ages and specifically relevant experience at none. Children see liquids poured into containers of different dimensions at all ages – and are not ordinarily told at any age that the amount of liquid remains the same after pouring as before. Why, then, would they consistently have one concept of liquid quantity conservation at age five and a different one at age seven?

Recognition of the unwelcome side effects of the one-to-one depictions of cognitive growth has led to a new generation of research that focuses directly on changes in children's thinking. This research has documented large-scale variability in children's thinking and suggests that the variability contributes directly to cognitive growth.

Pervasive Variability

Variability in children's thinking exists at every level – not just between children of different ages, or between different children of the same age, but also within an individual solving a set of related problems, within an individual solving the same problem twice, and even within an individual on a single trial.

Variability within an individual solving related problems

Detailed analyses of tasks on which one-to-one correspondences between age and way of thinking have been postulated indicate that children's thinking is generally much more variable than past depictions have suggested. To cite an example from language development, rather than young children passing through a stage in which they always over-regularize past tense forms (e.g., saying "goed" and "eated" rather than "went" and "ate"), children at all ages between two and a half and five years produce both substantial numbers of overregularized forms and substantial numbers of correct ones. The variability throughout this age range is present for a single child followed throughout the period, as well as for groups of children sampled at a single age. Adding to the variability, children often produce more than one incorrect form of a given verb; on different occasions, a given child will say, "I ate it," "I eated it," and "I ated it" (Kuczaj, 1977).

Similar variability has been found in the development of memory strategies. Contrary to the widely cited model that five-year-olds do not rehearse and eight-year-olds do, trial-by-trial assessments indicate that the majority of children of both ages sometimes do and sometimes do not rehearse (McGilly & Siegler, 1990). The percentage of trials on which they rehearse increases with age, but, again, there is variability throughout the age range.

Conceptual development evidences the same pattern. Despite claims that five-year-olds think of number conservation solely in terms of the lengths of the rows, trial-by-trial assessments indicate that most five-year-olds sometimes rely on the lengths of the rows, sometimes rely on the type of transformation, and sometimes use other strategies such as counting or pairing (Siegler, 1993). Again, the frequency of reliance on these ways of thinking changes with age, but most five-year-olds' judgments and verbal explanations indicate several different ways of thinking about the concept.

Development of problem-solving skills provides yet more evidence for such within-subject cognitive variability. Contradicting models in which preschoolers are said to use the sum strategy (counting from 1) to solve simple addition problems and in which first through third graders are said to use the min strategy (counting from the larger addend, as when solving 3 + 6 by counting "6, 7, 8, 9") to solve them, children of all these ages use a variety of strategies. In one study, most children presented a set of addition problems used at least three different strategies on different problems, and most children examined in a more extensive microlongitudinal study used at least five distinct strategies (Siegler & Jenkins, 1989).

Variability within an individual solving a single problem twice

The variability within individual children cannot be reduced to children using different strategies on different problems. Even presented the identical problem twice within a single session, or on two successive days, children use different strategies on roughly one third of the pairs of trials in addition, time-telling, and block-building tasks (Siegler & McGilly, 1989; Siegler & Shrager, 1984; Wilkinson, 1982). This variability within individuals within problems cannot be explained by learning; in these studies, children used the strategy that appeared more advanced almost as often for the first presentation of a problem as for the second (roughly 45% vs. 55%).

Variability within a single trial

In the limiting case, variability has been found even within an individual solving a particular problem on a single trial. This type of variability has been reported by investigators interested in the relation between children's hand gestures and verbal explanations. In these studies, children often express one type of understanding through the gestures and a quite different understanding through the explanations (Church & Goldin-Meadow, 1986; Goldin-Meadow & Alibali, in press). For example, on number conservation problems, children may express a reliance on relative lengths of the rows in their hand gestures, while at the same time verbally expressing reliance on the type of transformation, or vice versa.

These findings suggest that cognitive change is better thought of in terms of changing distributions of ways of thinking than in terms of sudden shifts from one way of thinking to another. The types of descriptions of change that emerge from such analyses are illustrated in figures 1 and 2. Figure 1 shows changes in three children's addition strategies over a three-month period (Siegler & Jenkins, 1989); figure 2 shows changes in a child's map-drawing strategies over a two-year period (Feldman, 1980). Similar changes in distributions of strategies have been found in studies of conceptual understanding, memory strategies, problem solving, and language. In all these domains, cognitive development involves changing distributions of approaches, rather than discontinuous movements from one way of thinking to another.

Variability and Cognitive Change

Variability is not just an incidental feature of thinking; it appears to play a critical role in promoting cognitive change. Several types of evidence converge on this conclusion. One comes from observations of children in the process of discovering new strategies. Both the trials immediately before a discovery and the trial on which the discovery is made frequently involve especially variable behavior – disfluencies, unclear references, long pauses, and unusual gestures (Siegler & Jenkins, 1989). A second type of empirical evidence linking variability to cognitive change involves analyses of which children are most likely to make discoveries. Children whose verbal explanations and gestures reflect different initial misunderstandings of number conservation and of numerical equivalence problems $(a + b + c = \_ + c)$ are more likely to make discoveries subsequently than are children whose explanations and gestures reflect the same initial misunderstanding (Church & Goldin-Meadow, 1986; Goldin-Meadow & Alibali, in press). Similarly, children whose pretest explanations reflect varied ways of thinking are more likely to learn from instruction regarding the meaning of the equal sign in

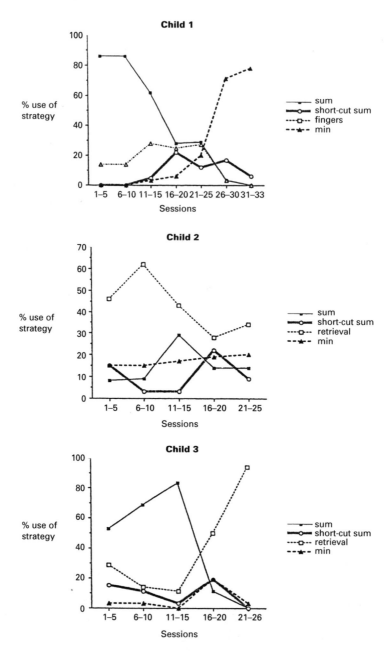

Figure 1 Changes in distributions of addition strategies of three children over roughly 30 sessions conducted over a three-month period. Notice the variability that is present within each child's performance within each block of sessions, as well as the changes in distributions of strategy used over the course of the study.

Source: Data from Siegler & Jenkins, 1989.

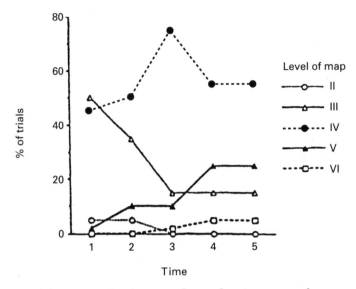

Figure 2 Changes in distributions of map-drawing approaches across five sessions, conducted over a two-year period. Higher numbers indicate more advanced levels of map drawing; thus, Level IV maps are more advanced than Level III ones.

Source: Data from Feldman, 1980.

mathematics than are children whose pretest explanations reflect crisp, specific misunderstandings (Graham & Perry, 1993).

A different type of evidence for the contribution of variability to cognitive change comes from formal models of development. Theorists who differ in many particular assumptions have found that modeling change requires both mechanisms that produce variability and mechanisms that produce adaptive choices among the variants. Connectionist models of development are based on connection strengths among processing units varying at all points in learning, from initial, randomly varying strengths to final, asymptotic levels; change occurs through redistributions of the varying connection strengths. Dynamic systems models also treat variability as a fundamental property of development; they aim to explain how local variability gives rise to global regularities. Similarly, recent symbolic-processing models of development focus on how varying strategies, analogies, and other higher-order units come to be used increasingly in the situations in which they are most effective.

At a less formal level, operant conditioning models, evolutionarily based models, and generate-and-test models are all based on the assumption that change occurs through selection processes operating on omnipresent, spontaneously produced variability in behavior (e.g., see Campbell, 1974; McClelland & Jenkins, 1991; Smith & Thelen, in press; Skinner, 1981).

A striking empirical finding about the variability in children's thinking, and one that is important for its ability to contribute to cognitive development, is the constrained quality of the variations that children generate. Far from conforming to a trial-and-error model, in which all types of variations might be expected, the new approaches that children attempt consistently conform to the principles that define legal strategies in the domain (except when children are forced to solve problems for which they do not possess any adequate strategy). For example, in a 30-session study of preschoolers' discovery of new addition strategies, none of the children ever attempted strategies that violated the principles underlying addition (Siegler & Jenkins, 1989). They invented legitimate new strategies, such as the min strategy, but never illegitimate ones, such as adding the smaller addend to itself or counting from the larger addend the number of times indicated by the first addend. The question is how they limit their newly generated strategies to legal forms.

One possibility is that even before discovering new strategies, children often understand the goals that legitimate strategies in the domain must satisfy. Such understanding would allow them, without trial and error, to discriminate between legitimate new strategies that meet the essential goals and illegitimate strategies that do not. A very recent study revealed that children possessed such knowledge in both of the domains that were examined – simple addition and tic-tac-toe (Siegler & Crowley, in press). In simple addition, children who had not yet discovered the min strategy nonetheless judged that strategy (demonstrated by the experimenter) to be as smart as the strategy they themselves most often used – counting from 1 – and significantly smarter than an equally novel but illegitimate strategy that the experimenter demonstrated. In tic-tac-toe, children rated a novel strategy that they did not yet use – forking – as even smarter than the strategy they themselves usually employed – trying to complete a single row or column. Ability to anticipate the value of untried strategies may promote cognitive growth by filtering out unpromising possibilities and thus channeling innovations in potentially useful directions.

Conclusions

Thinking is far more variable than usually depicted. In the past, researchers have usually ignored such variability or viewed it as a bother. This stance has led to subjects being given practice periods, not so that especially variable behavior in those periods can be studied, but so that it can be discarded, in order that it not obscure the more orderly patterns in later performance. When such variability has been explicitly noted at all, it has usually been viewed as an unfortunate limitation of human beings, a kind of design defect, something to be overcome through practice. Computers, robots, and other machines not subject to this flaw can perform many tasks more accurately than people can. Presumably, people's performance would also be enhanced if it were less variable.

This view of variability as detracting from efficient performance misses at least half the story, though. The variability of cognition and action allows us to discover a great deal about the environments toward which the thinking and action are directed. Our difficulty in reproducing the way we pronounced a word in an unfamiliar foreign language may lead to some even less adequate pronunciations in the short run, but in the longer run may lead us to generate and then learn better pronunciations. Likewise, our inability to give a colloquium in the same words twice, even when we want to, may lead to some parts being less clear than in the best of our previous presentations, but it also allows us to observe audience reaction to new lines of argument and to learn which ones are best received. In general, cognitive variability may lead to performance never incorporating on any one occasion all the best features of previous performance, but also may be critical to our becoming increasingly proficient over time.

If cognitive variability does indeed facilitate learning, it would be adaptive if such variability were most pronounced when learning, rather than efficient performance, is most important – that is, in infancy and early childhood. This appears to be the case. Across many domains, expertise brings with it decreasingly variable performance. To the extent that young children are "universal novices," their lack of expertise alone would lead to their performance being more variable than that of older children and adults. A number of cognitive neuroscientists have hypothesized that above and beyond such effects of practice, the process of synaptogenesis, which results in children from roughly birth to age seven having far more synaptic connections than older children and adults, may contribute both to the high variability of early behavior and to young children's special ability to acquire language, perceptual skills, and other competencies under abnormal organismic and environmental conditions (Goldman-Rakic, 1987; Greenough, Black, & Wallace, 1987). That is, young children's greater variability at the neural level seems to allow them to learn useful behaviors under a greater range of circumstances. The general lesson seems to be that explicitly recognizing the great variability of infants' and young children's thinking, and attempting to explain how it is generated and constrained, will advance our understanding of the central mystery about cognitive development – how change occurs.

References

Campbell, D. T., Evolutionary epistemology. In *The Philosophy of Karl Popper*, Vol. 14, Schilpp, P. A. Ed. Open Court, La Salle, IL (1974). Skinner, B. F., Selection by consequences. *Science, 213*, 501–504 (1981).

Church, R. B., and Goldin-Meadow, S. The mismatch between gesture and speech as an index of transitional knowledge. *Cognition, 23*, 43–71 (1986).

Feldman, D. H. *Beyond universals in cognitive development*. Ablex, Norwood, NJ, 1980.

Goldin-Meadow, S., and Alibali, M. W. Transitions in concept acquisition: Using the hand to read the mind. *Psychological Review* (in press).

Goldman-Rakic, P. S. Development of cortical circuitry and cognitive function. *Child Development, 58*, 601–622 (1987).

Graham, T., and Perry, M. Indexing transitional knowledge. *Developmental Psychology, 29*, 779–788 (1993).

Greenough, W. T., Black, J. E., and Wallace, C. Experience and brain development. *Child Development, 58*, 539–559 (1987).

Kuczaj, S. A. The acquisition of regular and irregular past tense forms. *Journal of Verbal Learning and Verbal Behavior, 16*, 589–600 (1977).

McClelland, J. L., and Jenkins, E. Nature, nurture, and connections: Implications of connectionist models for cognitive development. In *Architectures for intelligence*, Van Lehn, K. Ed. Erlbaum, Hillsdale, NJ (1991).

McGilly, K., and Siegler, R. S. The influence of encoding and strategic knowledge on children's choices among serial recall strategies. *Developmental Psychology, 26*, 931–941 (1990).

Siegler, R. S. A microgenetic study of number conservation. Manuscript in preparation, Carnegie Mellon University, Pittsburgh (1993).

Siegler, R. S., and Crowley, K. Goal sketches constrain children's strategy discoveries. *Cognitive Psychology* (in press).

Siegler, R. S., and Jenkins, E. *How children discover new strategies*. Erlbaum, Hillsdale, NJ (1989).

Siegler, R. S., and McGilly, K. Strategy choices in children's time-telling. In *Time and human cognition: A life span perspective*, Levin, I., and Zakay, D. Eds. Elsevier Science, Amsterdam (1989).

Siegler, R. S., and Shrager, J. Strategy choices in addition and subtraction: How do children know what to do? In *The origins of cognitive skills*, Sophian, C. Ed. Erlbaum, Hillsdale, NJ (1984).

Smith, L. B., and Thelen, E., Eds. *Dynamical systems in development: Applications*. Bradford Books, Cambridge, MA (in press).

Wilkinson, A. C. Partial knowledge and self-correction: Developmental studies of a quantitative concept. *Developmental Psychology, 18*, 876–893 (1982).

FOUR

Information Processing and Connectionism

Introduction

Kim Plunkett's article begins with an apparent paradox in developmental psychology. Young infants, who are in full command of the ability to reach and grasp objects, fail to retrieve an object which is partially or fully concealed, even though we know that they are aware of the continued existence of the object. Plunkett describes a computational model, consisting of a complex neural network, that helps to solve this apparent paradox: simply, the model predicts that infants will learn to reach for visible objects prior to reaching for hidden objects, even though the model "knows" that the hidden object continues to exist. This example of model building "seems to support the initial insight that children's object representations develop in a fragmentary fashion" and the model's predictions provide a close match with the performance of infants on actual tasks.

Connectionist modeling often seems to give us insights into the ways in which cognitive development takes place. Plunkett describes four insights that these models provide: (1) learning can often be more simple than we imagine; (2) small and gradual changes in knowledge, awareness, and skills can often lead to apparent qualitative changes in behavior, so that changes in functioning that appear to reflect qualitative differences may, in fact, be determined by quantitative changes; (3) different areas of development (different domains) can emerge both from domain-specific and domain-general learning capacities; (4) "small is beautiful," that is, starting with a limited learning ability can actually work to enhance learning – "The ignorance and apparent inadequacies of the immature organism may, in fact, be highly beneficial for learning the solutions to complex problems. Small is beautiful."

Plunkett continues with connectionist accounts of learning the past tense of verbs and other aspects of language development. One of the most important contributions of connectionist models to our understanding of development is to suggest that many behavioral changes that have been thought of as discontinuities in development, thereby indicating the onset of a new stage or phase of development, can often be more easily explained and interpreted as a result of the accumulated effect of many small quantitative changes in a simple, nonlinear learning mechanism.

Connectionist modeling directly addresses the nature/nurture debate in that it explores the issue of what innate specification (the "initial state" of the organism) might mean, in order to get learning off the ground and to direct the course of development. What is certain is that connectionist accounts of development are here to stay! Such models give insights into what might develop, and how changes in behavior and thinking might occur. They can often suggest critical experiments, and they challenge existing models of the course of cognitive development.

Further reading

Elman, J., Bates, E., Karmiloff-Smith, A., Johnson, M., Parisi, D., & Plunkett, K. (1996). *Rethinking innateness: Development in a connectionist perspective.* Cambridge, MA: MIT Press.

Development in a Connectionist Framework: Rethinking the Nature–Nurture Debate

Kim Plunkett

A Developmental Paradox

Two findings in developmental psychology stand in apparent conflict. Piaget (1952) has shown that at a certain stage in development, children will cease in their attempts to reach for an object when it is partially or fully covered by an occluder. This finding is observed in children up to the age of about six months and is interpreted to indicate that the object concept is not well established in early infancy. The object representations that are necessary to motivate reaching and grasping behavior are absent. In contrast, other studies have shown that young infants will express surprise when a stimulus array is transformed in such a way that the resulting array does not conform to reasonable expectations. For example, change in heart rate, sucking or GSR (galvanic skin response) is observed when an object, previously visible, fails to block the path of a moving drawbridge, or a locomotive fails to reappear from a tunnel or has changed color when it reappears (Baillargeon, 1993; Spelke et al., 1994). These results are interpreted as indicating that important representations of object properties such as form, shape, and the capacity to block the movement of other objects are already in place by four months of age. The conflict in these findings can be stated as follows: Why should the infant cease to reach for a partially or fully concealed object when it already controls representational characteristics of objects that confirm the stability of object properties over time, and that predict the interaction of those represented properties with objects that are visible in the perceptual array?

One answer to this conflict is that Piaget grossly underestimated young children's ability to retrieve hidden objects. However, this answer is no resolution to the conflict: Piaget's findings are robust. Alternatively, one might question Piaget's interpretation of his results. Young infants know a lot about the permanent properties of objects, but recruiting object representations in the service of a reaching task requires additional sensorimotor skills which have little to do with the infant's understanding of the permanence of objects. Again, this response must be rejected. Young infants who are in full command of the skill to reach and grasp a visible object still fail to retrieve an object which is partially or fully concealed (von Hofsten, 1989). Motor skills are not the culprit here. The capacity to relate object knowledge to other domains seems to be an important part of object knowledge itself. Object knowledge has to be accessed and exercised.

A resolution

A resolution of the conflict can be found in considering some fundamental differences in the nature of the two types of task that infants are required to perform. In experiments that measure "surprise" reactions to unusual object transformations such as failure to reappear from behind an occluder, the infant is treated as a passive observer (Baillargeon, 1993). In essence, the infant is evaluated for its expectations concerning the future state of a stimulus array. Failure of expectation elicits surprise. In the Piagetian task, the infant is required to actively transform the stimulus array. To achieve this, not only must the infant know where the object is but she must be able to coordinate that information with knowledge about the object's identity – typically, the infant reaches for objects she wants. We suppose that this coordination is relatively easy for visible objects, because actions are supported by externally available cues. However, when the object is out of sight, the child has to rely on internal representations of the object's identity and position. We assume that the internal representations for object position and identity develop separately. This assumption is motivated by recent neurological evidence that spatial and featural information is processed in separate channels in the human brain – the so-called "what" and "where" channels (Ungerlieder & Mishkin, 1982). In principle, the child could demonstrate knowledge of an object's position without demonstrating knowledge about its identity, or vice versa. Surprise reactions might be triggered by failure of infant expectations within either of these domains. For example, an object may suddenly change its featural properties or fail to appear in a predicted position. Internal representations are particularly important when the object is out of sight. Hence, we might expect infants to have greater difficulty performing tasks that involve the coordination of spatial and featural representations – such as reaching for hidden objects – when these representations are only partially developed.

Building a model

The resolution outlined in the previous section constitutes a theory about the origins of infants' surprise reactions to objects' properties (spatial or featural) which do not conform to expectations and attempts to explain why these surprise reactions precede the ability to reach for hidden objects even though they possess the motor skills to do so. Mareschal, Plunkett, & Harris (1999) have constructed a computational model that implements the ideas outlined in this theory (see figure 1). The model consist of a complex neural network that processes a visual image of an object that can move across a flat plane. Different types of objects distinguished by a small number of features appear on the plane one at a time. These objects may or may not disappear behind an occluder. All objects move with a constant velocity so that if one disappears behind an occluder, it will eventually reappear on the other side. Object velocities can vary from one presentation to the next.

The network is given two tasks. First, it must learn to predict the next position of the moving object, including its position when hidden behind an occluder. Second, the network must learn to initiate a motor response to reach for an object, both when visible and when hidden. The network is endowed with several information-processing capacities that enable it to fulfill these tasks. The image of the object moving across the plane is processed by two separate modules. One module learns to form a spatially invariant representation of the object so that it can recognize its identity irrespective of its position on the plane (Foldiak, 1991). The second module learns to keep track of the object but loses all information about the object's identity (Ungerlieder & Mishkin, 1982). This

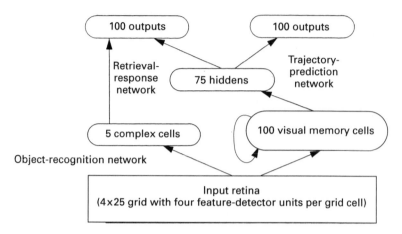

Figure 1   The modular neural network (Mareschal et al., 1999) used to track and initiate reaching responses for visible and hidden objects. An object-recognition network and a visual-tracking network process information from an input retina. The object-recognition network learns spatially invariant representations of the objects that move around the retina. The visual-tracking network learns to predict the next position of the object on the retina. The retrieval-response network learns to integrate information from the other two modules in order to initiate a reaching response. The complete system succeeds in tracking visible objects before it can predict the reappearnce of hidden objects. It also succeeds in initiating a reaching response for visible objects before it learns to reach for hidden objects.

second module does all the work that is required to predict the position of the moving object. However, in order to reach for an object, the network needs to integrate information about the object's identity and its position. Both modules are required for this task. Therefore, the ability to reach can be impeded either because the representations of identity and position are not sufficiently developed or because the network has not yet managed to properly integrate these representations in the service of reaching.

Given the additional task demands imposed on the network for reaching it would seem relatively unsurprising to discover that the network learns to track objects before it learns to reach for them. The crucial test of the model is whether it is able to make the correct predictions about the late onset of reaching for hidden objects relative to visible objects. In fact, the model makes the right predictions for the order of mastery in tracking and reaching for visible and hidden objects. It quickly learns to track and reach for visible objects, tracking being slightly more precocious than retrieval. Next, the network learns to track occluded objects as its internal representations of position are strengthened and it is able to "keep track" of the object in the absence of perceptual input. However, the ability to track hidden objects together with the already mastered ability to reach for visible objects does not guarantee mastery of reaching for hidden objects. The internal representations that control the integration of spatial and featural information require further development before this ability is mastered.

Evaluating the model

Notice how this modeling endeavor provides a working implementation of a set of principles that constitute a theory about how infants learn to track and reach for visible and hidden objects. It identifies a set of tasks that the model must perform and the information-processing capacities required to perform those tasks. All these constitute a set of assumptions that are not explained by the model. However, given these assumptions, the model is able to make correct predictions about the order of mastery of the different tasks. The model implements a coherent and accurate theory (although not necessarily true – the assumptions might be wrong). However, this model, just like any other, has a number of free parameters which the modeler may "tweak" in order to achieve the appropriate predictions. It is necessary to derive some novel predictions which can be tested against new experimental work with infants, in order to evaluate the generality of the solution the model has found. This model makes several interesting predictions including improved tracking skills at higher velocities and imperviousness to unexpected feature changes while tracking. The first experimental prediction has been confirmed (see Mareschal, Harris, & Plunkett, 1997) while the second prediction is currently being tested. This instance of model building and evaluation thus seems to support the initial insight that children's object representations develop in a fragmentary fashion, and that the development of these fragments of knowledge shape infant performance on various tasks in line with their manner of involvement in the tasks concerned.

Connectionist Insights

The model described in the previous section is an example of a computer simulation that uses the learning capabilities of artificial neural networks to construct internal representations of a training environment in the service of several tasks (reaching and tracking). Neural networks are particularly good at extracting the statistical regularities of a training environment and exploiting them in a structured manner to achieve some goal. They consist of a well-specified architecture driven by a learning algorithm. The connections or weights between the simple processing units that make up the network are gradually adapted over time in response to localized messages from the learning algorithm. The final configuration of weights in the network constitutes what it knows about the environment and the tasks it is required to perform.

Connectionist modeling provides a flexible approach to evaluating alternative hypotheses concerning the start state of the organism (or what we may think of as its innate endowment), the effective learning environment that the organism occupies, and the nature of the learning procedure for transforming the organism into its mature state. The start state of the organism is modeled by the choice of network architecture and computational properties of the units in the network. There is a wide range of possibilities that the developmentalist can choose from. The effective learning environment is determined by the manner in which the modeler chooses to define the task for the network. For example, the modeler must decide upon a representational format for the pattern of inputs and outputs for the network, and highlight the manner in which the network samples patterns from the environment. These decisions constitute precise hypotheses about the nature of the learning environment. Finally, the modeler must decide how the network will learn. Again, a wide variety of learning algorithms are available to drive weight adaptation in networks. Any particular connectionist model embodies a set of decisions governing all of these factors, which are crucial for specifying clearly one's theory of development. Quite small changes in one of the choices can result in dramatic changes in the performance of the model – some of them quite unexpected. Connectionist modeling offers a rich space for exploring a wide range of developmental hypotheses.

In the remainder of this article I will briefly review some connectionist modeling work that has explored some important areas in the hypothesis space of developmental theories. I aim to underscore four main lessons or insights that these models have provided:

1   When constructing theories in psychology, we use behavioral data from experiments or naturalistic observation as the objects that our explanations must fit. We attempt to infer underlying mechanisms from overt behavior. Connectionist modeling encourages us to be suspicious of the explanations we propose. Often, networks surprise us with the simplicity of the solution they discover to apparently complex tasks – sometimes leading us to the conclusion that learning may not be as difficult as we thought.

2   When we see new forms of behavior emerging in development, we are tempted to conclude that some radical change has occurred in the mechanisms governing that behavior. Connectionist modeling has shown us that small and gradual internal changes in an organism can lead to dramatic nonlinearities in its overt behavior – new behavior need not mean new mechanisms.

3   Theories of development are often domain specific. Behaviors that are discrete and associated with distinguishable modalities promote explanations that do not reach beyond the specifics of those modalities or domains. These encapsulated accounts often emphasize the impoverished character of the learning environment and lead to complex specifications of the organism's start state. Connectionist models provide a framework for investigating the interaction between modalities and a formalism for entertaining distributed as well as domain-specific accounts of developmental change. This approach fosters an appreciation of developing systems in which domain-specific representations emerge from a complex interaction of the organism's domain-general learning capacities with a rich learning environment.

4   Complex problems seem to require complex solutions. Mastery of higher cognitive processes appears to require the application of complex learning devices from the very start of development. Connectionist modeling has shown us that placing limitations on the processing capacity of developing systems during early learning can actually enhance their long-term potential. The ignorance and apparent inadequacies of the immature organism may, in fact, be highly beneficial for learning the solutions to complex problems. Small is beautiful.

Inferring Mechanisms from Behavior

Children make mistakes. Developmentalists use these mistakes as clues to discover the nature of the mechanisms that drive correct performance. For example, in learning the past tense forms of irregular verbs or plurals of irregular nouns, English children may sometimes overgeneralize the "-ed" or "s" suffixes to produce incorrect forms like "hitted" or "mans." These errors often occur after the child has already produced the irregular forms correctly, yielding the well-known U-shaped profile of development.

A dual-mechanism account

A natural interpretation of this pattern of performance is to suggest that early in development, the child learns irregular forms by rote, simply storing in memory the forms that she hears in the adult language. At a later stage, the child recognizes the regularities inherent in the inflectional system of English and reorganizes her representation of the past tense or plural system to include a qualitatively new device that does the work of adding a suffix, obviating the need to memorize new forms. During this stage, some of the original irregular forms may get sucked into this new system and suffer inappropriate generalization of the regular suffix. Finally, the child must sort out which forms cannot be generated with the new rule-based device. They do this by strengthening their memories for the irregular forms which can thereby block the application of the regular rule and eliminate overgeneralization errors (Pinker & Prince, 1988) (see figure 2).

This account of the representation and development of past-tense and plural inflections in English assumes that two qualitatively different types of mechanism are needed to capture the profile of development in young children – a rote memory system to deal with the irregular forms and a symbolic rule system to deal with the rest. The behavioral dissociation between regular and irregular forms – children make mistakes on irregular forms but not on regular forms – make the idea of two separate mechanisms very appealing. Double dissociations between regular and irregular forms in disordered populations add to the strength of the claim that separate mechanisms are responsible for different types of errors: in some language disorders children may preserve

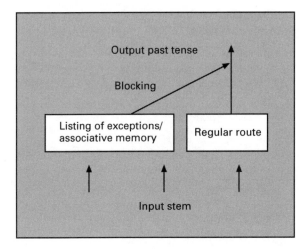

Figure 2   The dual-route model for the English past tense (Pinker & Prince, 1988). The model involves a symbolic regular route that is insensitive to the phonological form of the stem and a route for exceptions that is capable of blocking the output from the regular route. Failure to block the regular route produces the correct output for regular verbs but results in overgeneralization errors for irregular verbs. Children must strengthen their representation of irregular past-tense forms to promote correct blocking of the regular route.

performance on irregular verbs but not on regular, while in other disorders the opposite pattern is observed.

Although the evidence is consistent with the view that a dual-route mechanism underlies children's acquisition of English inflectional morphology, this is no proof that the theory is correct. There may be other types of mechanistic explanations for these patterns of behavior and development. Connectionist modeling offers a tool for exploring alternative developmental hypotheses.

Single-mechanism account

One of the earliest demonstrations of the learning abilities of neural networks was for English past-tense acquisition. Rumelhart & McClelland (1986) suggested that the source of children's errors in learning past-tense forms was to be found in their attempts to systematize the underlying relationship that holds between the verb's stem and its past-tense

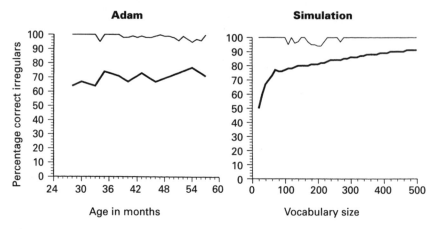

Figure 3   Network overregularization errors on irregular verbs as found in the Plunkett & Marchman (1993) simulation compared to those produced by one of 83 children analyzed by Marcus et al. (1992). The thick line indicates the percentage of regular verbs in the child's/network's vocabulary at various points in learning. Note the initial period of error-free performance and overall low error rate characteristic of the developmental profiles for the model and child. Plunkett and Marchman also demonstrated that the *types* of errors that occurred in the model closely resembled the types of errors produced by the children studied by Marcus et al.

form. For most verbs in English, the sound of the stem does not affect the past-tense form. You just add "ed" on the end. However, there is a small subset of verbs which exhibit a different relationship between stem and past-tense form. For example, there is a set of no-change verbs where the stem and past-tense forms are identical (*hit → hit*). All these verbs end in an alveolar consonant (/t/ or /d/). Other verbs undergo a particular type of vowel change (*ring → rang, sing → sang*), apparently triggered by the presence of the rhyme *-ing* in the stem. Neural networks are particularly good at picking up on these types of regularities, so Rumelhart & McClelland trained a simple network to produce the past-tense forms of verbs when presented with their stems. The details of the learning procedure and network architecture are not important here (see Plunkett (1995) for a detailed review of this and related models).

What is important is to note that Rumelhart & McClelland were successful in training the network to perform the task and that *en route* to learning the correct past-tense forms of English verbs, the network made mistakes that are similar to the kind of mistakes that children make during the acquisition of inflectional morphology. Furthermore, the network did not partition itself into qualitatively distinct devices during the process of learning – one for regular verbs and one for irregular verbs. The representation of both verb types seemed to be distributed throughout the entire matrix of connections in the network. Nevertheless, a behavioral dissociation between regular and irregular verbs was observed in the network. Most of its errors occurred on irregular verbs.

More recently, Marchman (1993) has shown that damage to a network trained on the past-tense problem results in further dissociations between regular and irregular forms: production of irregular forms remains intact while production of regular verbs deteriorates, mimicking patterns of performance observed in disordered populations. As with the Rumelhart & McClelland model, the representation of regular and irregular verbs was distributed throughout the network, i.e., there was no evidence of dissociable mechanisms.

As it turns out, there were a lot of fundamental design problems with the Rumelhart & McClelland model that made it untenable as a realistic model of children's acquisition of the English past tense (Pinker & Prince, 1988). Some of these problems have been fixed, some haven't (MacWhinney & Leinbach, 1991; Plunkett & Marchman, 1991, 1993; Cottrell & Plunkett, 1994). However, the basic insight that the original model offered still remains: The observation of behavioral dissociations in some domain of performance does not necessarily imply the existence of dissociable mechanisms driving those dissociations in behavior. Behavioral dissociations can emerge as the result of subtle differences in the graded representations constructed by these networks for different types of tasks.

Of course, just because one can train a network to mimic children's performance in learning the past tense of English verbs, does not mean that children learn them the same way as the network. The relatively simple learning system that Rumelhart & McClelland and other researchers have used to model children's learning may underestimate the complexity of the resources that children bring to bear on this problem. However, the neural network model does show that, in principle, children could use a relatively simple learning system to solve this problem. The modeling work has thereby enriched our understanding of the range and types of mechanism that might drive development in this domain.

Discontinuities in Development

Developmentalists often interpret discontinuities in behavior as manifesting the onset of a new stage or phase of development (Piaget, 1955; Karmiloff-Smith, 1979; Siegler, 1981). The child's transition to a new stage of development is usually construed as the onset of a new mode of operation of the cognitive system, perhaps as the result of the maturation of some cognitively relevant neural subsystem. For example, the vocabulary spurt that often occurs toward the end of the child's second year has been explained as the result of an insight (McShane, 1979), in which the child discovers that objects have names. Early in development, the child lacks the necessary conceptual machinery to link object names with their referents. The insight is triggered by a switch that turns on the naming machine. Similar arguments have been offered to explain the developmental stages through which children pass in mastering the object concept, understanding quantity and logical relations.

It is a reasonable supposition that new behaviors are caused by new events in the child, just as it is reasonable to hypothesize that dissociable behaviors imply dissociable mechanisms. However, connectionism teaches us that new behaviors can emerge as a result of gradual changes in a simple learning device. It is well known that the behavior of dynamical systems unfolds in a nonlinear and unpredictable fashion. Neural networks are themselves dynamical systems, and they exhibit just these nonlinear properties.

Plunkett, Sinha, Møller, & Strandsby (1992) trained a neural network to associate object labels with distinguishable images. The images formed natural (though overlapping) categories so that images that looked similar tended to have similar labels. The network was constructed so that it was possible to interrogate it about the name of an object when only given its image (call this production) or the type of image when only given its name (call this comprehension).

Network performance during training resembled children's vocabulary development during their second year. During the early stages of training, the network was unable to produce the correct names for most objects – it got a few right but improvement was slow. However, with no apparent warning, production of correct names suddenly increased until all the objects in the network's training environment were correctly labeled. In other words, the network went through a vocabulary spurt (see figure 4). The network showed a similar improvement of performance for comprehension, except that the vocabulary spurt for comprehension preceded the productive vocabulary spurt. Last but not least, the network made a series of under- and overextension errors *en route* to masterful performance (such as using the word "dog" exclusively for the family pet or calling all four-legged animals "dog") – a phenomenon observed in young children using new words (Barrett, 1995).

There are several important issues that this model highlights. First, the pattern of behavior exhibited by the model is highly nonlinear *despite the fact that the network architecture and the training environment remain constant throughout learning.* The only changes that occur in the network are small increments in the connections that strengthen the association between an image and its corresponding label. No new mechanisms are needed to explain the vocabulary spurt. Gradual changes within a single learning device are, in principle, capable of explaining this profile of development. McClelland (1989) has made a similar point in the domain of children's developing understanding of weight/distance relations for solving balance beam problems (Siegler, 1981).

Second, the model predicts that comprehension precedes production. This in itself is not a particularly radical prediction to make. However, it is an emergent property of the network that was not "designed in" before the model was built. More important is the network's prediction that there should be a nonlinearity in the receptive direction, i.e., a vocabulary spurt in comprehension. When the model was first built, there was no indication in the literature as to the precision of this prediction. The prediction has since been shown to be correct (Reznick & Goldfield, 1992). This model provides a good example of how a computational model can be used not only to evaluate hypotheses about the nature of the mechanisms underlying some behavior but also to generate predictions about the behavior itself. The ability to generate novel predictions about behavior is important in simulation work as it offers a way to evaluate the generality of the model in understanding human performance.

The behavioral characteristics of the model are a direct outcome of the interaction of the linguistic and visual representations that are used as inputs to the network. The nonlinear profile of development is a direct

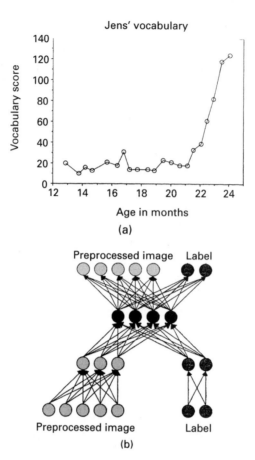

Figure 4   (a) Profile of vocabulary scores typical for many children during their second year – taken from Plunkett (1995). Each data point indicates the number of different words used by the child during a recording session. It is usually assumed that the "bumps" in the curve are due to sampling error, though temporary regressions in vocabulary growth cannot be ruled out. The vocabulary spurt that occurs around 22 months is observed in many children. It usually consists of an increased rate of acquisition of nominals – specifically names for objects (McShane, 1979). (b) Simplified version of the network architecture used in Plunkett et al., 1992. The image is filtered through a retinal preprocessor prior to presentation to the network. Labels and images are fed into the network through distinct "sensory" channels. The network is trained to reproduce the input patterns at the output – a process known as autoassociation. Production corresponds to producing a label at the output when only an image is presented at the input. Comprehension corresponds to producing an image at the output when only a label is presented at the input.

consequence of the learning process that sets up the link between the linguistic and visual inputs, and the asymmetries in production and comprehension can be traced back to the types of representation used for the two types of input. The essence of the interactive nature of the learning process is underscored by the finding that the network learns less quickly when only required to perform the production task. Learning to comprehend object labels at the same time as learning to label objects enables the model to learn the labels faster.

It is important to keep in mind that this simulation is a considerable simplification of the task that the child has to master in acquiring a lexicon. Words are not always presented with their referents and even when they are it is not always obvious (for a child who doesn't know the meaning of the word) what the word refers to. Nevertheless, within the constraints imposed upon the model, its message is clear: New behaviors don't necessarily require new mechanisms, and systems integrating information across modalities can reveal surprising emergent properties that would not have been predicted on the basis of exposure to one modality alone.

Small is Beautiful

The immature state of the developing infant places her at a decided disadvantage in relation to her mature, skilled caregivers. In contrast, the newborn of many other species are endowed with precocious skills at birth. Why is *Homo sapiens* not born with a set of cognitive abilities that match the adult of the species? This state of affairs may seem all the more strange given that we grow very few new neurons after birth and even synaptic growth has slowed dramatically by the first birthday. In fact, there may be important computational reasons for favoring a relatively immature brain over a cognitively precocious endowment.

A complete specification of a complex nervous systems would be expensive in genetic resources. The programming required to fully determine the precise connectivity of any adult human brain far exceeds the information capacity in the human genome. Much current research in brain development and developmental neurobiology points to a dramatic genetic underspecification of the detailed architecture of the neural pathways that characterize the mature human brain –

particularly in the neocortex. So how does the brain know how to develop? It appears that evolution has hit upon a solution that involves a trade-off between nature and nurture: You don't need to encode in the genes what you can extract from the environment. In other words, use the environment as a depository of information that can be relied upon to drive neural development.

The emergence of neural structures in the brain is entirely dependent upon a complex interaction of the organism's environment and the genes' capacity to express themselves in that environment. This evolutionary engineering trick allows the emergence of a complex neural system with a limited investment in genetic prewiring. Of course, this can have disastrous consequences when the environment fails to present itself. On the other hand, the flexibility introduced by genetic underspecification can also be advantageous when things go wrong, such as brain damage. Since information is available in the environment to guide neural development, other brain regions can take over the task of the damaged areas. Underspecification and sensitivity to environmental conditions permit a higher degree of individual specialization and adaptation to changing living conditions. Starting off with a limited amount of built-in knowledge can therefore be an advantage if you're prepared to take the chance that you can find the missing parts elsewhere.

There are, however, other reasons for wanting to start out life with some limits on processing capacity. It turns out that some complex problems are easier to solve if you first tackle them from an oversimplistic point of view. A good example of this is Elman's (1993) simulation of grammar learning in a simple recurrent network (see figure 5). The network's task was to predict the next word in a sequence of words representing a large number of English-like sentences. These sentences included long-distance dependencies, i.e., embedded clauses which separated the main noun from the main verb. Since English verbs agree with their subject nouns in number, the network must remember the number of the noun all the way through the embedded clause until it reaches the main verb of the sentence. For example, in a sentence like "The boy with the football that his parents gave him on his birthday chases the dog," the network must remember that "boy" and "chases" agree with each other. This is the type of phenomenon which Chomsky (1959) used to argue against a behaviorist approach to language.

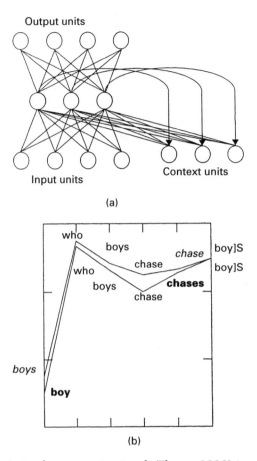

Figure 5 (a) A simple recurrent network (Elman, 1993) is good at making predictions. A sequence of items is presented to the network, one at a time. The network makes a prediction about the identity of the next item in the sequence at the output. Context units provide the network with an internal memory that keeps track of its position in the sequence. If it makes a mistake, the connections in the network are adapted slightly to reduce the error. (b) When the input consists of a sequence of words that make up sentences, the network is able to represent the sequences as trajectories through a state space. Small differences in the trajectories enable the network to keep track of long-distance dependencies.

Even after a considerable amount of training, the network did rather poorly at predicting the next word in the sequence – as do humans (cf. "The boy chases the ???"). However, it did rather well at predicting the grammatical category of the next word. For example, it seemed to know when to expect a verb and when to expect a noun, suggesting that it had learned some fundamental facts about the grammar of the language to which it had been exposed. On the other hand, it did very badly on long-distance agreement phenomena, i.e., it could not predict correctly which form of the verb should be used after an intervening embedded clause. This is a serious flaw if the simulation is taken as a model of grammar learning in English speakers, since English speakers clearly are able to master long-distance agreement.

Elman discovered two solutions to this problem. The network could learn to master long-distance dependencies if the sentences to which it was initially exposed did not contain any embedded clauses and consisted only of sequences in which the main verb and its subject were close together. Once the network had learned the principle governing subject–verb agreement under these simplified circumstances, embedded clauses could be included in the sentences in the training environment and the network would eventually master the long-distance dependencies. Exposure to a limited sample of the language helped the network to decipher the fundamental principles of the grammar which it could then apply to the more complex problem. This demonstration shows how "motherese" might play a facilitatory role in language learning (Snow, 1977).

Elman's second solution was to restrict the memory of the network at the outset of training while keeping the long-distance dependencies in the training sentences. The memory constraint made it physically impossible for the network to make predictions about words more than three or four items downstream. This was achieved by resetting the context units in the recurrent network and is equivalent to restricting the system's working memory. When the network was constrained in this fashion it was only able to learn the dependencies between words that occurred close together in a sentence. However, this limitation had the advantage of preventing the network from being distracted by the difficult long-distance dependencies. So again the network was able to learn some of the fundamental principles of the grammar. The working memory of the network was then gradually expanded so that it had an opportunity to learn the long-distance dependencies. Under these conditions, the network succeeded in predicting the correct form of verbs after embedded clauses.

The initial restriction on the system's working memory turned out to have beneficial effects: Somewhat surprisingly, the network succeeded in learning the grammar underlying word sequences when working memory started off small and was gradually expanded, while it failed when a full working memory was made available to the network at the start of training.

The complementary nature of the solutions that Elman discovered to the problem of learning long-distance agreement between verbs and their subjects highlights the way that nature and nurture can be traded off against one another in the search for solutions to complex problems. In one case, exogenous environmental factors assisted the network in solving the problem. In the other case, endogenous processing factors pointed the way to an answer. In both cases, though, the solution involved an initial simplification in the service of long-term gain. In development, big does not necessarily mean better.

Current Shortcomings

One-trial learning

Children and adults learn quickly. For example, a single reference to a novel object as a *wug* may be sufficient for a child to use and understand the term appropriately on all subsequent occasions. The connectionist models described in this paper use learning algorithms which adjust network connections in a gradualistic, continuous fashion. An outcome of this computational strategy is that new learning is slow. To the extent that one-trial learning is an important characteristic of human development, these connectionist models fail to provide a sufficiently broad basis for characterizing the mechanisms involved in development.

There are two types of solution that connectionist modelers might adopt in response to these problems. First, it should be noted that connectionist learning algorithms are not inherently incapable of one-trial learning. The rate of change in the strength of the connections in a network is determined by a parameter called the learning rate. Turning up the learning rate will result in faster learning for a given input pattern. For example, it is quite easy to demonstrate one-trial learning in a network that exploits a Hebbian learning algorithm. However, a side effect of using high learning rates is that individual training patterns can interfere with each other, sometimes resulting in undesirable instabilities in the network. Of course, interference is not always undesirable and may help us explain instabilities in children's performance such as in their acquisition of the English past tense. Generally, though, *catastrophic interference* between training patterns (when training on one pattern completely wipes out the traces of a previously trained pattern) is undesirable. One way to achieve one-trial learning without catastrophic interference is to ensure that the training patterns are orthogonal (or dissimilar) to each other. Many models deliberately choose input representations that fulfill this constraint.

An alternative response to the problem of one-trial learning in networks is to suggest that in some cases it is illusory, i.e., when individuals demonstrate what is apparently entirely new learning, they are really exploiting old knowledge in novel ways. Vygotsky (1962) coined the term *zone of proximal development* to describe areas of learning where change could occur at a fast pace. Piaget (1952) used the notion of *moderate novelty* in a similar fashion. The performance of networks can change dramatically over just a couple of learning trials. For example, the Plunkett et al. (1992) simulation of vocabulary development exhibited rapid vocabulary growth after a prolonged period of slow lexical learning. The McClelland (1989) balance beam simulation shows similar stagelike performance. In both cases, the networks gradually move toward a state of readiness that then suddenly catapults them into higher levels of behavior. Some one-trial learning may be amenable to this kind of analysis. It seems unlikely, however, that all one-trial learning is of this kind.

Defining the task and the teacher

Some network models are trained to carry out a specific task that involves a teacher. For example, the Rumelhart & McClelland (1986) model of past-tense acquisition is taught to produce the past-tense form of the verb when exposed to the corresponding stem. These are called supervised learning systems. In these simulations, the modeler must justify the source of the teacher signal and provide a rationale for the task the network is required to perform. Other models use an unsupervised form of learning such as auto-association (Plunkett et al., 1992) or prediction (Elman, 1993; Mareschal et al., 1999). In these models, the teacher signal is the input to the network itself. In general, connectionist modelers prefer to use unsupervised learning algorithms. They involve fewer assumptions about the origins of the signal that drive learning. However, some tasks seem to be inherently supervised. For example, learning that a dog is called a *dog* rather than a *chien* involves exposure to appropriate supervision. Nevertheless, it is unclear how the brain goes about conceptualizing the nature of the task to be performed and identifying the appropriate supervisory signal. Clearly, different parts of the brain end up doing different types of things. One of the challenges facing developmental connectionists is to understand how neural systems are able to define tasks for themselves in a self-supervisory fashion and to orchestrate the functioning of multiple networks in executing complex behavior.

Biological plausibility

Throughout this paper I have tried to demonstrate how connectionist models can contribute to our understanding of the mechanisms underlying linguistic and cognitive development. Yet the learning algorithms employed in some of the models described here are assumed to be biologically implausible. For example, backpropagation (Rumelhart, Hinton, & Williams, 1986) involves propagating error backward through the layers of nodes in the network. However, there is no evidence indicating that the brain propagates error across layers of neurons in this fashion, and some have argued that we are unlikely to find such evidence (Crick, 1989).

There is a considerable literature concerning the appropriate level of interpretation of neural network simulations. For example, it is often argued that connectionist models can be given an entirely functionalist interpretation and the question of their relation to biological neural networks left open for further research. In other words, the vocabulary of connectionist models can be couched at the level of software rather than hardware, much like the classical symbolic approach to cognition. Many developmental connectionists, however, are concerned to understand the nature of the relationship between cognitive development and changes in brain organization. Connectionist models that admit the use of biologically implausible components appear to undermine this attempt to understand the biological basis of the mechanisms of change.

Given the success of connectionist approaches to modeling development, it would seem wasteful to throw these simulations into the wastebasket of the biologically implausible. Clearly, the most direct way forward is to implement these models using biologically plausible learning algorithms, such as Hebbian learning. Nevertheless, there are several reasons for tentatively accepting the understanding achieved already through existing models. First, algorithms like backpropagation may not be that implausible. The neurotransmitters that communicate signals across the synaptic gap are still only poorly understood but it is known that they communicate information in both directions. Furthermore, information may be fed backward through the layered system of neurons in the cortex – perhaps exploiting the little understood back-projecting neurons in the process.

A second, related proposal assumes that algorithms like backpropagation belong to a family of learning algorithms, all of which have similar computational properties and some of which have biologically plausible implementations. The study of networks trained with backpropagation could turn out to yield essentially the same results as networks trained with a biologically plausible counterpart. There is some support for this point of view. For example, Plaut & Shallice (1993) lesioned a connectionist network trained with backpropagation and compared its behavior with a lesioned network originally trained using a contrastive Hebbian learning algorithm. The pattern of results obtained were essentially the same for both networks. This result does not obviate the need to build connectionist models that honor the rapidly expanding body of knowledge relating to brain structure and systems. However, it does suggest that given the rather large pockets of ignorance concerning brain structure and function, we should be careful about jettisoning our hard-won understanding of computational systems that may yet prove to be closely related to the biological mechanisms underlying development.

Some Lessons

A commonly held view has been that connectionism involves a *tabula rasa* approach to human learning and development. It is unlikely that any developmental connectionist has ever taken this position. Indeed, it is difficult to imagine what a *tabula rasa* connectionist network might look like. All the models reviewed in this article assume a good deal of built-in architectural and processing constraints to get learning off the ground. In some cases, such as the Rumelhart & McClelland model of the past tense, the initial constraints are quite modest. In others, such as the Mareschal et al. model of visual tracking and reaching, the initial architectural and computational assumptions are rather complex. These modeling assumptions, together with the task definition, imply a commitment to the ingredients that are necessary for learning to begin.

What is needed to get learning off the ground? We have seen that there are two main sources of constraint:

1   The initial state of the organism embodies a variety of architectural and computational constraints that determine its information-processing capabilities.
2   Environmental structure supports the construction of new representational capacities not initially present in the organism itself.

Modeling enables us to determine whether a theory about the initial state of the organism can make the journey to the mature state, given a well-defined training environment. Modeling also enables us to investigate the minimal assumptions about the initial state that are needed to make this journey.

A minimalist strategy may not necessarily provide an accurate picture of the actual brain mechanisms that underlie human development. However, it provides an important potential contrast to theories of the initial state that are based on arguments from the poverty of the stimulus. Investigating the richness of the stimulus shifts the burden away from the need to postulate highly complex, hard-wired information-processing structures. A minimalist strategy may also provide valuable insights into alternative solutions that the brain may adopt when richer resources fail.

Theories about the initial state of the organism cannot be dissociated from theories about what constitutes the organism's effective environment. Release two otherwise identical organisms in radically different environments and the representations they learn can be quite disparate. Connectionist modeling offers an invaluable tool for investigating these differences, as well as examining the necessary conditions that permit the development of the emergent representations that we all share.

Note

This manuscript was produced while the author was engaged in a collaborative book project with Jeff Elman, Liz Bates, Mark Johnson, Annette Karmiloff-Smith, and Domenico Parisi. The content of this manuscript has been influenced profoundly by discussions with them. The reader is strongly recommended to consult Elman et al. (1996) for a more wideranging and detailed discussion of the issues raised here.

References

Baillargeon, R. (1993). The object concept revisited: New directions in the investigation of infant's physical knowledge. In C. E. Granrud (Ed.), *Visual perception and cognition in infancy* (pp. 265–315). London, UK: LEA.

Barrett, M. D. (1995). Early lexical development. In P. Fletcher & B. MacWhinney (Eds.), *The handbook of child language* (pp. 362–392). Oxford: Blackwell.

Chomsky, N. (1959). Review of Skinner's verbal behavior. *Language, 35*, 26–58.

Cottrell, G. W., & Plunkett, K. (1994). Acquiring the mapping from meanings to sounds. *Connection Science, 6*(4), 379–412.

Crick, F. H. C. (1989). The real excitement about neural networks. *Nature, 337*, 129–132.

Elman, J. L. (1993). Learning and development in neural networks: The importance of starting small. *Cognition, 48*(1), 71–99.

Elman, J., Bates, E., Karmiloff-Smith, A., Johnson, M., Parisi, D., & Plunkett, K. (1996). *Rethinking innateness: Development in a connectionist perspective.* Cambridge, MA: MIT Press.

Foldiak, P. (1991). Learning invariance in transformational sequences. *Neural Computation, 3*, 194–200.

Karmiloff-Smith, A. (1979). Micro- and macrodevelopmental changes in language acquisition and other representational systems. *Cognitive Science, 3*, 91–118.

MacWhinney, B., & Leinbach, A. J. (1991). Implementations are not conceptualizations: Revising the verb learning model. *Cognition, 40*, 121–157.

Marchman, V. A. (1993). Constraints on plasticity in a connectionist model of the English past tense. *Journal of Cognitive Neuroscience, 5*(2), 215–224.

Marcus, G. F., Ullman, M., Pinker, S., Hollander, M., Rosen, T. J., & Xu, F. (1992). Overregularization in language acquisition. *Monographs of the Society for Research in Child Development, 57*(4), Serial No. 228.

Mareschal, D., Harris, P., & Plunkett, K. (1997). The effect of linear and angular velocity on 2, 4 and 6 month olds' visual pursuit behaviour. *Infant Behavior and Development, 20*(4), 435–448.

Mareschal, D., Plunkett, K., & Harris, P. (1999). A computational and neuropsychological account of object-oriented behaviours in infancy. *Developmental Science, 2,* 306–317.

McClelland, J. L. (1989). Parallel distributed processing: Implications for cognition and development. In R. G. M. Morris (Ed.), *Parallel distributed processing: Implications for psychology and neurobiology.* Oxford: Clarendon Press.

McShane, J. (1979). The development of naming. *Linguistics, 17,* 879–905.

Piaget, J. (1952). *The origins of intelligence in the child.* New York: International Universities Press.

Piaget, J. (1955). Les stades du developpement intellectuel de l'enfant et de l'adolescent. In P. O. et al. (Eds.), *Le problème des stades en psychologie de l'enfant.* Paris: Presses Univer. France.

Pinker, S., & Prince, A. (1988). On language and connectionism: Analysis of a Parallel Distributed Processing Model of language acquisition. *Cognition, 29,* 73–193.

Plaut, D. C., & Shallice, T. (1993). Deep dyslexia: A case study of connectionist neuropsychology. *Cognitive Neuropsychology, 10*(5), 377–500.

Plunkett, K. (1995). Connectionist approaches to language acquisition. In P. Fletcher & B. MacWhinney (Eds.), *Handbook of child language* (pp. 36–72). Oxford: Blackwell.

Plunkett, K., & Marchman, V. (1991). U-shaped learning and frequency effects in a multi-layered perceptron: Implications for child language acquisition. *Cognition, 38,* 43–102.

Plunkett, K., & Marchman, V. (1993). From rote learning to system building: Acquiring verb morphology in children and connectionist nets. *Cognition, 48,* 1–49.

Plunkett, K., Sinha, C. G., Møller, M. F., & Strandsby (1992). Symbol grounding or the emergence of symbols? Vocabulary growth in children and a connectionist net. *Connection Science, 4,* 293–312.

Reznick, J. S., & Goldfield, B. A. (1992). Rapid change in lexical development in comprehension and production. *Developmental Psychology, 28,* 406–413.

Rumelhart, D. E., Hinton, G. E., & Williams, R. J. (1986). Learning internal representations by error propagation. In D. E. Rumelhart, J. L. McClelland, & PDP Research Group (Eds.), *Parallel distributed processing: Explorations in the microstructure of cognition: Vol 1. Foundations* (pp. 318–362). Cambridge, MA: MIT Press.

Rumelhart, D. E., & McClelland, J. L. (1986). On learning the past tense of English verbs. In J. L. McClelland & D. E. Rumelhart (Eds.), *Parallel distributed processing: Explorations in the microstructure of cognition.* Cambridge, MA: MIT Press.

Siegler, R. (1981). Developmental sequences within and between concepts. *Monographs of the Society for Research in Child Development, 46,* Whole No. 2.

Snow, C. E. (1977). Mothers' speech research: From input to interaction. In C. E. Snow & C. A. Ferguson (Eds.), *Talking to children: Language input and acquisition.* Cambridge, UK: Cambridge University Press.

Spelke, E. S., Katz, G., Purcell, S. E., Ehrlich, S. M., & Breinlinger, K. (1994). Early knowledge of object motion: Continuity and inertia. *Cognition, 51,* 131–176.

Ungerlieder, L. G., & Mishkin, M. (1982). Two cortical visual systems. In D. J. Ingle, M. A. Goodale, & J. Mansfield (Eds.), *Analysis of visual behavior.* Cambridge, MA: MIT Press.

von Hofsten, C. (1989). Transition mechanisms in sensori-motor development. In A. de Ribaupierre (Ed.), *Transition mechanisms in child development: The longitudinal perspective* (pp. 223–259). Cambridge, UK: Cambridge University Press.

Vygotsky, L. (1962). *Thought and language.* Cambridge, MA: MIT Press.

FIVE

Motor Learning and Development

Introduction

For more than half a century, developmental psychologists thought that motor development was no more than an unfolding of a preprogrammed sequence as a result of the maturation of children's motor systems (to allow them, for instance, to carry their own weight when standing) and of their nervous systems; thus, children's motor skills were considered to be outside the realm of cognitive development research. In the last two decades, with the use of new technology and imaginative methods, Thelen and her colleagues have provided evidence to suggest that both notions are wrong. Take coordinated walking as an example. It was long believed that the coordinated alternating stepping exhibited by newborns was simply a reflex that was "turned off" around three to four months of age by an innate program of motor development. The same program was thought to be responsible for the reappearance of walking by 12–14 months of age.

In now classic studies, Thelen elicited coordinated stepping in infants after its disappearance by placing their legs under water or on a treadmill. This suggests that infants are able to carry out patterned motor behaviors at any age provided that sufficient environmental support is provided. The present article is another clever demonstration that motor development is not determined by a genetically programmed biological clock that dictates when and how a motor skill should appear. Rather, children learn to achieve motor coordination "on the spot"; coordinated motor patterns are the result of children's active integration of their cognition of the task at hand (or "at foot") and their existing motor skills, all within the constraints of a specific task context.

Data from research on how children learn to use their limbs have led Thelen and her colleagues to postulate that children's motor skills are developed in the same manner as their other cognitive abilities. This postulation forms the basis of a new, controversial theory of cognitive development: dynamic systems theory (for a comprehensive discussion, see Thelen & Smith, 1994).

Reference

Thelen, E., & Smith, L. B. (1994). *A dynamic systems approach to the development of cognition and action.* Cambridge, MA: MIT Press.

Further reading

Bogartz, R. S. (1994). The future of dynamic systems models in developmental psychology in the light of the past. *Journal of Experimental Child Psychology, 58,* 289–319.

Smith, L. B., & Thelen, E., eds (1993). *A dynamic systems approach to development: Applications.* Cambridge, MA: MIT Press.

Three-Month-Old Infants Can Learn Task-Specific Patterns of Interlimb Coordination

Esther Thelen

At three months of age, human infants cannot reach, sit, or crawl, and their limb movements appear jerky and uncontrolled. Yet within the next few months, they acquire these fundamental motor skills, and by the end of the first year, they are adept at grabbing things and moving around. Traditionally, the appearance of such motor milestones has been attributed to autonomous brain maturation (e.g., Goldman-Rakic, 1987; Konner, 1991; McGraw, 1945). In the past few years, however, developmentalists have proposed an alternative view: that even simple motor skills are learned by infants through a process of continually modifying their current abilities to the requirements of a task (Freedland & Bertenthal, 1994; Gibson, 1988; Goldfield, Kay, & Warren, 1993; Thelen et al., 1993). Such a view has refocused attention to the processes and mechanisms by which infants assemble solutions to changing opportunities in the environment and to how infants remember and generalize what they have learned. This study demonstrates that such a learning process is in place as early as three months of age, before functionally specific limb movements are normally seen. In particular, I show that when faced with a novel and attractive task, three-month-olds can assemble new and more adapted patterns of movement. I suggest that this process of discovering better solutions underlies the development of all motor skills.

An essential component of all motor-skill acquisition is the ability to coordinate the movements of the limbs. Some tasks, like crawling or walking, require complex patterns of limb alternation. Others, like catching a large ball, involve moving both limbs simultaneously to the correct positions in space. And still others, like holding a container while removing the lid, demand that one arm be held still and steady while the other performs a rotational movement.

Although for adults the coordination patterns involved in walking, catching, and opening jars are highly practiced and seemingly automatic, for infants, these patterns must be learned. Indeed, infants face the same problem as do adults who are learning new skills such as cello playing, tap dancing, or skiing. The problem for both is how to modify what the body can already do to fit the new task. This, in turn, requires some knowledge of the current patterns, the flexibility to generate different patterns, and the ability to select movements appropriate to the perceived and intended goal.

The notion that new movements arise from modifying current abilities is critical. In dynamic terms, we can speak of an organism's *coordination tendencies* (Corbetta & Thelen, 1994), *intrinsic dynamics* (Zanone & Kelso, 1991), or *comfort states* (Kugler & Turvey, 1987): All of these terms refer to coordination patterns that are easy and preferred under particular circumstances. The coordination tendencies reflect the organism's structure, its history, and its energetic status. At any point in life, new skills may involve unlearning the customary patterns as much as finding the new ones. Tap dancing is hard, for example, because it is inimical to the coordination tendencies of legs, which prefer to move in an alternating gait with particular heel-toe patterns.

There is abundant evidence that although their movements are not skilled and often seemingly without specific goals, even young infants have preferred patterns of interlimb coordination. Sometimes these patterns greatly support and facilitate later skills, but just as often they interfere. For example, the tendency to alternate legs, as seen in spontaneous kicking (Thelen, 1985) and in stepping elicited by a treadmill (Thelen, 1986), clearly lays a basis for later walking. This same tendency, however, makes jumping and skipping more difficult to learn. Likewise, although the early preference for moving both arms simultaneously (Corbetta & Thelen, 1993) is conducive to catching a large ball, it must be unlearned to open a bottle.

In this report, I address the nature of the process by which infants discover new motor patterns through modifying their current interlimb dynamics to fit the demands of a desired task. The study uses a *microge-*

netic method (Vygotsky, 1978) whereby learning is facilitated in an experimental session as an analog to how such learning may take place in real life over longer time scales. In particular, the study uses the potent paradigm of *conjugate reinforcement*, used elegantly by Rovee-Collier and her colleagues to study infant memory (Rovee-Collier, 1991). In this procedure, infants' legs are attached with a ribbon to an overhead mobile. Because their leg kicks are reinforced by the movements and sounds of the mobile, infants learn and remember an increased rate of kicking. Fisher and I (Thelen & Fisher, 1983) subsequently found that when reinforced, infants also increase the amplitude and velocity of kicks.

Because motor development requires changes of coordination as well as of movement frequency and vigor, it is important to ask when and how infants can learn and remember new patterns of movement. Indeed, Rovee-Collier, Morrongiello, Aron, and Kupersmidt (1978) reported that infants differentially increased the kick rate of the particular leg harnessed to the mobile, thus gaining "maximum control over the activity of the mobile with a minimum of energy expenditure" (p. 332). In the present study, I used the conjugate procedure to demonstrate how infants may shift coordination patterns in response to a novel context, also to produce a maximally efficient response. To do this, I simulated a real-life learning situation by making it more efficient to use a normally nonpreferred pattern. When there is no particular task condition, or when one leg is reinforced by a mobile, three-month-old infants usually kick either with both legs in alternation or with a single leg. Simultaneous, or in phase, kicking is seen less commonly (Thelen, 1985). To test whether infants could modify this preference, I yoked their legs together with a soft piece of elastic that permitted single- or alternate-leg kicking, but made simultaneous kicking much more effective for vigorous activation of the mobile because full excursions otherwise required stretching the elastic. I asked whether, over the course of the experiment, infants would discover the effectiveness of the simultaneous pattern and learn to use it in preference to the initially more stable configuration of interlimb alternation.

Method

The subjects were 24 three-month-old infants, 15 boys and nine girls, who were recruited by follow-ups of published birth announcements.

Five additional infants were recruited but did not complete the experiment because of fussiness, and data from two infants were not used because of technical problems. The study was conducted in a mobile laboratory van driven to each infant's home. The infant lay supine in a portable crib in a small room in the van that had light, neutral walls and minimally distracting features. The infant could not see a parent or experimenter during the session. A commercial infant mobile with painted wooden elements was suspended above the crib. During reinforcement conditions, I attached the infant's left leg to the stand holding the mobile by a monofilament thread sewn to an elastic ankle cuff. During nonreinforcement conditions, the thread was moved to an empty stand so that the infant's movements did not activate the mobile. To yoke the legs together, I used a 5.5-cm piece of sewing elastic attached to soft foam ankle cuffs held on by a strip of Velcro. Each entire session was videotaped with a single camera for subsequent two-dimensional digitization of the leg movements using the Peak Performance Movement Analysis System (Peak Performance Technologies, Inc., Englewood, Colorado). Parents were given a videotape of the session and a small gift for participating.

Infants wore diapers and T-shirts and two black 2.5-cm-diameter yarn balls taped on to their shins. The balls provided the points used by the Peak System to track the excursions of the legs. Infants were assigned successively to one of four experimental groups, based on whether the legs were yoked together (Y) or free (F) during three conditions: baseline (4 min, no reinforcement), acquisition (10 min, reinforcement), and extinction (2 min, no reinforcement). The patterns for the groups were as follows: Group 1, YYF; Group 2, FYF; Group 3, FFF; and Group 4, YFF. The conditions tested the effectiveness of yoking the legs alone and in combination with reinforcement of leg kicks.

Experimenters digitized the movements of both right and left marked legs for each 16-minute session at 60 Hz, resulting in a continuous time-series of the x, y coordinates of the excursions of the legs. The time-series were smoothed with a 6-Hz recursive Butterworth filter. All subsequent analyses used the excursions of the legs only in the x-direction, which was flexion toward and extension away from the infant's trunk. Although infants sometimes lowered and lifted their legs, they moved them primarily toward and away from the body. Adduction and abduction were rare. The displacement time-series and their associated velocities were analyzed and plotted in 30-second segments.

To test whether infants learned the contingency and the effect of yoking on the rate of movements of each leg, I first subjected the time-series of each leg to a computer program that detected *movement units*. A movement unit (MU) is a single event of acceleration and deceleration (Brooks, Cooke, & Thomas, 1973); for instance, in a simple kick, the flexion and extension are each one MU. An MU was counted when the increasing velocity exceeded a first threshold set to exclude very small movements and when the decreasing velocity went below a second threshold set to capture significant slowing down and reversal of direction. Two observers set these thresholds by comparing velocity profiles with movements on video in six infants; after agreement, the same thresholds were used for all infants. The program also calculated the peak velocity associated with each MU.

The second analysis determined whether yoking changed the patterns of leg coordination, that is, whether the legs moved more synchronously, or in alternation, or in some other pattern. Quantifying patterns of bilateral coordination in infants over 16 minutes of movement presents a challenge because the patterns are always changing. To capture these shifting relations, I performed a moving-window correlation on the x-displacements of both legs, with a one-second window (60 video fields) and a step of one video field, or 17 ms. Each 30-second segment thus yielded 1,755 r values (see Corbetta & Thelen, 1993, for details). For each window, a correlation of +1 indicated both legs moving toward and away from the body exactly in phase, a correlation of −1 indicated alternating or antiphase motions, and correlations around 0 meant the movements were unrelated, as when one leg was kicking and the other was still. As an index of synchrony in each segment, I chose the percentage of the 1.755 r values that equaled or exceeded $r = .4$. (See the appendix for details on correlations when both legs showed no movement.)

All the results are based on averaged values for two-minute blocks during baseline and acquisition, and for one-minute blocks during extinction to examine time-related changes in the short extinction period.

Results

First, I asked whether, as in previous work, infants increased the rate and vigor of their movements and whether there were differences in

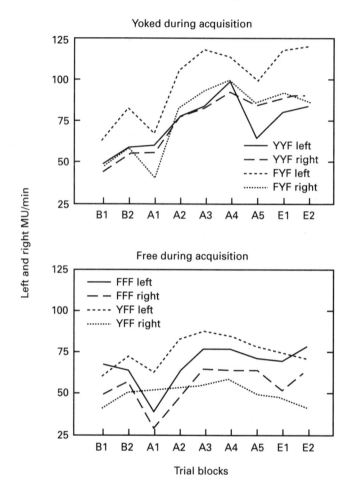

Figure 1 Mean rate of movement in movement units/minute (MU/min) for four experimental groups. (See the text for an explanation of the four groups.) The top panel shows data for Groups 1 and 2, both yoked during acquisition; the bottom panel shows data for Groups 3 and 4, free during acquisition. B = baseline, A = acquisition, E = extinction. Baseline and acquisition trial blocks are two minutes; extinction blocks are one minute.

responses for right and left legs. Subsequently, I tested for differences in patterns of coordination.

All groups learned the contingency and increased their movements. Figure 1 depicts the average number of MUs per minute for the right and

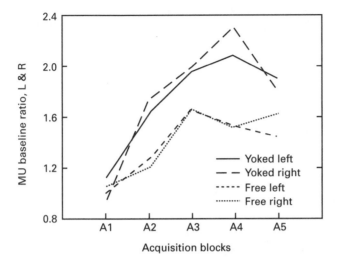

Figure 2 Mean rate of movement during learning trials expressed as a ratio of the baseline rate. Data for Groups 1 and 2 (yoked during acquisition) are collapsed, as are data for Groups 3 and 4 (free during acquisition). MU baseline ratio is the number of movement units in each acquisition block divided by the average number of movement units in baseline for left and right legs.

left legs for each of the four experimental groups. A repeated measures analysis of variance (ANOVA) yielded a significant effect for trial block ($F[8, 160] = 8.34, p < .001$) and leg ($F[1, 20] = 27.11, p < .001$), and a group-by-leg interaction ($F[3, 20] = 3.26, p < .05$).

Because there was such a wide range of initial rates of movement (ranges in baseline from 3 to 156 MU/min), and in lateral preference (note, e.g., FYF's strong left bias), I also normalized the MU rate by establishing a ratio, for each infant, of MUs per minute for each trial block divided by the infant's average MUs per minute for baseline. Then I tested the effect on this ratio of yoked versus free movement during acquisition and extinction, collapsing Groups 1 and 2 (yoked during acquisition) and Groups 3 and 4 (free during acquisition). Figure 2 shows the mean ratios for the two resultant groups during each two-minute acquisition block. A repeated measures ANOVA with these dependent variables yielded a significant effect of acquisition block ($F[6, 132] = 6.39$, $p < .001$), a nearly significant group-by-block interaction ($F[6, 132] = 2.09, p = .059$), and a significant group-by-leg-by-block interaction

($F[6, 132] = 2.45, p = .028$). Yoked infants increased their movements more over their baseline rates in both legs compared with free infants. Thus, I did not find response differentiation, that is, increased kicking in the reinforced leg versus the nonreinforced leg. However, because Rovee-Collier et al. (1978) reported response differentiation only late in the training session, I also tested as a *post hoc* test the two groups' movement ratios only in extinction. Paired *t* tests between legs showed that neither group had a significant difference between movements in right and left legs.

Next, I examined the velocity of the movements. Infants increased the vigor of their kicking, as indexed by the average peak velocity. A repeated measures ANOVA yielded a significant effect for trial block ($F[7, 147] = 5.82, p < .001$) and for leg ($F[1, 21] = .014, p = .014$), but no interactions. Although the left leg moved faster overall, I also tested the specific prediction that in unyoked infants, the left leg (the leg tied to the mobile) would kick faster than the right leg in extinction. This prediction was borne out: Paired *t* tests showed that although for the yoked group the average peak velocity of the two legs did not differ significantly, during extinction, the free group kicked faster with their left legs than with their right legs ($t = 4.30, p < .001$).

Thus, as expected, infants kicked more and faster when reinforced. They also used more directionally coordinated patterns of the two legs. Figure 3 depicts the percentage of correlation windows equal to or greater than $r = .4$ for each group over the entire session. A repeated measures ANOVA yielded a significant effect for trial block ($F[8, 160] = 4.63, p < .001$) and a significant group-by-block interaction ($F[24, 160] = 2.51, p < .001$). To account for the interaction, I conducted a *post hoc* test, collapsing the groups who were yoked and those who were free during acquisition and testing them over acquisition alone. This yielded a significant effect of group ($F[1, 22] = 11.48, p = .003$), with the yoked group's leg displacements consistently more correlated than the free group's during acquisition. The percentage of time when the two legs moved in the same direction dropped dramatically during both extinction blocks, when the yoke was removed.

Discussion

This study demonstrates that three-month-old infants were able to shift their patterns of interlimb coordination to efficiently accomplish a novel, experimentally imposed task. When their legs were tethered together, infants quickly learned to shift the prevalence of in-phase movements, and they steadily increased the proportion of the more effective pattern. Although infants whose legs were not yoked also kicked more frequently and faster to activate the mobile, their proportion of in-phase movements declined over acquisition. In contrast to the yoked groups, the infants whose legs were free during acquisition kicked faster only with the single leg attached to the mobile. Although I did not replicate Rovee-Collier et al.'s (1978) demonstration of differentiation in movement frequency, this result may be due to different methods and thresholds of counting movements. The method used in this study was sensitive to even small movements toward and away from the torso, not just those vigorous enough to be perceived as "kicks." Thus, if the response differentiation involved larger amplitudes and velocities in the reinforced leg and concurrently smaller and slower movements in the nonreinforced leg, the current method would detect velocity differences, but not necessarily frequency differences.

Many studies have shown that infants increase the frequency of leg movements under the conjugate reinforcement procedure (Rovee-Collier, 1991), as well as the force and amplitude of those movements (Thelen & Fisher, 1983). The control of the initiation of a movement and of its relative force and speed is critical for acquiring skill. But these modulations must also be applied differentially between the limbs and within the segments of a limb in order to produce a smoothly coordinated response. This study demonstrated that even at three months, infants can assemble and maintain a pattern of interlimb coordination when given a particular task constraint. The role of the task constraint is critical: When the yoke was removed during extinction, infants quickly lost the simultaneous pattern (fig. 3), although they continued a high rate of movement. This finding suggests that the bilateral pattern was assembled "on line" in response to the leg tether.

What was the effect of the tether? The elastic yoke made the kicking task different in two ways. First, it constrained the action of each individual leg so that in alternating or single-leg patterns, more forceful movements would be necessary to activate the mobile vigorously. (It should be noted again that although the tether constrained single-leg movement, it by no means prevented it. Infants could, and sometimes did, choose to move the mobile with one-leg kicks, although the full range of motion was diminished.) But equally important, I believe, is the fact that the yoking provided additional proprioceptive information

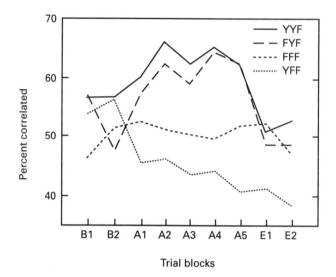

Figure 3   The percentage of moving-window correlations at .4 and above for two-leg displacement toward and away from the body in the four experimental groups. (See the text for an explanation of the four groups.) B = baseline, A = acquisition, E = extinction. Baseline and acquisition trial blocks are two minutes; extinction blocks are one minute.

about the dynamic status of the legs. That is, as each leg moved, information about the force and direction of the movement was transmitted to the opposite leg through the dynamic tug on the leg. Perhaps it is this additional information that facilitated the very rapid learning of bilateral coordination in the yoked groups. Indeed, yoking alone, even in the absence of reinforcement, appeared to facilitate coordination, as seen in Group 1's especially rapid learning. When the yoke disappeared, infants reverted to more common patterns.

In everyday learning of new motor skills, tasks and constraints also appear and disappear. Opportunities for action depend on the presence of desired objects, suitable support surfaces, postures available to the infant, helping social support, and so on. But although any particular set of opportunities may be unique, similar categories of opportunities must be commonplace. Thus, in Gibsonian terms, a certain class of objects affords reaching or mouthing, or certain surfaces afford crawling upon. What is important for understanding development is how infants discover and learn new patterns in a specific situation, as demonstrated in this experiment; how those patterns are remembered; and then how classes of solutions are generalized to novel, but similar situations. Just as the conjugate reinforcement paradigm has illuminated the general nature of infant memory, it may also prove useful for investigating the learning and remembering of motor patterns. Such studies will contribute to an emerging view of infants as active participants in their own motor-skill acquisition, in which developmental change is engendered through infants' everyday problem-solving activities.

Appendix

There were rare times during the sessions when infants did not move at all. Because no movement in both legs created a misleading +1.0 correlation, we removed from the files those data points where both the displacement and the velocity traces from the right and left legs were flat, indicating no movement. The following table reports, for each group and condition, the number of subjects from whom data were cut followed by the total percentage of time deleted:

Table A1   Number of subjects from whom data were deleted and percentage of time deleted

		Condition	
Group	Baseline	Acquisition	Extinction
1	2/0.3	4/3.0	0/0.0
2	5/3.6	5/2.5	4/15.7
3	4/4.1	6/1.8	2/1.6
4	5/3.6	5/1.9	3/3.8

References

Brooks, V. B., Cooke, J. C., & Thomas, J. S. (1973). The continuity of movements. In R. B. Stein, K. G. Pearson, R. S. Smith, & J. B. Redford (Eds.), *Control of posture and locomotion* (pp. 257–272). New York: Plenum.

Corbetta, D., & Thelen, E. (1993). Shifting patterns of interlimb coordination in infants' reaching: A case study. In S. P. Swinnen, H. Heuer, J. Massion, & P. Casaer (Eds.), *Interlimb coordination: Neural, dynamical and cognitive constraints* (pp. 413–438). New York: Academic Press.

Corbetta, D., & Thelen, E. (1994). Developmental origins of bimanual coordination: A dynamic perspective. Manuscript submitted for publication.

Freedland, R. L., & Bertenthal, B. I. (1994). Developmental changes in interlimb coordination: Transition to hands-and-knees crawling. *Psychological Science, 5*, 26–32.

Gibson, E. J. (1988). Exploratory behavior in the development of perceiving, acting, and the acquiring of knowledge. *Annual Review of Psychology, 39*, 1–41.

Goldfield, E. C., Kay, B. A., & Warren, W. H., Jr. (1993). Infant bouncing: The assembly and tuning of action systems. *Child Development, 64*, 1128–1142.

Goldman-Rakic, P. S. (1987). Development of control circuitry and cognitive function. *Child Development, 58*, 601–622.

Konner, M. (1991). Universals of behavioral development in relation to brain myelination. In K. R. Gibson & A. C. Petersen (Eds.), *Brain maturation and cognitive development: Comparative and cross-cultural perspectives* (pp. 181–223). New York: Aldine de Gruyter.

Kugler, P. N., & Turvey, M. T. (1987). *Information, natural law, and the self-assembly of rhythmic movement.* Hillsdale, NJ: Erlbaum.

McGraw, M. B. (1945). *The neuromuscular maturation of the human infant.* New York: Columbia University Press.

Rovee-Collier, C. (1991). The "memory system" of prelinguistic infants. In A. Diamond (Ed.), *The development and neural bases of higher cognitive functions. Annals of the New York Academy of Sciences, 608*, 517–536.

Rovee-Collier, C. K., Morrongiello, B. A., Aron, M., & Kupersmidt, J. (1978). Topographic response differentiation and reversal in 3-month-old infants. *Infant Behavior and Development, 1*, 323–333.

Thelen, E. (1985). Developmental origins of motor coordination: Leg movements in human infants. *Developmental Psychobiology, 18*, 1–22.

Thelen, E. (1986). Treadmill-elicited stepping in seven-month-old infants. *Child Development, 57*, 1498–1506.

Thelen, E., Corbetta, D., Kamm, K., Spencer, J. P., Schneider, K., & Zernicke, R. F. (1993). The transition to reaching: Mapping intention and intrinsic dynamics. *Child Development, 64*, 1058–1098.

Thelen, E., & Fisher, D. M. (1983). From spontaneous to instrumental behavior: Kinematic analysis of movment changes during very early learning. *Child Development, 54*, 129–140.

Vygotsky, L. S. (1978). *Mind in society: The development of higher psychological processes.* Cambridge, MA: Harvard University Press.

Zanone, P. G., & Kelso, J. A. S. (1991). Experimental studies of behavioral attractors and their evolution with learning. In J. Requin & G. E. Stelmach (Eds.), *Tutorials in motor neuroscience* (pp. 121–133). Dordrecht, The Netherlands: Kluwer Academic Publishers.

SIX

Attention

Introduction

How children's attention develops is largely a mystery. To date, little research has been conducted to answer this question, the present article being one of the rare exceptions. The authors – Mark Johnson, a cognitive developmentalist who specializes in infancy research, and Michael Posner and Mary Rothbart, cognitive psychologists who specialize in adult attention – teamed up to examine whether four-month-olds are capable of covert, as opposed to overt, attention. Overt attention refers to the deployment of attention that is consistent with observable gaze behavior (eye direction or head orientation); covert attention refers to the deployment of attention that is independent of, or different from, overt gaze behavior. For example, sometimes we may look at one thing but our attention is on something else. Studying the early development of covert attention is not only important for understanding the origin of attention but also for understanding human consciousness and how it develops, a question that, I predict, will be the biggest challenge in cognitive science in the twenty-first century.

Further reading

Johnson, M. H. (1998). Developing an attentive brain. In Raja Parasuraman (ed.), *The attentive brain* (pp. 427–43). Cambridge, MA: MIT Press.

Posner, M. I. (1995). Attention in cognitive neuroscience: An overview. In Michael S. Gazzaniga (ed.), *The cognitive neurosciences* (pp. 615–24). Cambridge, MA: MIT Press.

Facilitation of Saccades Toward a Covertly Attended Location in Early Infancy

Mark H. Johnson, Michael I. Posner, and
Mary K. Rothbart

Covert visual attention refers to mechanisms of attention involved in shifting between spatial locations or objects independently of eye and head movements (Allport, 1989; Posner & Petersen, 1990). One source of evidence for covert attention in adults is the effect of cuing attention to a particular spatial location: A briefly presented cue serves to draw covert attention to a peripheral location, resulting in the subsequent facilitation of simple manual response time to indicate the appearance of the target (Maylor, 1985; Posner & Cohen, 1980, 1984), choice manual response time to indicate the location of the target (Maylor, 1985), and latency to make a saccadic eye movement toward that location (Posner, Rafal, Choate, & Vaughan, 1985).

In the majority of these studies, subjects have been presented with 80% valid trials (in which the target appears in the location indicated by the cue) and 20% invalid trials (in which the target appears in the location opposite to the cue). However, a variety of other frequencies of valid and invalid trials have been studied. For example, if a peripheral cue indicates that the target will appear with an 80% probability at a location on the opposite side, adult subjects show a brief temporary facilitation at the cued location. This result indicates that subjects initially shift covert attention to the cued location before shifting it to the expected location of the target (Posner, Cohen, & Rafal, 1982).

It has recently been shown that infants four months of age can learn a relationship between an arbitrary central cue and the peripheral location at which an attractive target stimulus is presented. The infants move their eyes in anticipation of the target, and do so significantly more to the cued location than to the noncued location (Clohessy, 1993; Johnson, Posner, & Rothbart, 1991). How do these anticipatory eye movements occur? One possibility is that the infants form a direct association between the cue stimulus and an eye movement. Another is that this association involves shifts of covert attention similar to those observed in studies with adults involving central (endogenous) cues such as arrows pointing to the left or right location. That is, an association is formed between the cue and a direction of covert orienting. Eye movements then follow the covert shift (Fischer & Breitmeyer, 1987). Similar difficulties of interpretation arise with other studies of visual orienting in infants. Several recent studies have examined the effect of presenting an extremely brief peripheral cue prior to attractive target stimuli. While infants rarely make eye movements toward such brief cues, from four months of age, they are faster to respond (make a saccade) to a target when it appears in the (valid) cued location than in an uncued location (Hood & Atkinson 1991; Johnson, in press; Johnson & Tucker, 1993). While these studies demonstrate that young infants show facilitation of eye movements as a result of the cue presentation, it remains unclear whether the facilitation is due to a direct effect on the eye movement system or to a covert shift of attention.

In the present experiment, we attempted to obtain stronger evidence for covert shifts of attention in infants by training them to make a saccade in the direction opposite to that in which the cue appeared. To do this, we presented infants with a series of trials resembling so-called countersaccade tasks (Hallett, 1978) in adults. In these trials, a cue reliably appeared in the peripheral location (right or left) opposite from that in which the target would appear. If infants were able to perform this task, we could test whether they were covertly orienting to the cue by including occasional test trials in which the target unexpectedly appeared in the same location as the cue. In these trials, the target would have to appear quickly enough after the cue to ensure that attention was still at that location. In the adult key-press studies, when the cue indicates a high probability of an opposite target, facilitation at the cued location lasts for only about 150 ms. Occasional probe trials with the target appearing at a very brief interval after the cue at the cued location allowed us to dissociate predictive saccade planning (Haith, Hazan, & Goodman, 1988) from covert shifts of attention. If the infants were forming a simple visual association between the cue and the eye movement program, they would be expected to show a slower reaction time than normal to make a saccade to the unexpected location (since after training, the cue would directly activate a saccade in the opposite direction). In contrast, if covert shifts of attention were occurring, infants would be expected to show faster reaction times to make a saccade when the target appeared in the same spatial location as the cue (since covert attention was drawn to the cue location, resulting in a temporary facilitation of actions, including eye movements, toward that location) even though this location was unexpected.

Subjects

The 32 subjects for the experimental condition were four-month-olds (range = 115–136 days) with no known birth or other complications. The data from another 13 infants were discarded because of excessive fussing, drowsiness, or lack of sufficient trials for analysis. Ten four-month-old subjects participated in the control condition, with the data from another five subjects being discarded because of fussing or insufficient attention to the stimuli. Equal numbers of males and females were tested. As evidenced by the number of spontaneous smiles, most infants appeared to enjoy the procedure.

Procedure

The babies sat in a baby chair 75 cm from the center of three color monitors. Displays on these monitors were contolled by a Macintosh IIci microcomputer. Each trial began with the presentation of a fixation display on the central screen. The display was multicolored and dynamic, was accompanied by an auditory stimulus, and served to ensure that the infant was looking at the central screen at the beginning of each trial. The stimulus, which was composed of looming squares expanding and contracting with a regular bleeping sound, subtended 5° of visual angle.

The experimenter could see the infant by means of a video camera mounted above the display screens. When the infant was judged to be looking at the fixation pattern, the experimenter pressed a key.

The training phase of the experiment consisted of the first 12 trials, which were all the type of trial referred to as a training trial (see figure 1a). On these trials, the fixation stimulus remained on following the key press. After approximately one second, a peripheral cue stimulus appeared on one of the two side screens (29° to the right or left). Whether the peripheral stimulus appeared to the right or to the left of the fixation stimulus was determined by a pseudorandom schedule. The cue stimulus was identical on both sides: a flashing green diamond (3° in width) that was presented for 100ms. Following the offset of both the central stimulus and the cue, there was a 400-ms gap before the presentation of the target stimulus on the side screen (right or left) opposite from that in which the cue had appeared. The target stimulus was composed of a dynamic, multicolored, rotating-cogwheel shape. When the infant shifted gaze toward the target, the trial was terminated and the next one begun by presentation of the central fixation stimulus.

After 12 training trials, the test phase of the experiment began. This next phase of 20 trials was divided into five blocks of four trials each. Three of these blocks, the test blocks, contained both training trials and test trials (two of each type). Trials were randomly assigned within these blocks, and these test blocks were interleaved among blocks composed entirely of training trials: Thus, infants were exposed to six test trials within the last 20 trials of the experiment.

The test trials were identical to the training trials up to the offset of the cue and central attractor stimulus. The target stimulus then appeared in the same spatial location as the cue after an interval of 100 ms (see figure 1b).

Infants in the control group were exposed to a procedure that was identical to the above in all respects except that in all 32 of the trials, the cue stimulus was presented on both sides. There was then either a 100- or a 400-ms delay before target presentation on either the right or the left. Trial types were assigned following a pseudorandom schedule balanced within blocks of four trials each (see figure 1c).

Videotapes of infants' eye movements during the experiment were subsequently coded by persons not directly involved in the testing. Only

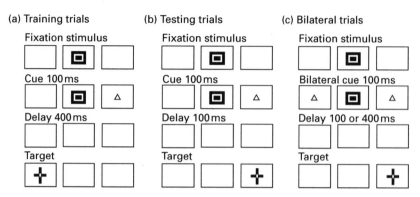

Figure 1   The sequence of stimulus presentation on the three screens for (a) training trials, (b) test trials, and (c) control group trials.

trials in which a direct saccade was made from the fixation stimulus to the target were included in the computation of median reaction time (RT). Coders recorded the time (in video frames) between the onset of the target stimulus and the start of an eye movement. Reliability between coders was very good (.96 to .99 correlation between three coders over 96 trials). Median RTs for the training trials (in the training phase), the test trials, and the training trials from the test blocks were calculated for each infant in the experimental group and for the 100- and 400-ms delay trials in the control group.

Results

Experimental group

Less than 15% of trials in the first four training trials involved a saccade to the cue stimulus prior to the appearance of the target. Thus, the cue stimulus did not normally result in the generation of a saccade. Table 1 shows the mean of median RTs to make a saccade toward the target for the first and second eight training trials during the experiment. There was a reduction in the mean median RT between the first and second of these training blocks for the experimental group.

Less than 15% of training trials in the test block involved a saccade to the cue stimulus prior to the appearance of the target. In figure 2, we show the difference in the mean of median RTs to orient toward the

Table 1 *The mean of median RTs to make a saccade toward the target*

Group	First 8 trials	Second 8 trials
Experimental (training trials)	508 ms	486 ms
Control (400-ms trials only)	467 ms	480 ms

target when it appeared in the test location, as opposed to its expected (training) location on the opposite screen. An analysis of variance with repeated measures performed on the medians revealed a significant main effect of trial type ($F[1, 30] = 6.16, p < .02$) but not sex of subject ($F[1, 30] = 3.92, p > .05$), and no significant interaction ($F[1, 30] = .114, p > .05$). Thus, both male and female infants showed a significant reduction in RTs to begin a saccade to the location in which the cue appeared, as compared with the normal training trials in which the target appeared on the opposite side. Note that the mean of median RT to make a saccade to the target in the test trials was considerably lower than in either of the blocks of training trials.

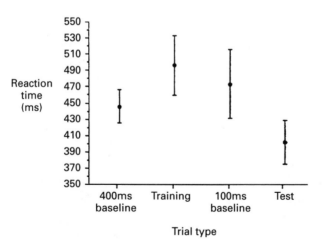

Figure 2 The means and standard errors of median RTs to orient toward the target stimulus for the training and test trials during the test blocks of the experiment. The equivalent figures for the 100- and 400-ms control group trials (baseline) are also shown.

Control group

The means of median RTs for the control group of infants for the 100- and 400-ms trials are also shown in figure 2. There was no significant difference between the RTs to make a saccade to the target in the 100- and 400-ms trials, indicating that differences found between the experimental and training trials are not attributable to the different interstimulus intervals.

Discussion

The mean median RT for responding toward the target in the cued location in the test trials was considerably lower than either the RT in the training trials or that of the appropriate (100-ms) baseline in the control group. This finding is consistent with infants making a covert shift to the cue, even when they may be planning a saccade in the opposite direction. This result replicates and strengthens previous claims in which covert shifts of attention were inferred from the effect of brief cues that were consistently followed by a target in the same spatial location (Hood & Atkinson, 1991; Johnson, in press; Johnson & Tucker, 1993). In these previous studies, however, the finding of facilitation to the cued location was also subject to the interpretation that the cue had its effect directly on the eye movement system by reducing the threshold for making a saccade. This interpretation is less plausible in the present study, in which infants were trained to make a saccade to the opposite location following presentation of the cue.

The significant reduction of RT to make a saccade toward the target during the test trials is, we believe, most consistent with the interpretation of facilitation toward a covertly attended location. This interpretation is consistent with the brain of the four-month-old infant being sufficiently mature to support covert shifts of visual attention. To date, no evidence for covert shifts of attention in infants under four months of age has been observed (for review, see Hood, in press; Johnson, in press), suggesting that the ability develops around this age. Both neuroanatomical (Conel, 1939–1967) and brain-scanning evidence relating to the postnatal growth of the human cortex suggest that the parietal lobes, a cortical region associated with covert attention (e.g., Posner & Petersen, 1990), is undergoing rapid development around four months of age. For example, results of a positron emission tomography study led Chugani, Phelps, and Mazziotta (1987) to conclude that parietal regions undergo their most rapid period of development between three and six months of age. Thus, we tentatively suggest that the maturation of parietal structures may be related to the ontogeny of covert visual attention.

The experimental group of infants showed a decrement in their RT to orient toward the target during the training trials (see table 1), which may be taken as evidence that they were learning the contingency present in the stimulus array. While this evidence is necessarily indirect, in other studies, reduction in RT has covaried with more direct measures of learning (Johnson et al., 1991). Further, the reduction in RT cannot be attributed to general experience in the task because this reduction was not seen in the control group of infants in this experiment (table 1) or in a similar experimental condition (with slightly different timing parameters) in which a single cue had no predictive validity (Johnson & Tucker, 1993).

If infants in the experimental group were learning about the relation between the cue and target during the training trials, why did the mean median RT of these infants in training trials never go below the RT of infants in the control group (who did not have a predictive cue)? It is evident from the longer RT at the start of the training session than in the equivalent control group trials (508 vs, 467 ms) that there is a considerable RT cost to orienting away from a single cue, even after a 400-ms delay. In a number of infant and adult studies, orienting in the direction opposite from the cue results in RTs greater than baseline level, and in the present study, we suggest that this cost interacts with the effects of learning. That is, the learning effect may be superimposed on a generally slowed RT due to covert shifts in the opposite direction. If this analysis is correct, the reduction in RT observed in the training trials in this task may not be directly attributable to covert shifts of attention. Rather, covert shifts and learning may independently influence saccade generation. In the case of the training trials in this study, the two factors are in opposition. Thus, while covert shifts of attention influence eye movements, they are not necessarily responsible for the learning and anticipatory effects resulting from repeated presentations of sequences of visual stimuli (Haith et al., 1988).

Clearly, a number of developments in visual orienting and attention abilities occur during the first few months of life. We hypothesize that the onset of the ability to shift covert attention is one factor responsible for the transition from an infant responsive to its environment in an automatic manner to an infant capable of following its own agenda by directing its attention under volitional control.

References

Allport, A. (1989). Visual attention. In M. I. Posner (Ed.), *Foundations of cognitive science* (pp. 631–682). Cambridge, MA: MIT Press.

Chugani, H. T., Phelps, M. E., & Mazziotta, J. C. (1987). Positron emission tomography study of human brain functional development. *Annals of Neurology*, *22*, 487–497.

Clohessy, A. B. (1993). Anticipatory eye movements in infants and adults: Using visual cues to predict event locations. Unpublished doctoral dissertation, University of Oregon, Eugene.

Conel, J. L. (1939–1967). *The postnatal development of the human cerebral cortex* (Vols. I–VIII). Cambridge, MA: Harvard University Press.

Fischer, B., & Breitmeyer, B. (1987). Mechanisms of visual attention revealed by saccadic eye movements. *Neuropsychologia*, *25*, 73–83.

Haith, M. M., Hazan, C., & Goodman, G. S. (1988). Expectation and anticipation of dynamic visual events by 3.5-month-old babies. *Child Development*, *59*, 467–479.

Hallett, P. E. (1978). Primary and secondary saccades to goals defined by instructions. *Vision Research*, *18*, 1270–1296.

Hood, B. (in press). Visual selective attention in the human infant: A neuroscientific approach. *Advances in Infancy Research*.

Hood, B., & Atkinson, J. (1991, May). *Shifting covert attention in infants*. Paper presented at the meeting of the Society for Research in Child Development, Seattle.

Johnson, M. H. (in press). Visual attention and the control of eye movements in early infancy. In C. Umilta & M. Moscovitch (Eds.), *Attention and performance XV: Conscious and nonconscious information processing*. Cambridge, MA: MIT Press.

Johnson, M. H., Posner, M. I., & Rothbart, M. K. (1991). Components of visual orienting in early infancy: Contingency learning, anticipatory looking, and disengaging. *Journal of Cognitive Neuroscience*, *3*, 335–344.

Johnson, M. H., & Tucker, L. A. (1993). The ontogeny of covert visual attention: Facilitatory and inhibitory effects. *Abstracts of the Society for Research in Child Development*, *9*, 424.

Maylor, E. A. (1985). Facilitatory and inhibitory components of orienting in visual space. In M. I. Posner & O. M. Marin (Eds.), *Attention and performance XI* (pp. 189–203). Hillsdale, NJ: Erlbaum.

Posner, M. I., & Cohen, Y. (1980). Attention and the control of movements. In G. E. Stelmach, & J. Requin (Eds.), *Tutorials in motor behavior* (pp. 243–257). Amsterdam: North-Holland.

Posner, M. I., & Cohen, Y. (1984). Components of visual orienting. In H. Bouma & D. G. Bouwhis (Eds.), *Attention and performance X: Control of language processes* (pp. 531–554). Hillsdale, NJ: Erlbaum.

Posner, M. I., Cohen, Y., & Rafal, R. D. (1982). Neural systems control of spatial orienting. *Philosophical Transactions of the Royal Society of London, 298B,* 187–198.

Posner, M. I., & Petersen, S. E. (1990). The attention system of the human brain. *Annual Review of Neuroscience, 13,* 25–42.

Posner, M. I., Rafal, R. D., Choate, L. S., & Vaughan, J. (1985). Inhibition of return: Neural basis and function. *Cognitive Neuropsychology, 2,* 211–228.

SEVEN

Perceptual Development

Introduction

What does the world look like in the eyes of infants? Do infants perceive the world the same way as we do? If they do not, how does their perceptual ability develop? William James (1890) believed that young infants are faced with a "big blooming and buzzing confusion" without any perceptual organization. Piaget (1956) posited that infants are born with impoverished perceptual abilities; their perception of the world develops slowly and is limited by their motor experiences. For example, Piaget once suggested that infants can only see things within their reach; only with increased mobility does their view of the world become more and more like that of adults.

Infancy research in the second half of the twentieth century has shown that both James and Piaget were wrong. Many empirical findings suggest that infants' perceptual abilities develop very rapidly, and in some cases this rapid development requires limited perceptual experiences. The results reported by Johnson nicely illustrate how rapidly children's perceptual abilities develop. While many infant researchers now agree that infants possess remarkable perceptual skills, the question of their origin remains controversial. Some researchers suggest that infants are born with relatively sophisticated knowledge about the physical world. Others, including Johnson, argue that they acquire such knowledge postnatally.

References

James, W. (1890). *The principles of psychology.* New York: Holt, Reinhart, & Winston.
Piaget, J. (1956). *The child's conception of space.* London: Routledge & Kegan Paul.

Further reading

Spelke, E. (1994). Initial knowledge: Six suggestions. *Cognition, 50,* 431–45.

Young Infants' Perception of Object Unity: Implications for Development of Attentional and Cognitive Skills

Scott P. Johnson

When we look at the world around us, we do not experience the surroundings as an unorganized patchwork of colors and shapes, but rather as occupied by segregated objects, each characterized by individual boundaries and surfaces. The fact that objects often occlude one another and commonly go in and out of sight seems to pose us little difficulty. We assume that most objects are continuous over space and time, that they do not generally disappear and reappear, and that one object does not necessarily end at another's boundary. This subjective experience is due to our facility at using the wide variety of visual cues available to us, as well as commonsense notions of object permanence.

How is it that even though infants are born with no visual experience, they are, after some span of time, able to visually parse the optic array into segregated objects? Some theories addressing this question have stressed innate core principles that specify the fundamental object properties such as object identity and spatiotemporal continuity (Spelke, 1990). Others have proposed that a protracted period of experience in observing and manipulating objects is necessary for development of these skills (Piaget, 1936/1952, 1937/1954). The studies reported here suggest that both of these views are incorrect. There is little evidence that infants are born equipped with sophisticated object perception abilities (contrary to theories invoking innate core principles), but there is rapid progress in perception of object boundaries, depth, and occlusion (arguing against the necessity of extended experience with objects). By the middle of the first year of life, infants seem to view objects in their surroundings in much the same way as do adults, by exploiting a variety of the visual cues available to them in the optic array.

Using Visual Information to Parse the Optic Array

Consider the problem that confronts a person who examines a scene visually. When a scene is viewed from a stationary vantage point, the accuracy of the perception of the relative distances of objects can be ascertained by attending to one or more of a variety of depth cues or to sources of information for the segregation of disparate surfaces in the visual array. These cues include linear perspective, relative and familiar size, height in the visual field, texture gradients, shading, shadows, and points of occlusion known as T-junctions, where the edge of a far surface is occluded by a near surface (Gibson, 1950). In addition, a person's two eyes pick up slightly different views of many objects, and most adults are able to use this binocular disparity as a cue to the distance of objects. Also, the lenses of the eyes accommodate appropriately via the ciliary muscles, and eye position converges and diverges as necessary, to focus on near and far objects. Finally, motion adds important information about depth. A person moving through the environment perceives retinal images of near objects to move past more quickly than images of far objects. This motion parallax is a cue to the relative distance of objects. Furthermore, the motion of objects viewed against a stationary background aids in segregation because the background is progressively occluded (deleted) and unoccluded (accreted) by the moving objects. These various cues are generally redundant in everyday experience, in that they are consistent in the information they provide about object distance, although there is variation in their individual reliability (Cutting & Vishton, 1995).

Young infants are confronted with the same optic array as are adults (although there may be limitations in visual acuity in very young infants). How do they respond to such a seemingly bewildering variety of visual cues? For that matter, how can we know what cues are used by young (prelingual) infants to parse the optic array? Is there a hierarchy of cues, such that one or more cues are used early, whereas the use of others awaits some period of development?

Infants' Parsing of the Optic Array: The Object Unity Task

One way in which these questions have been addressed is with displays depicting partly occluded subjects (Kellman & Spelke, 1983). For example, the display in figure 1a depicts two rod parts, moving back and forth, above and below a box. When adults view such a display, they typically assume the unity of the rod parts, perhaps in part because the visible rod parts are aligned and undergo common motion above and below the box.

To investigate infants' perception of object unity in this display, researchers use what is called a *habituation* procedure. The first step is to present the display to each infant repeatedly and determine the number of repetitions following which the infant's looking times become progressively shorter. This habituation is thought to reflect a decrement of interest on the infant's part. The next step is to follow habituation immediately with the presentation of a different (test) display. If the infant recovers interest immediately (i.e., looks longer at the display), the researcher concludes that the infant has noted the difference. However, if the infant's looking times continue to be short, the researcher concludes that either the infant does not note any difference between the habituation and test stimuli or the test stimulus is not sufficiently novel to elicit recovery. In the case of the rod-and-box display, preference for a broken rod, or two disjoint rod parts (fig. 1c), over a complete rod (fig. 1b) after habituation is taken to indicate that the infant perceived the two rod parts in the habituation display as belonging to a single, partly occluded object. That is, the complete rod is familiar; the broken rod, relatively novel. (A control rod-and-box display is also used, to assess whether there is an inherent preference for either test display. Typically, a control display contains two rod parts and a box, but only the top rod part moves while the bottom part remains stationary. All the studies reported here have employed such a control condition, and have found no consistent preference for either test display in any case.)

In summary, then, the logic used in interpreting infants' reactions to the stimuli used in the rod-and-box displays is as follows. An infant is habituated by presenting a sequence of rod-and-box displays until looking time declines. If, after habituation, the infant looks longer at the broken rod than at the complete rod, it is assumed that the rod parts in

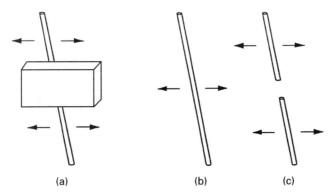

(a)   (b)   (c)

Figure 1 The rod-and-box procedure (after Kellman & Spelke, 1983). Individual infants are presented with the display shown in (a) until they habituate (i.e., the time they look at the display is less than half the original level, averaged over trials). Following habituation, infants are presented with complete-rod (b) and broken-rod (c) test displays, either on alternating trials or side by side.

the habituation stimulus were perceived as a complete, partly occluded rod. In contrast, if the infant looks longer at the complete rod, the rod parts in the habituation stimulus are assumed to have been perceived as disjoint objects. If there is no preference for either test display, it is assumed that the infant's perception of object unity may have been ambiguous. The experimenter manipulates visual cues in the habituation stimulus to determine the cues affecting the way in which infants parse the visual display into segregated objects.

How Do Young Infants Perceive Object Unity?

Early studies of the cues that support perception of object unity (Kellman & Spelke, 1983; Kellman, Spelke, & Short, 1986) concluded that common motion of the rod parts, relative to a stationary box and background, was the primary visual cue used by infants in determining that the rod parts belong to a unified object. This claim was based on the fact that infants who were four months of age preferred the broken rod over the complete rod after viewing displays in which both rod parts moved (either horizontally, vertically, or in depth) behind a stationary box. In contrast, these infants showed no preference for either test display after viewing habituation displays in which a box moved in front of a stationary rod, or both rod and box moved together, or there was no motion.

More recent studies also using rod-and-box displays have begun to call into question the notion that common motion uniquely supports young infants' perception of object unity. Note that if only common motion supports perception of object unity in young infants, then habituation to displays in which this cue is available should result in consistent posthabituation preference for the broken rod.

My colleagues and I began our investigations in this area by asking if three-dimensional depth cues are necessary to support young infants' perception of object unity (Johnson & Náñez, 1995). We presented two-dimensional (computer-generated) rod-and-box displays against a textured background to four-month-olds until habituation (see fig. 2a). Test displays of broken and complete rods followed in alternation. The rods and rod parts in the test displays moved back and forth in an identical manner. The infants consistently preferred the broken rod, suggesting that whatever cues remained in the display were sufficient to support four-month-olds' perception of object unity.

We next asked if accretion and deletion (i.e., progressive uncovering and covering) of background texture contributes to young infants' perception of object unity, perhaps as a supplementary depth cue (Johnson & Aslin, 1996). For this investigation, we used two-dimensional rod-and-box displays identical to those in the study just described but for a matte black background (no texture) (fig. 2b). Four-month-olds showed no consistent preference for either test display. This result may seem

---

Figure 2 Habituation and test displays, and looking times to test displays in experimental and control conditions, from studies of four-month-olds' perception of object unity. In the experimental displays, the rod parts moved back and forth together, and the box was stationary. In the control displays, only the top rod part moved while the bottom remained stationary. All displays were two-dimensional and computer-generated. The preferred test display is inferred to be novel relative to the habituation display. Displays and looking times are shown for rod-and-box displays with background texture and aligned rod edges (a), with no background texture and aligned rod edges (b), with background texture and nonaligned but relatable rod edges (c), and with background texture and nonaligned and nonrelatable rod edges (d).

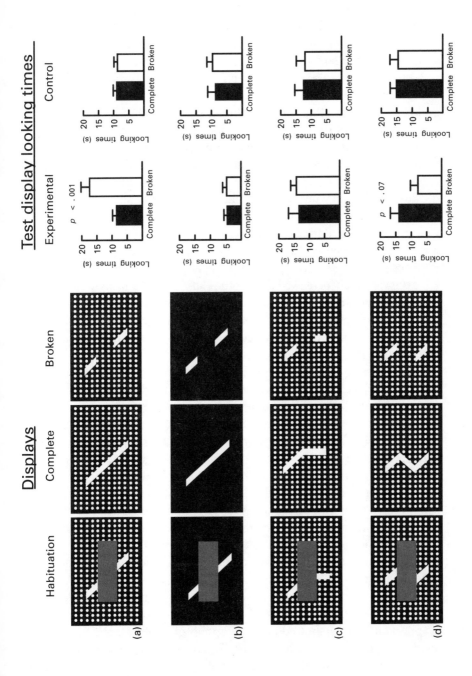

Test display looking times

somewhat counterintuitive, in that it is not immediately obvious how accretion and deletion of texture on the far surface (the background) contributes to determining if the rod parts are connected behind the near surface (the box).

We interpreted this result by appealing to an account of adults' perception of the connectedness of edges behind an occluder. Nakayama and his colleagues (Nakayama & Shimojo, 1990; Nakayama, Shimojo, & Silverman, 1989) noted that in order to segregate objects appropriately in an occlusion display, the viewer must determine in which depth plane each surface resides (*depth placement*), as well as discern the outer contours of each surface (*contour ownership*), realizing that the contours of some objects may be partly occluded. For example, in a rod-and-box display, the viewer must perceive that the box is closer than the rod and that the rod's boundary does not end at the top and bottom edges of the box. If either process is disrupted, then perception of the rod parts' unity may not occur. In the present study, it appears that the infants may not have appropriately perceived the depth relations in the display. Interestingly, four-month-olds have been found to perceive unity in three-dimensional displays without background texture (Slater et al., 1990). Thus, these infants used other cues (such as binocular disparity) to determine depth placement of the display elements.

Our next study explored the role of the alignment of rod edges in perception of object unity (Johnson & Aslin, 1996). We devised two displays in which the rod edges were nonaligned; the rod parts moved back and forth against a textured background. In one display (fig. 2c), the edges were oriented such that they were relatable (i.e., they would meet if extended behind the box, as in figure 3b; see Kellman & Shipley, 1991, for a formal definition of relatability). In the other display (fig. 2d), the edges were nonrelatable (see fig. 3c). The infants appeared to strongly rely on relatability as information for edge connectedness. When the rod edges were nonaligned but relatable, the pattern of posthabituation preference indicated ambiguity regarding their unity. However, when the rod edges were nonaligned and nonrelatable, the infants seemed to perceive the rod parts as disjoint, despite the common motion. Again, this result is consistent with a two-process account of perception of object unity, involving both depth placement and contour ownership. The previous study showed how disruption of depth placement interferes with perception of object unity. The results from the nonaligned-edge conditions in this study suggest that contour ownership also plays an important role in this process.

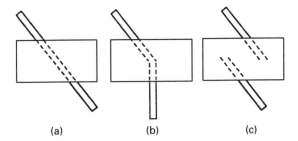

(a)   (b)   (c)

Figure 3 Rod-and-box arrangements demonstrating alignment and relatability. Edges are defined as relatable if they would meet at an obtuse angle if extended behind an occluder (see Kellman & Shipley, 1991, for details). In (a), the two rod parts are aligned. Additionally, they are relatable. The edges of the two rod parts would meet if extended behind the box (indicated by the dotted lines). In (b), the two rod parts are not aligned, but they are relatable. In (c), the rod parts are neither aligned nor relatable.

Accounting for Differences in Perception of Object Unity in Various Displays: The Threshold Model

How is it possible to reconcile the results from the earlier and later studies, which seem to disclose such different roles of individual visual cues in infants' perception of object unity? There does not seem to be a single cue, such as common motion, central to this process. Rather, perception of object unity appears to be determined by a variety of cues. Aslin and I (Johnson & Aslin, 1996) have proposed a *threshold model,* stipulating that perception of object unity occurs in infants when *sufficiency* of visual information meets *efficiency* of perceptual skills, cognitive skills, or both. That is, there must be an adequate number of cues available in an occlusion display, and infants must be sensitive to them, in order for object segregation to occur. Four-month-olds' perception of object unity in some displays but not others indicates that infants at this age are differentially sensitive to available cues. By adding or deleting individual cues in habituation displays, researchers can learn which cues a particular age group uses.

The threshold model is more descriptive than explanatory. It is not yet possible to predict from the model whether a particular set of cues in a given occlusion display will support perception of object unity for infants at a given age. However, the model is consistent with what is currently known about infants' parsing of the optic array, and we hope that further research will provide a more thorough outline of the development of cue use in infants.

The model is also consistent with recent theories of human visual perception that characterize the visual system as utilitarian (Ramachandran, 1988). That is, the visual system is designed to take advantage of whatever information is available at the time: Perception is akin to a "bag of tricks" that are used because they work, across real-world situations, well enough to be reasonably reliable. The often-cited apparent sophistication of infants' perceptual and cognitive skills (e.g., Baillargeon, 1993) may by partly due to the redundancy of the cues available in most situations. When cues are examined systematically, it does not seem surprising that perceptual skills are taxed, because redundancy is controlled.

The Emergence of Perception of Object Unity

Thus far, I have restricted the discussion to four-month-olds. Does perception of object unity at this young age imply contributions of innate principles underlying object perception (e.g., Spelke, 1990)? If so, one might expect newborn infants to perceive object unity in occlusion displays. However, newborns have been found to consistently prefer a complete rod to a broken rod after habituation to a rod-and-box display (Slater et al., 1990). This response pattern is the opposite of the one reported in four-month-olds, and suggests that some period of development is necessary for perception of object unity to emerge in infants.

Recently, Náñez and I investigated the emergence of perception of object unity by showing rod-and-box displays to two-month-old infants, asking whether their responses would be more similar to those of four-month-olds or newborn infants (Johnson & Náñez, 1995). Interestingly, the two-month-olds responded like neither of these age groups, instead showing an approximately equal preference for the two test displays (fig. 4a). This finding might be interpreted to indicate that two-month-olds are not fully capable of perceiving object unity, but recall the threshold model – it might be that with additional visual information, infants at this young age would be more likely to perceive the unity of the rod parts.

This hypothesis was tested in three ways, all of which involved simply showing more of the rod behind occluders that were reduced in size (Johnson & Aslin, 1995). In one display, the box was made smaller in height; in a second display, a vertical gap was placed in the box; and in a third display, the box contained two gaps displaced horizontally (figs. 4b, 4c, and 4d, respectively). Each display permitted more of the rod to be seen as it moved back and forth behind the box. In all three conditions, two-month-olds showed preferences for the broken rod, indicating early perception of object unity. These results support the threshold model. That is, it seems likely that the threshold for the level of visual information required for two-month-olds' perception of object unity is higher than the threshold of four-month-olds. When this requirement is met in displays that are richer in cues, the younger infants respond to unity.

What about even younger infants? Is it possible that the displays used previously to assess newborns' perception of object unity (i.e., Slater et al., 1990) were not sufficiently rich in cues to meet what might be expected to be a very high threshold? This question was recently addressed by showing newborns full-cue rod-and-box displays, rich in visual information in support of object unity (Slater, Johnson, Brown, & Badenoch, 1996). Specifically, the cues included common motion of the rod parts relative to a stationary box and background, color differences between surfaces (known to be discriminable by newborns), reduced size of the occluder, a large difference in depth between rod and box, and alignment of rod edges. However, even after habituation to the rich-cue display, the newborns showed a reliable preference for the complete rod. Thus, there is little evidence to suggest that they took advantage of the extra visual information available to perceive unity.

It may be that newborns lack not the perceptual skills, but rather the cognitive skills necessary to infer the hidden region of the rod. Although one might argue that cognitive skills are not involved in this task (if one takes object unity to be an object property that is available directly, much as shape, color, and depth are), I would argue that cognitive skills are in fact involved because the viewer must take account of an object part that cannot be seen directly. Indeed, the responses of newborns described here and elsewhere (Slater et al., 1990) are most consistent with newborns' perception of the separated rod surfaces as disjoint objects.

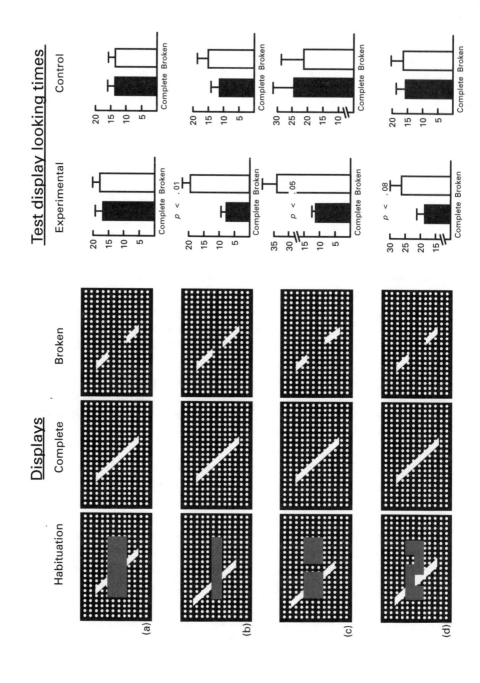

Test display looking times

Displays

Habituation | Complete | Broken

Experimental | Control

Figure 4   Habituation and test displays, and looking times to test displays in experimental and control conditions, from studies of two-month-olds' perception of object unity. Again, all displays were two-dimensional and computer-generated. Displays and looking times are shown for rod-and-box displays with background texture and aligned rod edges (a), with small boxes (b), with boxes having a single gap (c), and with boxes having a double gap (d). The displays in (a) are identical to those shown to four-month-olds (fig. 1a). In the single-gap and double-gap control conditions, the rod was not visible at any time in the gap.

◄───────────────────────────────────────

Concluding Remarks

The most interesting questions remaining involve how it is that infants develop perception of bounded, segregated, continuous objects after only a few months of visual experience. The studies of perception of object unity described in this review clarify many aspects of young infants' object perception skills, but the mechanisms underlying emergence of these fundamental abilities remain unknown. At this point, the data suggest that the visual system is opportunistic in its development, taking advantage of whatever information is available at the time. No doubt some mechanisms of development consist of rapid improvements in infants' attention to, and interpretation of, visual cues they encounter in their daily activities.

References

Baillargeon, R. (1993). The object concept revisited: New directions in the investigation of infants' physical knowledge. In C. E. Granrud (Ed.), *Visual perception and cognition in infancy* (pp. 265–315). Hillsdale, NJ: Erlbaum.

Cutting, J. E., & Vishton, P. M. (1995). Perceiving layout: The integration, relative potency, and contextual use of different information about depth. In W. Epstein & S. Rogers (Eds.), *Handbook of perception and cognition: Vol. 5. Perception of space and motion* (pp. 69–117). San Diego: Academic Press.

Gibson, J. J. (1950). *The perception of the visual world*. Boston: Houghton Mifflin.

Johnson, S. P., & Aslin, R. N. (1995). Perception of object unity in 2-month-old infants. *Developmental Psychology, 31*, 739–745.

Johnson, S. P., & Aslin, R. N. (1996). Perception of object unity in young infants: The roles of motion, depth, and orientation. *Cognitive Development, 11,* 161–180.

Johnson, S. P., & Náñez, J. E. (1995). Young infants' perception of object unity in two-dimensional displays. *Infant Behavior and Development, 18,* 133–143.

Kellman, P. J., & Shipley, T. F. (1991). A theory of visual interpolation in object perception. *Cognitive Psychology, 23,* 141–221.

Kellman, P. J., & Spelke, E. S. (1983). Perception of partly occluded objects in infancy. *Cognitive Psychology, 15,* 483–524.

Kellman, P. J., Spelke, E. S., & Short, K. R. (1986). Infant perception of object unity from translatory motion in depth and vertical translation. *Child Development, 57,* 72–86.

Nakayama, K., & Shimojo, S. (1990). Toward a neural understanding of visual surface representation. *Cold Spring Harbor Symposia on Quantitative Biology, 40,* 911–924.

Nakayama, K., Shimojo, S., & Silverman, G. H. (1989). Stereoscopic depth: Its relation to image segmentation, grouping, and the recognition of occluded objects. *Perception, 18,* 55–68.

Piaget, J. (1952). *The origins of intelligence in children* (M. Cook, Trans.). New York: International Universities Press. (Original work published 1936.)

Piaget, J. (1954). *The construction of reality in the child* (M. Cook, Trans.). New York: Basic Books. (Original work published 1937.)

Ramachandran, V. S. (1988). Interactions between motion, depth, colour and form: The utilitarian theory of perception. In C. Blakemore (Ed.), *Visual coding and efficiency (Essays in honour of H. B. Barlow)* (pp. 346–360). Cambridge, UK: Cambridge University Press.

Slater, A., Johnson, S. P., Brown, E., & Badenoch, M. (1996). Newborn infants' perception of partly occluded objects. *Infant Behavior and Development, 19,* 145–148.

Slater, A., Morison, V., Somers, M., Mattock, A., Brown, E., & Taylor, D. (1990). Newborn and older infants' perception of partly occluded objects. *Infant Behavior and Development, 13,* 33–49.

Spelke, E. S. (1990). Principles of object perception. *Cognitive Science, 14,* 29–56.

Further reading

Kellman, P. J. (1993). Kinematic foundations of infant visual perception. In C. E. Granrud (Ed.), *Visual perception and cognition in infancy* (pp. 121–173). Hillsdale, NJ: Erlbaum.

Spelke, E. S., & Van de Walle, G. A. (1993). Perceiving and reasoning about objects: Insights from infants. In N. Eilan, R. McCarthy, & B. Brewer (Eds.),

Spatial representation: Problems in philosophy and psychology (pp. 132–161). Cambridge, MA: Blackwell.

Yonas, A., & Granrud, C. E. (1985). The development of sensitivity to kinetic, binocular, and pictorial depth information in human infants. In D. J. Ingle, M. Jeannerod, & D. N. Lee (Eds.), *Brain mechanisms and spatial vision* (pp. 113–145). Dordrecht, Netherlands: Martinus Nijhoff.

EIGHT

Early Numerical Knowledge

Introduction

Cognitive development research, in a nutshell, studies how children think. Thinking, by definition, is a mental process that is private and not directly accessible to outside observers. How to get access to the inaccessible is the ultimate challenge for cognitive development research; ingenuity and inventiveness are needed for such an endeavor. Karen Wynn's paper is an excellent example of how methodological ingenuity and inventiveness can lead to a startling discovery: four-month-olds can count and even add and subtract small numbers!

The method used by Wynn is based on a phenomenon known to many people who like magic shows. When a magician pulls a rabbit out of an empty hat, we are not only entertained but also puzzled: How did she do it? What are the possible explanations of this apparently impossible feat? Cognitive development researchers pursue the puzzle even further: Why are we puzzled about a rabbit appearing from an empty hat but not puzzled about snow flakes falling from an empty sky? What do we do when we are puzzled? As it turns out, normally we look *longer* at the impossible event and show surprised expressions. The reason for our puzzlement is because the magician's trick violates our knowledge about how the world should operate. Conversely, if we do not have such expectations, then we should not be puzzled or surprised. In other words, we may spend the same amount of time looking at the magician's trick as looking at the falling snow.

This surprise test procedure has been applied by researchers to uncover infants' incredible early knowledge about physics (such as gravity, support, solidity etc.; Baillargeon, 1994). Wynn uses this procedure to study infants' numerical or mathematical understanding. In a typical experiment, she might show the infant one or two objects for a while. Then a screen appears in front of the object(s) and hides them.

While infants are watching, a hand appears that either removes an object from, or adds an object, behind the screen. Then the screen is removed to reveal the original display (i.e., as if nothing has been added or removed). This should be surprising to you if you understand addition and subtraction. The question that Wynn tries to answer is whether infants would be surprised as you are. Read on and be prepared to be surprised by her findings!

Reference

Baillargeon, R. (1994). How do infants learn about the physical world? *New Directions in Psychological Science, 3,* 133–40.

Further reading

Xu, F., & Carey, S. (1996). Infants' metaphysics: The case of numerical identity. *Cognitive Psychology, 30,* 111–53.

Infants Possess a System of Numerical Knowledge

Karen Wynn

A mathematical system can be characterized by a body of mathematical entities, along with a set of procedures for operating upon these entities to yield further information. For example, the system of euclidean geometry is composed of a set of geometrical entities (point, line, plane, angle, etc.), together with a system of inferential reasoning that can be applied over these entities to reveal further geometrical knowledge. Similarly, the natural numbers, in conjunction with arithmetical functions such as addition and multiplication, form another mathematical system.

My colleagues and I have been investigating human infants' numerical abilities. The picture emerging from this research is one of impressive early competence and suggests that a system of numerical knowledge may be part of the inherent structure of the human mind: Infants can mentally represent different numbers and have procedures for manipulating these numerical representations to obtain further numerical information. In this review, I summarize these empirical findings, describe a specific model for how infants might represent and reason about number, and discuss briefly how this initial system of knowledge may relate to later numerical knowledge.

Infants Can Represent Number

Infants can distinguish different small numbers of visual items, such as dots, points of light, and photographs of household objects. In studies showing this capacity, each infant is repeatedly presented with arrays containing a certain number of items, until the infant's looking time to the arrays decreases to a prespecified criterion (typically to half of his or her initial levels of looking). At this point, the infant is considered to be *habituated* to the stimuli. Following habituation, the infant is presented with new displays, some containing the original number of items and some containing a new number of items. It is well known that infants tend to look longer at things that are new or unexpected to them; therefore, if infants can distinguish between the two numbers, they should look longer at the displays containing the new number of items. It has been found that when infants are habituated to displays of two items, they then look longer when shown three items, and vice versa, showing that they can distinguish the two kinds of arrays. Under some conditions, infants in this type of experiment will also distinguish three items from four.[1]

Infants can enumerate other kinds of entities in addition to visual items. After being habituated to arrays of two objects, infants looked longer at a black disk when it emitted two sequential drumbeats than when it emitted three; infants habituated to arrays of three objects looked longer at the disk when it emitted three drumbeats than when it emitted two.[2] Thus, the infants not only enumerated both the objects and the drumbeats, but also recognized numerical correspondences between them. This finding indicates that infants' numerical representations are abstract ones that can apply to input from different perceptual modalities.

We have recently shown that six-month-olds can also enumerate physical actions in a sequence.[3] One group of infants was habituated to a puppet jumping two times, another to a puppet jumping three times. On each trial, the puppet jumped the required number of times, with a brief pause between jumps. Upon completing the jump sequence, the puppet stood motionless, and infants' looking time to the stationary puppet was measured. Following habituation, both groups of infants were presented with test trials in which the puppet sometimes jumped two times and sometimes jumped three times. Infants looked reliably longer at the puppet on trials containing the new number of jumps (fig. 1a). The structure of jump sequences ruled out the possibility that infants were responding on the basis of the tempo or overall duration of the sequences rather than number.

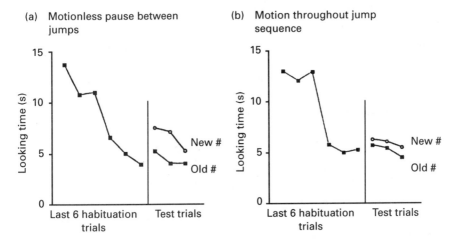

Figure 1 Six-month-olds' looking times on the last six habituation trials and on old- and novel-number test trials for jump sequences (a) in which interjump intervals were motionless and (b) in which the puppet was in continuous motion.

In a second, similar experiment, we asked whether infants could discriminate between two- and three-jump sequences when the puppet remained in constant motion throughout each sequence; between jumps, the puppet's head wagged from side to side in an exaggerated fashion. In these sequences, the individual actions of the puppet could not be defined through a low-level perceptual analysis (on the basis of, e.g., the presence or absence of motion), but required an analysis of the pattern of motion in the sequence. There is, in fact, more than one way to pick out distinct actions in such a sequence; for example, one might pick out the individual jumps as distinct from the head-wagging activity and count them, or one might pick out the repeating pattern of "jumping followed by head wagging" and count its repetitions. Thus, the identification of discrete actions within a continuous sequence of motion is a cognitive imposition. Nonetheless, infants again looked significantly longer at the novel-number test sequences (fig. 1b), indicating that they are able to parse a continuous sequence of motion into distinct segments on the basis of the structure of motion in the sequence, and to enumerate these segments. Thus, infants can enumerate complex, cognitively determined entities.

Visual items, sounds, and physical actions are all very different kinds of entities. Typically, in experiments of the kind just described, visual items or patterns are presented to infants simultaneously, enduring together through time and occupying different locations in space; thus, the identification of visual items requires primarily an analysis of spatial information. Sounds, in contrast, have no spatial extent (though a sound may emanate from a specific physical location, it is perceived independently of it), but typically occur at different points in time and endure only temporarily, so their identification relies primarily on an analysis of temporal information. Finally, actions consist of internally structured patterns of motion that unfold over time, and so their identification entails an integration of both spatial and temporal information. The fact that infants can enumerate entities with quite distinct properties, presented in different perceptual modalities, indicates that infants possess abstract, generalizable representations of small numbers, and that these representations are independent of the perceptual properties of specific arrays.

Infants Have Procedures that Support Numerical Reasoning

Possessing genuine numerical knowledge entails more than simply the ability to represent different numbers. A numerical system is composed not only of numbers, but also of procedures for manipulating these numbers to yield further numerical information. Infants might be able to determine numbers of entities without being able to reason about these numbers or to use them to make numerical kinds of inferences. If so, we would not want to credit infants with a system of numerical knowledge.

Studies conducted in my laboratory show that five-month-old infants are able to engage in numerical reasoning: They have procedures for manipulating their numerical representations to obtain information of the relationships that hold between them. In these experiments, the infant is shown a small collection of objects, which then has an object added to or removed from it. The resulting collection of objects that is subsequently shown to the infant is either numerically consistent or inconsistent with the addition or subtraction. Because infants look longer at outcomes that violate their expectations, if they are anticipating the number of objects that should result, they will look longer at inconsistent outcomes than at consistent ones.

In the first experiment,[4] one group of five-month-old infants was shown an addition situation in which one object was added to another identical object, and another group was shown a subtraction situation in which one object was removed from a collection of two objects. Infants in the 1 + 1 group saw one item placed into a display case. A screen then rotated up to hide the item, and the experimenter brought a second item into the display and placed it out of sight behind the screen (fig. 2, top). The 2 − 1 group saw two items placed into the display. After the screen rotated up to hide them, the experimenter's hand reentered the display, went behind the screen, and removed one item from the display (fig. 2, bottom). For both groups, the screen then dropped to reveal either one or two items. Infants' looking times to the displays were then recorded.

Pretest trials, in which infants were simply presented with displays of one and two items to look at, revealed no significant preference for one number over the other, and no significant difference in preference between the two groups. But there was a significant difference in the looking patterns of the two groups on the test trials: Infants in the 1 + 1 group looked longer at the result of one item than the result of two items; infants in the 2 − 1 situation looked longer at the result of two items that the result of one item (fig. 3).

In another experiment, infants were shown an addition of one item to another, and the final number of objects revealed was either two or three. Again, infants looked significantly longer at the inconsistent outcome of three objects than at the consistent outcome of two objects (fig. 4). (Pretest trials revealed no baseline preference to look at three items over two items.)

These results are robust; they have been obtained in other laboratories, using different stimuli and with variations in the procedure.[5] One study tested the possibility that infants were anticipating certain spatial locations to be filled and others empty, rather than anticipating the number of items in the display. One group of five-month-old infants was presented with 1 + 1 situations, and another group was presented with 2 − 1 situations; for both groups, the outcome was sometimes one object and sometimes two objects. All the objects were placed on a large revolving plate in the center of the display, which was occluded when the screen was raised. The objects were therefore in continuous motion, so no object retained a distinct spatial location throughout the experimental operation. Nonetheless, infants looked reliably longer at the

Sequence of events: 1 + 1 = 1 or 2

1. Object placed in case 2. Screen comes up 3. Second object added 4. Hand leaves empty

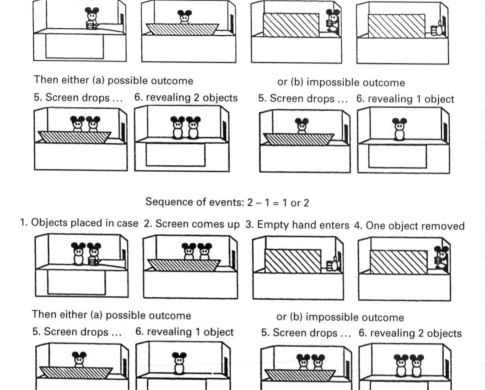

Then either (a) possible outcome   or (b) impossible outcome

5. Screen drops ... 6. revealing 2 objects   5. Screen drops ... 6. revealing 1 object

Sequence of events: 2 − 1 = 1 or 2

1. Objects placed in case 2. Screen comes up 3. Empty hand enters 4. One object removed

Then either (a) possible outcome   or (b) impossible outcome

5. Screen drops ... 6. revealing 1 object   5. Screen drops ... 6. revealing 2 objects

Figure 2 Sequence of events shown in Wynn,[4] Experiments 1 and 2. *Source*: Courtesy of *Nature*.

numerically incorrect outcomes, showing that they were computing over the number of objects, not over the filled-or-empty status of different spatial locations.[6]

A Mechanism for Determining and Reasoning about Number

The ability to discriminate small numbers of entities precisely, and in some cases to perform numerical operations over these numbers, has

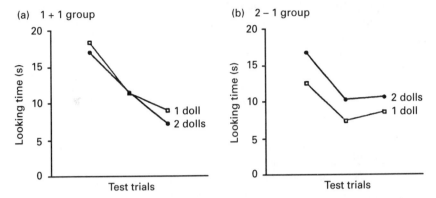

Figure 3   Five-month-olds' looking times to outcomes of one doll and two dolls following event sequences in which one doll was added to a display of one doll (a) or one doll was taken away from a display of two dolls (b).

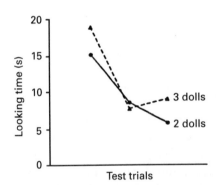

Figure 4   Five-month-olds' looking times to two versus three dolls after viewing a sequence of events in which one doll was added to a display of one doll.

been documented in a variety of warm-blooded vertebrate species as well as in human infants. This suggests that a common mechanism may have evolved to perform this function at a distant point in evolutionary history.[7]

The *accumulator* is a model of a mental mechanism for representing number, originally proposed to account for numerical abilities in rats.[8] The accumulator mechanism can account for both the ability to represent number and the ability to operate over these numerical representations.[1] This mechanism produces pulses at a constant rate; these pulses can be passed into an accumulator by the closing of a switch. For each entity that is to be counted, the switch closes for a fixed brief interval, passing the pulses into the accumulator during that interval. Thus, the accumulator fills up in equal increments, one increment for each entity counted (fig. 5). The final fullness level of the accumulator represents the number of items counted. The entire mechanism contains several accumulators and switches to allow the counting of different sets of entities simultaneously.

As the accumulator is a physical mechanism and random variability is inherent to any physical process, the exact fullness level of the accumulator will vary somewhat across different counts of the same number of items. This variability will increase with higher counts; therefore, larger numbers will be less discriminable from their neighbors than smaller numbers. This feature of the model may account for why infants' ability to discriminate adjacent numbers is limited to smaller numbers, and why they less reliably distinguish 3 from 4 than they do 2 from 3.

Because the entire fullness of the accumulator represents the number of the items counted, the magnitudinal relationships between the numbers are specified in these representations. For example, 4 is 2 more than 2, or twice as large; the accumulator's representation for 4 has two more increments than the representation for 2, so the accumulator is twice as full. If the mechanism provides procedures for operating over these representations, infants (and animals) will be able to appreciate some of these numerical relationships. Addition, for example, could be achieved by "pouring" the contents from an accumulator representing one value into an accumulator representing another value. Subtracting one value from another could also be achieved: If Accumulator A represents a given number and Accumulator B represents the value to be subtracted from it, the difference could be obtained by pouring out, one increment at a time, the contents of A into an empty third accumulator, C, until A and B are equally filled. At this point, C will represent the numerical difference of the values originally represented by A and B.

Relationship of this Initial System of Knowledge to Later Numerical Knowledge

Although an extensive body of numerical information is in principle accessible by virtue of the magnitudinal structure of the representa-

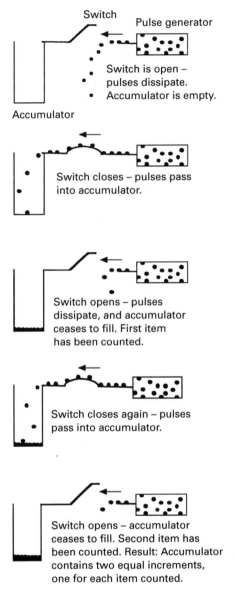

Figure 5 Schematic diagram of the states of Meck and Church's[8] accumulator mechanism as it enumerates two items. The resulting fullness level of the accumulator is the mental representation for 2.

tions produced by the accumulator, access to these facts requires procedures for manipulating the representations in appropriate ways, and there will be practical limits on how the outputs of the mechanism can be manipulated. The kind of procedure required for determining the product of two values, for example, will be much more complex than that for determining the sum of two values; and that required for determining, say, the cube of a value will be more complex still. Infants' knowledge is therefore limited by the procedures they have available for operating over the numerical representations generated by the accumulator mechanism.

There are also limits to the kinds of numerical entities the accumulator mechanism represents. It does not represent numbers other than positive integers. Interestingly, an understanding of numbers other than positive integers emerges only gradually and with much effort, both ontogenetically and culturally.[9] For example, children have great difficulty learning to think of fractions as numerical entities; to do so requires expanding their construal of numbers as values that represent discrete quantities of individual entities. This kind of conceptual expansion has also occurred repeatedly in the historical development of mathematics. Zero, for example, was not initially considered a number, but rather was introduced simply as a place-holder symbol representing an absence of values in a given position in place-value numeral notation (so as to be able to distinguish, e.g., 307 from 37). Only eventually did zero come to be considered a numerical entity in its own right, by virtue of becoming embedded in the number system as rules for its numerical manipulation were developed. The emergences of negative numbers, irrational numbers, complex numbers, and so on have followed similarly gradual progressions.

These facts suggest that the positive integers – the very values that the accumulator model is capable of representing – are psychologically privileged numerical entities. Just as the development of mathematics as a formal system required a conceptualization of numbers that went beyond the positive integers, individual children must undergo a similar (though not necessarily so extensive!) reconceptualization. Gaining a better understanding of how children do this is crucial for ultimately understanding the role that infants' initial foundation of numerical competence plays in the development of later knowledge.

Notes

1   For a comprehensive review of these findings, see K. Wynn, Evidence against empiricist accounts of the origins of numerical knowledge, *Mind & Language*, *7*, 315–332 (1992); K. Wynn, Origins of numerical knowledge, *Mathematical Cognition*, *1*, 35–60 (1995).

2   P. Starkey, E. S. Spelke, and R. Gelman, Numerical abstraction by human infants, *Cognition*, *36*, 97–128 (1990). When, as in this experiment, test stimuli and habituation stimuli are presented in different perceptual modalities, infants typically look longer at the matching stimuli in the new modality rather than the completely novel stimuli, possibly because the correspondence along a single dimension between two very different kinds of stimuli (e.g., pictures and sounds) is inherently interesting to infants.

3   K. Wynn, Infants' individuation and enumeration of actions, *Psychological Science* (in press).

4   K. Wynn, Addition and subtraction by human infants, *Nature*, *358*, 749–750 (1992).

5   We have extended these results, exploring infants' numerical expectations in further situations; see Wynn (1995), note 1. For replications by other researchers, see, e.g., R. Baillargeon, Physical reasoning in young infants: Seeking explanations for impossible events, *British Journal of Developmental Psychology*, *12*, 9–33 (1994); D. S. Moore, Infant mathematical skills? A conceptual replication and consideration of interpretation, manuscript submitted for publication (1995); T. J. Simon, S. J. Hespos, and P. Rochat, Do infants understand simple arithmetic: A replication of Wynn (1992), *Cognitive Development*, *10*, 253–269 (1995).

6   E. Koechlin, S. Dehaene, and J. Mehler, Numerical transformations in five month old human infants, manuscript submitted for publication (1995).

7   For review and discussion, see chapter 10 of C. R. Gallistel, *The organization of learning* (MIT Press, Cambridge, MA, 1990).

8   For a detailed description of the accumulator model and of experimental support for it, see W. H. Meck and R. M. Church, A mode control model of counting and timing processes, *Journal of Experimental Psychology: Animal Behavior Processes*, *9*, 320–334 (1983); see also C. R. Gallistel and R. Gelman, Preverbal and verbal counting and computation, *Cognition*, *44*, 43–74 (1992).

9   See, e.g., R. Gelman, Epigenetic foundations of knowledge structures: Initial and transcendent constructions, in *The epigenesis of mind: Essays on biology and cognition*, S. Carey and R. Gelman, Eds. (Erlbaum, Hillsdale, NJ, 1991); M. Kline, *Mathematical thought from ancient to modern times*, Vol. 1 (Oxford University Press, Oxford, UK, 1972).

NINE

Intentionality and Imitation

Introduction

The old saying "Monkey see, monkey do," stripping away its negative connotation, in fact celebrates an incredible cognitive ability of monkeys: the ability to imitate. Imitation is not a simple feat. It requires observers to watch the actions of a model and then to produce their own actions that match those of the model, normally without feedback. Although it is known that many primates imitate another's action, the process by which they do so remains controversial. Some theorists believe that primate imitation is simply a result of releasing an inborn action triggered by the model's action, while others argue that mental imagery has to be involved to accomplish a successful imitation.

Controversy notwithstanding, Meltzoff and his colleagues, over the last two decades, have produced startling evidence that human infants as young as a few days old are able to imitate an adult model's facial actions such as tongue protrusion, mouth opening, and lip protrusion shortly after the model displays the action. Around six months of age, infants can also begin to imitate actions involving objects. By 12 months of age they will reproduce a model's action without prior practice after a time delay of as long as four weeks. This suggests that infants hold a representation of the model's action in their long-term memory.

This article (edited for this reader) pushes the envelope even further: the evidence reported here shows that infants at 18 months of age do not passively copy whatever is displayed by the model; rather, they only produce the *intended*, unseen action of the model, not the model's *actual* action. In other words, 18-month-olds appear to "read" the model's mind!

Further reading

Meltzoff, A. N. (1996). The human infant as imitative generalist: A 20-year progress report on infant imitation with implications for comparative psychology. In C. M. Heyes & B. G. Galef, Jr. (eds), *Social learning in animals: The roots of culture* (pp. 347–70). San Diego, CA: Academic Press.

Meltzoff, A. N., & Moore, M. K. (1977). Imitation of facial and manual gestures by human neonates. *Science, 198,* 75–8.

Understanding the Intentions of Others: Re-Enactment of Intended Acts by 18-Month-Old Children

Andrew N. Meltzoff

A central topic in developmental cognitive science is to investigate how and when children develop a folk psychology or "theory of mind," the understanding of others as psychological beings having mental states such as beliefs, desires, emotions, and intentions (Astington & Gopnik, 1991a; Flavell, 1988; Harris, 1989; Leslie, 1987; Perner, 1991a; Wellman, 1990). It would be a world very foreign to us to restrict our understanding of others to purely physical terms (e.g., arm extensions, finger curlings, etc.). Failure to attribute mental states to people confronts one with a bewildering series of movements, a jumble of behavior that is difficult to predict and even harder to explain. At a rough level of approximation, this may be something like the state of children with autism (Baron-Cohen, Leslie, & Frith, 1985; Baron-Cohen, Tager-Flusberg, & Cohen, 1993). However, normal children give elaborate verbal descriptions of the unobservable psychological states of people, indicating that they relate observable actions to underlying mental states.

Recent research on children's understanding of mind has been focused on two differentiable questions: (a) Mentalism: How and when do children first begin to construe others as having psychological states that underlie behavior? (b) Representational model of mind: How and when do children come to understand mental states as active interpretations of the world and not simple copies or imprints of it? (Flavell, 1988; Forguson & Gopnik, 1988; Perner, 1991a; Wellman, 1990). One can be a mentalist without having a representational model of the mind, but being a representationalist entails being a mentalist. One has to understand that there is a mind or something like it before precise questions about the relation between mind and world can arise. A developmental ordering is suggested. It has been proposed that there is not a single "theory of mind," but rather a succession of different theories, in particular, an early mentalistic one that is replaced by a representational one (e.g., Gopnik, Slaughter, & Meltzoff, 1994; Gopnik & Wellman, 1992, 1994; Wellman, 1990, 1993).

The second question listed above has received the bulk of the empirical attention to date. [. . .]

The first question listed above concerns an earlier phase of development and has not received as much attention, but it is equally important. The experimental data that exist seem to suggest that even two-and-a-half- to three-year-olds are mentalists; they read below the surface behavior to understand the actions of persons. Wellman and Estes (1986) reported that three-year-olds distinguish between mental and physical entities. Bartsch and Wellman (1989) found that three-year-old children used beliefs and desires to explain human action. Lillard and Flavell (1990) showed that three-year-olds have a preference for construing human behavior in psychological terms. In their study a series of pictures was shown to children and described in both behavioral and mental state terms. For example, children were shown a picture of a child sitting on the floor (back to the viewer), and this was described as a child "wiping up" and "feeling sad" about his spilled milk. A duplicate picture was then given to the child, who was asked to explain the scene in his or her own terms. The results showed that three-year-olds were more likely to choose mentalistic descriptions than behavioral ones. This attribution of mental states by three-year-olds is compatible with research described by Gelman and Wellman (1991) and Wellman and Gelman (1988) showing that three- to four-year-old children tend to postulate unobservable "insides and essences" of things earlier than classically believed (Piaget, 1929).

Philosophers have argued that among the varied mental states we ascribe to persons, beliefs are particularly complex (e.g., Searle, 1983). This is because they are the representational states *par excellence*. As defined by philosophers, beliefs always involve representations or interpretations of the world rather than simply attitudes toward it or relations with it; however, other mental states such as desires and intentions may easily be construed nonrepresentationally and so may be easier to understand (Astington & Gopnik, 1991b; Flavell, 1988; Gopnik & Wellman, 1994; Perner, 1991b; Wellman, 1990, 1993). Mental states such as desire and intention may be particularly good topics to investigate if one is interested in the earliest roots of children's understanding of mind.

Empirical work supports this view. [. . .] Wellman (1990, 1993; Wellman & Woolley, 1990) suggested that a "belief psychology" grows out of a prior "desire psychology," and he and others have pushed back the earliest instances of children's understanding of mind, as measured by way of desire tasks, to two to three years of age.

To date, most of the techniques for assessing children's "theory of mind" have relied on verbal report. This makes it difficult to test children before about two to two and a half years old. There is a keen interest among both psychologists and philosophers (Campbell, 1994, 1995; Fodor, 1992; Goldman, 1992, 1993; Gordon, 1994) in the aboriginal roots of children's understanding of mind. Several nonverbal abilities in infancy have been proposed as candidates, including symbolic play and metarepresentation (Leslie, 1987, 1988), joint attention and social referencing (Baron-Cohen, 1991; Butterworth, 1991; Wellman, 1990), and crossmodal representation of others as "like me" coupled with body imitation (Meltzoff, 1990a; Meltzoff & Gopnik, 1993; Meltzoff & Moore, 1995).

There is a rather large gap between these roots and the abilities examined in standard theory-of-mind experiments with two-and-a-half- to four-year-olds. This gap is due, in part, to the lack of a technique for exploring the relevant questions in children too young to give verbal reports. One aim of the current research is to develop a nonverbal test that can be used to pose such questions. The issue investigated here was children's understanding of the intentions of others, something more akin to desires than beliefs. The test used was called the *behavioral re-enactment procedure.*

The behavioral re-enactment procedure capitalizes on toddlers' natural tendency to pick up behavior from adults, to re-enact or imitate what they see (Meltzoff, 1988a, 1988b, 1990b, 1995; Piaget, 1962). However, it uses this proclivity in a new way. In the critical test situation in Experiment 1, children were confronted with an adult who merely demonstrated an "intention" to act in a certain way. Importantly, the adult never fulfilled this intention. He tried but failed to perform the act, so the end state was never reached. It remained unobserved by the child.

To an adult, it was easy to "read" the actor's intention. The experimental question was whether children interpreted this behavior in purely physical terms or whether they too read through the literal body movements to the underlying goal or intention of the act. The children, who were too young to give verbal reports, informed us how they represented the event by what they chose to re-enact. Another group of children followed the same experimental protocol and were tested in an identical fashion except that they saw the full target act. Various control groups were tested. Children's tendency to perform the target act was compared in several situations: after they saw the act demonstrated, after the target act was intended but not achieved, and after the target act was neither shown nor intended. The results suggest that 18-month-old children understand something about the intentions of others: They performed the acts the adult intended to do even though the adult's acts failed.

Experiment 2 compared children's reactions to a person versus an inanimate object. An inanimate device was built that traced the same movements through space as the human hand. The dual aims of this study were to test whether these spatial patterns might in and of themselves suggest a goal state and to explore the limits of the types of entities that may be construed as having psychological properties like intentions. The movements of the inanimate device did not lead children to produce the target acts.

Taken together, the experiments show that 18-month-old children already situate people within a psychological framework. They have adopted a key element of a folk psychology: People (but not inanimate objects) are understood within a framework that includes goals and intentions. The issue now raised for theory, and considered in the conclusions, is whether 18-month-olds impute mental states as the causes of behavior or whether they are in a transitional phase that serves to link the newborn's more embryonic notion of person (Meltzoff & Moore, 1995) to the full-blown mentalism of the three-year-old.

Experiment 1
Method

Children

The participants were 40 18-month-old children (M = 18.02 months, SD = .10; range: 542–554 days old). [. . .]

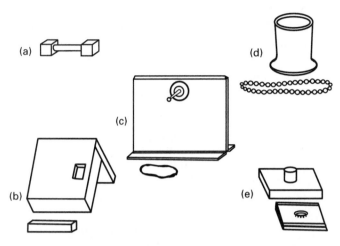

Figure 1   The five test objects: (a) dumbbell, (b) box and stick tool, (c) prong
and loop, (d) cylinder and beads, and (e) square and post.

Test environment and apparatus

The test was conducted in a room at the university that was unfurnished
save for the equipment and furniture needed for the experiment. The
child was tested while seated on his or her parent's lap in front of a rec-
tangular table ($1.2 \times .8$ m), the top surface of which was covered in black
contact paper. A video camera behind and to the left of the experimenter
recorded the infant's head, torso, and a portion of the table top in front
of the child where the test objects were manipulated. [. . .]

Test materials

Five objects served as test stimuli (figure 1). The child could not have
seen or played with these objects before, because they were specially constructed in the laboratory and were not commercially available. (Some
parts in the stimuli were store-bought items, but these components were
used in unusual ways.)
     [. . .]

Design

The children were randomly assigned to one of four independent groups
with ten children per group. There were two demonstration groups and

two control groups: Demonstration (target), Demonstration (intention), Control (baseline), and Control (adult manipulation). Within each group the test objects were presented in five different orders such that each object occurred equally often in each position. One male and one female child were assigned to each order. Thus, order and sex of infant were counterbalanced both within and between groups.

Procedure

On arrival at the university, the children and their families were escorted to a waiting room where they completed the necessary forms. They were then brought to the test room where parent and child were seated at the table across from the experimenter. The experimenter handed the children an assortment of rubber toys to explore. After the infant seemed acclimated with the room and the experimenter, usually about one to three minutes, the warm-up toys were withdrawn and the study began.

Demonstration (target).   For the children in this group the experimenter modeled a specific target act with each of the five objects. Each object was kept hidden before it was brought to the table for its demonstration and was returned to the hidden container before the next object was presented. For each stimulus, the target act was repeated three times in approximately 20 seconds and was then placed on the table directly in front of the infant. A 20-second response period was timed starting from when the infant touched the object. At the end of this response period, the first object was removed, and the second presentation was modeled following the same time procedure, and so on for the five test objects. The demonstrations were presented out of reach of the children so they could not touch or play with the toy but were confined to observing the event. The experimenter never used words related to the task such as "push button," "do what I do," or "copy me," but the experimenter was permitted to gain the child's attention by calling his or her name, saying "look over here," "oh, see what I have," or "it's your turn." The experimenter maintained a friendly demeanor throughout the demonstrations and did not express joy at successfully performing the act.

For the dumbbell, the act demonstrated was to pick it up by the wooden cubes and pull outward with a very definite movement so that the toy came apart into two halves. For the box, the act demonstrated was to pick up the stick tool and use it to push in the button, which then activated the buzzer inside the box. For the square, the act demonstrated was to pick up the plastic square and put the hole over the dowel. For the prong, the act demonstrated was to raise the nylon loop up to the prong and drape it over it. (The screen on which the prong was mounted was put perpendicular to the children on their left side.) For the cylinder, the act demonstrated was to raise the beads up over the opening of the cylinder and then to lower them down into the opening so that they were deposited on the bottom of the container.

Demonstration (intention). For this group the experimenter did not demonstrate the target acts. None of the final goal states was achieved. Instead, the experimenter was seen to try but fail to achieve these ends. The experimenter modeled the intention to perform these acts, but not the target acts themselves. Save for this critical difference, the remainder of the procedure for this group was identical to the group that saw the full target: The intention to produce the act was modeled three times and was followed by a 20-second response period for each test object so that the temporal factors were equated with the children who saw the target. The experimenter did not provide linguistic or facial expressions of failure. To an adult, the multiple, effortful tries effectively conveyed the intention to perform the target act, in line with Heider's (1958) descriptions of cues to intention in adult perceivers.

For the dumbbell, the experimenter picked it up by the wooden cubes, just as he had done in the Demonstration (target) condition. It appeared that the experimenter was trying to pull the ends outward. However, he failed to do so because as he pulled, one of his hands slipped off the end of the object. The direction of slippage alternated from left, to right, to left over the three stimulus presentations (the spatial terms are all referenced from the child's viewpoint). Thus there was no object transformation, and the goal state was never achieved. All that was visible were the experimenter's attempts to pull it apart.

For the box, the experimenter used the stick tool and tried to push the button. However, the experimenter always missed. Thus the affordance of the box was never seen; there was no activation of the buzzer, and the goal state of touching the button with the tool was never witnessed. Each of the three misses was spatially different: First, the stick tool missed off the left, next it missed to the right, and on the third attempt it was too high. In each case the tip of the tool came down on the top surface of the box.

For the prong device, the experimenter tried but failed in his attempt to put the nylon loop over the prong. He picked up the loop, but as he approached the prong he released it inappropriately so that it "accidentally" dropped to the table surface each time. First, the loop was released slightly too far to the left, then too far to the right, and finally too low, where it fell to the table directly below the prong. The goal state of draping the nylon loop over the prong was not demonstrated.

For the cylinder, the experimenter attempted to deposit the beads into the cylinder, but failed. First, he raised the loop of beads over the cylinder and lowered them down so that just the tip of the beads crossed the edge of the top lip. The beads were then released such that they fell to the table outside the cylinder. The second attempt consisted of suspending the beads slightly too far in front of the cup so that they again fell to the table top when released. Third, the experimenter gathered the beads up into his loosely closed hand and scraped his hand over the opening of the cylinder such that the beads fell outside the cylinder instead of into it. The child thus did not see the beads deposited in the cylinder but saw three failed attempts at doing so.

For the plastic square, the experimenter picked it up and attempted to put it on the dowel. However, he did not align it properly. It was tilted slightly toward the child, and the hole was not aligned directly over the dowel. The first time the hole undershot the dowel and remained on the left, the second time it overshot it to the right, and the third time the hole was spatially in front of the dowel. The children never saw the goal state of putting the square over the dowel.

Five different acts were used, providing some assessment of generality. The dumbbell involved an "effort" to pull an object, but the object itself remained completely untransformed. The prong-and-loop device involved moving one object (the loop) in a behavioral sequence that to the adult was explained by an underlying cause – the attempt to drape the loop over the prong. It seemed possible that some tasks might be more easily understood than others. [. . .] The idea was to test whether any (or all) of these acts could be understood from seeing a failed attempt; the range of acts would help explore whether particular tasks were easier than others at this age.

Control (baseline). A baseline control group was included to assess the likelihood that the target acts used in the demonstration groups would occur in the spontaneous behavior of the children independent of the adult model. The adult demonstration was excluded, but all other aspects of the procedure remained the same: The experimenter handed the child the test stimuli one at a time and timed a 20-second response period for each object. [. . .]

Control (adult manipulation).   In the two demonstration groups (both the target and intention) the children saw the experimenter pick up and handle the test objects. It could be argued that children may be more likely to manipulate and explore objects that the experimenter has handled. The baseline group controlled for the spontaneous production of the target actions but would not take care of controlling for any non-specific effects of seeing the adult manipulate the objects. Therefore, a second control group was also included. In this group, the experimenter manipulated the test objects for the same length of time as in the demonstration groups. The only difference between this group and the two demonstration groups was that he neither demonstrated the target acts nor even the intention to produce them. He picked up and handled the objects but refrained from those activities. If the children produce more target behaviors in the demonstration groups than in this control it cannot be attributed to seeing the adult handle the objects, because handling time by the experimenter was equated. The combination of both baseline and adult-manipulation controls provides an excellent assessment of whether the specific content of the adult demonstration is influencing the behavior of the children.
   [. . .]

Scoring

The response periods for all four groups were identical inasmuch as each infant had a series of five 20-second response periods. To ensure blind scoring of the data, a new videotape was made by deleting all the warm-up and presentation periods. It contained only the response periods and thus contained no artifactual clue as to the children's test group. It was scored in a random order by a coder who was kept unaware of the test group of the children.
   The operational definitions of performing the target acts were the following. For the dumbbell a "yes" was scored if the infant pulled the object apart. For the box a "yes" was scored if the infant used the stick tool to push the button and activate the buzzer. For the prong a "yes"

was scored if the nylon loop was put over the prong so that the prong protruded through it. For the cylinder a "yes" was scored if the beads were lowered all the way into the cylinder. For the plastic square a "yes" was scored if the infant placed the plastic square over the wooden dowel so that the dowel protruded through the hole.

[...]

Results and Discussion

The results suggest that 18-month-old children can understand the intended acts of adults even when the adult does not fulfill his intentions. Each child was presented with five objects, and for statistical analyses each was assigned a score ranging from 0 to 5 according to how many target acts he or she produced. Table 1 displays the mean number of target acts produced as a function of experimental group. The data were analyzed with a one-way analysis of variance (ANOVA). The results showed that the number of target acts varied significantly as a function of experimental group, with more target acts in the demonstration groups than the controls, $F (3, 36) = 22.95$, $p < .0001$. Follow-up pairwise comparisons using the Tukey honestly significant difference procedure showed that number of target acts produced by infants in the target demonstration ($M = 3.80$, $SD = .92$) and intention ($M = 4.00$, $SD = 1.15$) groups did not significantly differ from each other and that each group produced significantly more target acts than infants in the baseline ($M = 1.20$, $SD = 1.32$) and adult-manipulation ($M = 1.00$, $SD = .82$) control groups, which also did not significantly differ from each other. Nonpara-

Table 1 Number of children producing target acts as a function of group

Group	Number of target acts					
	0	1	2	3	4	5
Control (baseline)	4	3	0	3	0	0
Control (adult manipulation)	3	4	3	0	0	0
Demonstration (intention)	0	0	2	0	4	4
Demonstration (target)	0	0	1	2	5	2

metric analyses of the data (Kruskal–Wallis and Mann–Whitney *U*s) yielded identical results.

It is striking that the Demonstration (target) and Demonstration (intention) groups did not significantly differ from one another. Of the 50 trials (10s × 5 trials each) administered to the Demonstration (target) group, 38 resulted in the target act, which is similar to the 40 for the Demonstration (intention) group. A more qualitative examination of the videotapes supported this point. Infants in the intention group did not go through a period of trial and error with the test objects but directly produced the target act just as those who saw the full target had done. This can be captured by the latency to produce the target acts in the intention and target demonstration groups, which did not significantly differ from one another ($F < 1.0$) and were respectively 5.10 s ($SD = 2.74$) and 3.97 s ($SD = 2.70$). These short latencies support the impression gained from the videotapes that infants did not engage in extensive error correction and produced the targets rather directly.

Can children interpret the adult's behavior right from the first encounter? The results show that 80% of the children (eight of ten for each demonstration group) produced the target act with the first object as compared with only 20% (five of 20) in the control groups, x^2 (1, N = 40) = 10.03, $p < .005$. These data are informative because they show that prolonged exposure to these displays is not necessary; they can be interpreted even when they occur on the first trial.

Each test object was analyzed individually to assess the generality of the phenomenon and the range of events over which it works. Table 2 provides the complete data set, broken down object by object. For statistical analysis the two Demonstration groups (target and intention) were collapsed and compared with the collapsed Controls (baseline and adult-manipulation) because the expected frequencies were too small for a four-cell analysis (Siegel, 1956). The results from the 2 × 2 contingency tables comparing the number of children who produced the target response for each object (a dichotomous yes or no score) as a function of experimental treatment (Demonstration or Controls) showed that the demonstration was significantly more effective in eliciting the target behavior for each of the objects considered individually. The chi-square values were as follows (all $df = 1$, $N = 40$, one-tailed): dumbbell, 12.60, $p < .001$; box, 14.73, $p < .001$; prong, 14.44, $p < .001$; cylinder, 12.22, $p < .001$; and square, 2.98, $p < .05$. If one analyzes the controls versus the intention group alone, a similar pattern emerges for each

Table 2 Proportion of children producing target acts as a function of test objects and group

	Group			
Test object	Control (baseline)	Control (adult-manipulation)	Demonstration (intention)	Demonstration (target)
Dumbbell	.20	.40	.80	1.00
Box	.40	.10	.90	.90
Prong	.10	.20	.90	.70
Cylinder	.30	.20	.90	.80
Square	.20	.10	.50	.40
M	.24	.20	.80	.76

object, with significance values ranging from $p < .001$ to $p = .056$ (for the square). The results suggest that the phenomenon is not limited to one or two acts but is reasonably general, applying to all five of the acts tested. The only object that seemed to cause any difficulty was the plastic square, and re-examination of the videotapes indicated that this task strained the manual dexterity of the 18-month-olds. The children in both the intention and target act groups had motor skills difficulty in fitting the hole over the dowel (six children failed in the Demonstration [target] group and five failed in the Demonstration [intention] group).

[. . .]

Experiment 2

The results of Experiment 1 indicated that young children can pick up information from the failed attempts of human actors. One question that arises is whether the children are responding solely to the physics of the situation (the movements that are traced in space) or whether a psychological understanding of the human actor is involved. What would children do if they saw the same movements produced by an inanimate device? Do the spatial transformations in and of themselves suggest the target act? A device was built that mimicked the movements

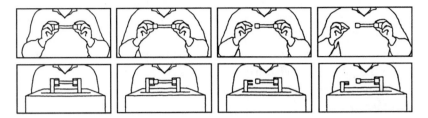

Figure 2 Human demonstrator (top panel) and mechanical device mimicking these movements (bottom panel) used in Experiment 2. Time is represented by successive frames left to right.

of the actor in the Demonstration (intention) group. The device did not look human, but it had a pincer that "grasped" the dumbbell on the two ends (just as the human did) and then pulled outward. These pincers then slipped off the cubes (just as the human hand did). The pattern of movements and the slipping motions were closely matched to the human hand movements, as described below (see figure 2).

Method

Children

The participants were 60 18-month-old children ($M = 18.08$ months, $SD = .13$; range = 541–555 days old). [. . .]

Test materials

The test object was the dumbbell shown in figure 1. For the human model group, the demonstration was performed by a human in the same way as already described in Experiment 1: Demonstration (intention). In the inanimate model group the demonstration was presented by a mechanical device (see figure 2). This device consisted of a small box with an open back panel. Through this opening the experimenter invisibly controlled two upright mechanical arms. Each mechanical arm consisted of a vertical piece with two horizontal finger/pincers at its end. The dumbbell was held between the pincers in the same way that it was held by the human fingers. The mechanical arms traced the same movements outward as the human arms did. Like the human actor, the mechanical device failed to pull apart the dumbbell, and the pincers slid off the ends of the dumbbell just as the human fingers did. An interesting detail is that the pincers were under slight spring tension. Therefore, when the pincer slid off the end, the two pincers came together just as the human fingers did when the adult's hand slipped off the end of the dumbbell. [. . .]

Design

The children were randomly assigned to one of two independent groups with 30 children per group: Human Demonstration (intention) and Inanimate Demonstration (mechanical slippage). Sex of child was counterbalanced within each group.

Procedure

[. . .]

Results

The children were visually riveted by both displays; visual attention to the displays exceeded 98% of the presentation period for both treatment groups. The children did not seem to be more frightened by one display than the other. There was no social referencing (turning around toward the parent) and no fussing by any of the children during the presentation periods.

Children did not seem to react differently when watching the human versus machine. The question can now be posed as to whether they interpreted the presentations differently. The data showed that they did. The groups significantly differed in their tendency to produce the target act. The children were six times more likely to produce the target act after seeing the human attempt to pull it apart (60% did so) than they were after seeing the demonstration by machine (10%). The corresponding contingency table analyzing group (human or machine) × response (yes or no) was significant, $x^2(1, N = 60) = 14.36$, $p < .0005$.

General Discussion

The goals of this research were both methodological and substantive. The first goal was to develop a procedure that could be used to pose "theory-of-mind" questions at ages younger than children could be queried through verbal means. The more substantive issues were to investigate (*a*) whether 18-month-olds understand the acts of others within a psychological framework that includes goals and intentions and (*b*) the limits of the types of entities that are interpreted within this framework. Is it tied to people?

Behavioral re-enactment procedure

A behavioral re-enactment procedure was developed to pose questions concerning the understanding of intention, but it would seem to have wider applicability than to intention alone. The test mandates that children formulate action plans on the basis of their interpretation of events. The response is a productive measure. Such re-presentation in action is not as informative as a verbal description, but it does entail that the children "tell" us how they saw things (rather than our making inferences from a more passive measure, such as increased or decreased attention in a habituation procedure).

The re-enactment technique capitalizes on past findings that toddlers can be induced to reproduce adults' behavior (Meltzoff, 1988a, 1988b, 1993, 1995; Piaget, 1962). The normal task was modified to differentiate between a surface versus more abstract construal of an event. It asked whether infants could go beyond duplicating what was actually done and would instead enact what the adult intended to do. By analogy, if adults are asked to repeat what was said, they often paraphrase rather than quote, and we glean much from what they leave out, magnify, and transform. Like adults, infants are not little taperecorders or videorecorders. The re-enactment procedure uses infants' nonverbal reconstructions of events to investigate their interpretive structures, here to explore their folk psychological framework.

Understanding intention in infancy

In Experiment 1, one group saw the adult perform a target act, Demonstration (target), and as expected, they re-enacted the same target.

Another group provided a more novel test. They never saw the adult perform the actual target act. For example, the adult tried to pull apart a toy but failed to do so because his hand slipped off as he attempted to pull it apart. In another case the adult strove to push a button with a stick tool but failed in his attempts. In a third, the adult intended to put a loop over a prong but under- and overshot the target, and the loop ineffectually fell to the table.

The terms "tried," "strove," and "intended" are used because that is how adults would code the behavior. This is a mentalistic way of describing things. The question is whether the infants also construe it this way. Or do they see things in a less psychological manner? Perhaps in more purely physical terms?

In Experiment 1, two control groups were included. [. . .] The significant difference between the treatment and control groups shows that infants' behavior was based on their perception of the adult's acts. They used the adult as a source of information about what to do with the objects, and their behavior was guided by the nature of the particular acts the adult did.

[. . .]

To underscore why the results reported here are relevant to the development of folk psychology, it is helpful to distinguish between seeing the behaviors of others in purely physical versus psychological terms. The former will be called *movements* or *motions* and the latter human *acts*. The behavior of another person can, of course, be described at either (or both) of these levels. We can say "Sally's hand contacted the cup, the cup fell over" or "Sally intended to pick up the cup." Strict behaviorists insist on the former because what is in the respondent's mind is unobservable. Cognitive and social psychologists prefer the latter description. The current research suggests that by 18 months of age children are not strict behaviorists. They do not see the behavior of others merely in terms of "hold the dumbbell and then remove one hand quickly," but rather see an "effort" at pulling. They do not see the demonstration as "loop falls to one side of prong and then the other side," but rather as an attempt to drape it over the prong. They show us how they see or interpret these events by re-enacting them for us. Infants apparently represent the behavior of people in a psychological framework involving goals and intended acts, instead of purely physical movements or motions. Borrowing language from perceptual psychology, one might say they code human behavior in terms of the "distal stimulus" (the intended act) instead of the "proximal cues" (the surface behavior and literal limb movements). Human behavior is seen as purposive.

Experiment 2 investigated whether there was something special about a person, or whether 18-month-olds would make similar attributions to the movements of an inanimate device. It is central to our adult conceptions of the world that there are two differentiable causal frameworks: (*a*) a physical causality for explaining the behavior of things and (*b*) a psychological causality for explaining the behavior of people. We can make errors in our attributions, and inanimate devices can be built that strain our normal distinctions (can computers have intentional states?). However, one doesn't generally ask the desk to move across the room – one shoves it. One doesn't believe the car key was "trying" to hide (even if it's absent whenever there is an important appointment). Similarly, one doesn't think that an errant arrow was actually trying to hit the bullseye but failed (that ascription is made of the archer), or that the pendulum of a grandfather clock is attempting to strike the side of the cabinet but missing. Intentions and goals are the types of things that are used to explain the behavior of persons, not things. In my terms, we see the bodily movements of people and interpret them in terms of acts, and we see the movements of things and interpret them as such, as movements or motions. Explanations for the latter lie in the domain of physics and for the former in the domain of psychology.

The outcome of Experiment 2 was that the 18-month-olds did not tend to produce the target act when a mechanical device slipped off the ends of the dumbbell, but they did produce the target act when the human hand slipped off the ends of the same toy. Evidently the goal, or to use more careful language, the end state ("dumbbell apart") was not suggested by the movement patterns alone when considered from a purely physical perspective. The findings provide evidence that 18-month-olds have a differentiation in the kinds of attributions they make to people versus things.

How might this tendency to treat humans within such a psychological framework arise in the child? Two accounts can be suggested. The first is rooted in Fodor's (1987, 1992) conjecture that humans have an innately specified belief–desire psychology. This was elaborated in Leslie's suggestion that there is a "theory of mind module" (Leslie, 1987, 1988, 1991; Leslie & Roth, 1993). Armed with the data reported here showing "intention-reading" in 18-month-olds, it could be proposed that there is an innate tendency for attributing intentions to humans (see also Premack, 1990). Fodor would certainly be comfortable with intention-reading as part of the innate belief–desire psychology. It would be interesting if children with autism, that is, children who have profound deficits in other aspects of understanding the minds of others (Baron-Cohen, 1990; Baron-Cohen et al., 1985; Harris, 1993; Leslie & Roth, 1993), showed deficits on the kinds of tasks reported here.

I have previously tested newborns' reactions to human faces and discussed innate aspects of social cognition, their initial construal of what a person is, and how persons differ from things (Meltzoff & Moore, 1983, 1992, 1994, 1995). Like Fodor, I am a nativist; but I prefer a special brand of nativism that has been called starting-state nativism versus Fodorian final-state or modularity nativism (Gopnik, 1993; Gopnik & Wellman, 1994; Meltzoff & Gopnik, 1993). Starting-state nativism embraces innate psychological structure, but it also embraces development (Gopnik et al., 1994; Gopnik & Wellman, 1994; Meltzoff, 1990b; Meltzoff & Moore, 1995).

Why suggest development? First, the rudimentary understanding of human goals and intentions does not entail a grasp of more complex mental states such as "belief" (Searle, 1983), and hence not a full-blown belief–desire psychology. Others have reported a developmental progression from understanding desires to understanding beliefs (Astington & Gopnik, 1991b; Gopnik, 1993; Perner, 1991b; Wellman, 1990, 1993). The present results would add that there is some understanding of intention at 18 months, and that like the case of simple desires, this could be accomplished without understanding beliefs *per se*. Moreover, there are two sides to intentional action, and there may be developmental changes in understanding both. One involves the nature of the goals that are brought about, that is, the causal consequences on the world; the other involves the relation between the mind and actions.

[. . .]

Regarding intentional action – the relation between mind and action – a distinction needs to be drawn between (*a*) the end states of a purely physical pattern, (*b*) goals of acts, and (*c*) intentions as mental states. The present data allow us to infer more than (*a*), but do not allow us to say with assurance whether infants were using (*b*) or (*c*). Let us see what is at stake in these distinctions.

Young infants can "go beyond the stimulus," using past information to project the future. They visually extend the trajectories of moving objects in anticipating re-encounters with them (Bower, 1982; Meltzoff & Moore, 1995; Moore, Borton, & Darby, 1978; Spelke & Van de Walle, 1993). They anticipate where to look when shown an alternating pattern of flashing lights (Haith, Hazan, & Goodman, 1988). One wonders whether the infants in the experiments reported here were merely projecting the next step of a physical sequence.

The findings indicate more than this, although the argument is a delicate one. The actions in the Demonstration (intention) group did not, strictly speaking, form a progression. The infants were shown three failed attempts, but each failed in a different way (usually equidistant from the desired end) that was not incrementally related to the target act (by experimental design). This is different from anticipating that an object that was seen along a trajectory at a, b, c, will next be at d, or that a light with the alternating pattern of a, b, a, b will next flash at a. Thus, in Experiment 1 the stick missed to the left, then the right, and then too high. Couldn't the next step be a miss that was too low, to complete the pattern? If the movements *qua* movements specified the next step, why wasn't it suggested when the movements were traced by the mechanical device? The infants in this experiment not only went beyond the surface stimulus, but they also went beyond the stimulus in a particular way that relied on human goals or intentions, not solely physics.

We now need to consider more closely what is meant by *intention*. Searle (1983) differentiated at least two broad types of intentions. He called *prior intentions* those mental states that occur in the mind of the actor in advance of the action being performed that can be described in the form "I will do *x*." One can have a prior intention but not perform any behavior at all (e.g., if the prior intention is not actually fulfilled). These are to be distinguished from *intentions in action*, which are what is involved at the moment of purposely performing a particular bodily movement (vs. when it happens accidently or reflexively). One can have a spur of the moment intention in action, without a prior intention to have it. Every purposeful bodily movement involves an intention in action, but only some intentions in action involve prior intentions. Searle has argued that one needs at least these two varieties of intention to describe adult understanding. Astington (1991) showed that both are entailed in the five-year-old's understanding.

It seems doubtful that 18-month-olds, let alone newborns, contemplate the prior intentions of others. These mental states are very far upstream, as it were. It is possible, however, that the 18-month-olds in these studies were manifesting an understanding of intentions in action. Infants' understanding of intention in action would allow them to make sense of what would otherwise be rather odd behavior on the part of the adult. It would organize the surface behaviors and allow the infant to see them as "failed attempts" that stemmed from one underlying cause.

However, a thoroughgoing developmental analysis must recognize that even intentions in action are, for the adult, invisible mental states imputed to the mind of the actor. Children in these studies may have imputed such states, or they may have stopped short and simply interpreted the goals of the actions. Infants may think that human acts have goals without yet ascribing underlying mental states in the mind of the actor as the cause of these goals. The results from Experiment 2 demonstrate that physical movements performed by a machine are not ascribed the same meaning as when performed by a person. Therefore, even a weak reading of the data suggests that infants are thinking in terms of goals that are connected to people and not to things. This is tantamount to saying that the infants are construing behavior in terms of a psychological framework including goals of acts, if not the intentions of actors.

The raw fact that 18-month-old children can succeed on the tasks reported here, that they can make sense of a failed attempt, indicates that they have begun to distinguish the surface behavior of people (what they actually do) from another deeper level. This differentiation lies at the core of our commonsense psychology. It underlies fluid communication (Baldwin & Moses, 1994; Bruner, 1983; Grice, 1957; Tomasello & Barton, 1994) as well as our moral judgments. This distinction is also important for understanding even very simple human behaviors. The current experiments suggest that 18-month-olds also understand the actions of others in terms of psychology, not solely physics. In this sense, 18-month-olds have already adopted the basic tenet of folk psychology.

References

Astington, J. W. (1991). Intention in the child's theory of mind. In D. Frye & C. Moore (Eds.), *Children's theories of mind: Mental states and social understanding* (pp. 157–172). Hillsdale, NJ: Erlbaum.

Astington, J. W., & Gopnik, A. (1991a). Developing understanding of desire and intention. In A. Whiten (Ed.), *Natural theories of mind: Evolution, development and simulation of everyday mindreading* (pp. 39–50). Cambridge, MA: Basil Blackwell.

Astington, J. W., & Gopnik, A. (1991b). Theoretical explanations of children's understanding of the mind. *British Journal of Developmental Psychology, 9*, 7–31.

Baldwin, D. A., & Moses, L. J. (1994). Early understanding of referential intent and attentional focus: Evidence from language and emotion. In C. Lewis & P. Mitchell (Eds.), *Children's early understanding of mind: Origins and development* (pp. 133–156). Hillsdale, NJ: Erlbaum.

Baron-Cohen, S. (1990). Autism: A specific cognitive disorder of "mind-blindness." *International Review of Psychiatry, 2*, 81–90.

Baron-Cohen, S. (1991). Precursors to a theory of mind: Understanding attention in others. In A. Whiten (Ed.), *Natural theories of mind: Evolution, development and simulation of everyday mindreading* (pp. 233–251). Cambridge, MA: Basil Blackwell.

Baron-Cohen, S., Leslie, A. M., & Firth, U. (1985). Does the autistic child have a "theory of mind"? *Cognition, 21*, 37–46.

Baron-Cohen, S., Tager-Flusberg, H., & Cohen, D. J. (1993). *Understanding other minds: Perspectives from autism.* New York: Oxford University Press.

Bartsch, K., & Wellman, H. M. (1989). Young children's attribution of action to beliefs and desires. *Child Development, 60*, 946–964.

Bower, T. G. R. (1982). *Development in infancy* (2nd ed.). San Francisco: W. H. Freeman.

Bruner, J. S. (1983). *Child's talk: Learning to use language.* New York: W. W. Norton.

Butterworth, G. (1991). The ontogeny and phylogeny of joint visual attention. In A. Whiten (Ed.), *Natural theories of mind: Evolution, development and simulation of everyday mindreading* (pp. 223–232). Cambridge, MA: Basil Blackwell.

Campbell, J. (1994). *Past, space, and self.* Cambridge, MA: MIT Press.

Campbell, J. (1995). The body image and self-consciousness. In J. Bermúdez, A. J. Marcel, & N. Eilan (Eds.), *The body and the self* (pp. 29–42). Cambridge, MA: MIT Press.

Flavell, J. H. (1988). The development of children's knowledge about the mind: From cognitive connections to mental representations. In J. W. Astington, P. L. Harris, & D. R. Olson (Eds.), *Developing theories of mind* (pp. 244–267). New York: Cambridge University Press.

Fodor, J. A. (1987). *Psychosemantics: The problem of meaning in the philosophy of mind.* Cambridge, MA: MIT Press.

Fodor, J. A. (1992). A theory of the child's theory of mind. *Cognition, 44*, 283–296.

Forguson, L., & Gopnik, A. (1988). The ontogeny of common sense. In J. W. Astington, P. L. Harris, & D. R. Olson (Eds.), *Developing theories of mind* (pp. 226–243). New York: Cambridge University Press.

Gelman, S. A., & Wellman, H. M. (1991). Insides and essence: Early understanding of the non-obvious. *Cognition, 213–244.*

Goldman, A. I. (1992). Empathy, mind, and morals. *Proceedings and Addresses of the American Philosophical Association, 66,* 17–41.

Goldman, A. I. (1993). The psychology of folk psychology. *Behavioral and Brain Sciences, 16,* 15–28.

Gopnik, A. (1993). How we know our minds: The illusion of first-person knowledge of intentionality. *Behavioral and Brain Sciences, 16,* 1–14.

Gopnik, A., Slaughter, V., & Meltzoff, A. N. (1994). Changing your views: How understanding visual perception can lead to a new theory of the mind. In C. Lewis & P. Mitchell (Eds.), *Children's early understanding of mind: Origins and development* (pp. 157–181). Hillsdale, NJ: Erlbaum.

Gopnik, A., & Wellman, H. M. (1992). Why the child's theory of mind really is a theory. *Mind and Language, 7,* 145–171.

Gopnik, A., & Wellman, H. M. (1994). The theory theory. In L. A. Hirschfeld, & S. A. Gelman (Eds.), *Mapping the mind: Domain specificity in culture and cognition* (pp. 257–293). New York: Cambridge University Press.

Gordon, R. M. (1994, April). *Sympathy, simulation, and the impartial spectator.* Paper presented at the Mind and Morals Conference, St. Louis, MO.

Grice, H. P. (1957). Meaning. *Philosophical Review, 66,* 377–388.

Haith, M. M., Hazan, C., & Goodman, G. S. (1988). Expectation and anticipation of dynamic visual events by 3.5-month-old babies. *Child Development, 59,* 467–479.

Harris, P. L. (1989). *Children and emotion: The development of psychological understanding.* Oxford, UK: Basil Blackwell.

Harris, P. L. (1993). Pretending and planning. In S. Baron-Cohen, H. Tager-Flusberg, & D. Cohen (Eds.), *Understanding other minds: Perspectives from autism* (pp. 228–246). New York: Oxford University Press.

Heider, F. (1958). *The psychology of interpersonal relations.* New York: Wiley.

Leslie, A. M. (1987). Pretense and representation: The origins of "theory of mind." *Psychological Review, 94,* 412–426.

Leslie, A. M. (1988). Some implications of pretense for mechanisms underlying the child's theory of mind. In J. W. Astington, P. L. Harris, & D. R. Olson (Eds.), *Developing theories of mind* (pp. 19–46). New York: Cambridge University Press.

Leslie, A. M. (1991). The theory of mind impairment in autism: Evidence for a modular mechanism of development? In A. Whiten (Ed.), *Natural theories of mind: Evolution, development and simulation of everyday mindreading* (pp. 63–78). Cambridge, MA: Basil Blackwell.

Leslie, A. M., & Roth, D. (1993). What autism teaches us about metarepresentation. In S. Baron-Cohen, H. Tager-Flusberg, & D. J. Cohen (Eds.), *Understanding other minds: Perspectives from autism* (pp. 83–111). New York: Oxford University Press.

Lillard, A. S., & Flavell, J. H. (1990). Young children's preference for mental state versus behavioral descriptions of human action. *Child Development*, *61*, 731–741.

Meltzoff, A. N. (1988a). Infant imitation after a 1-week delay: Long-term memory for novel acts and multiple stimuli. *Developmental Psychology*, *24*, 470–476.

Meltzoff, A. N. (1988b). Infant imitation and memory: Nine-month-olds in immediate and deferred tests. *Child Development*, *59*, 217–225.

Meltzoff, A. N. (1990a). Foundations for developing a concept of self: The role of imitation in relating self to other and the value of social mirroring, social modeling, and self practice in infancy. In D. Cicchetti & M. Beeghly (Eds.), *The self in transition: Infancy to childhood* (pp. 139–164). Chicago: University of Chicago Press.

Meltzoff, A. N. (1990b). Towards a developmental cognitive science: The implications of cross-modal matching and imitation for the development of representation and memory in infancy. In A. Diamond (Ed.), *The development and neural bases of higher cognitive functions. Annals of the New York Academy of Sciences, Vol. 608* (pp. 1–31). New York: New York Academy of Sciences.

Meltzoff, A. N. (1993). Molyneux's babies: Cross-modal perception, imitation, and the mind of the preverbal infant. In N. Eilan, R. McCarthy, & B. Brewer (Eds.), *Spatial representation: Problems in the philosophy and psychology* (pp. 219–235). Cambridge, MA: Basil Blackwell.

Meltzoff, A. N. (1995). What infant memory tells us about infantile amnesia: Long-term recall and deferred imitation. *Journal of Experimental Child Psychology*, *59*, 497–515.

Meltzoff, A. N., & Gopnik, A. (1993). The role of imitation in understanding persons and developing a theory of mind. In S. Baron-Cohen, H. Tager-Flusberg, & D. Cohen (Eds.), *Understanding other minds: Perspectives from autism* (pp. 335–366). New York: Oxford University Press.

Meltzoff, A. N., & Moore, M. K. (1983). Newborn infants imitate adult facial gestures. *Child Development*, *54*, 702–709.

Meltzoff, A. N., & Moore, M. K. (1992). Early imitation within a functional framework: The importance of person identity, movement, and development. *Infant Behavior and Development*, *15*, 479–505.

Meltzoff, A. N., & Moore, M. K. (1994). Imitation, memory, and the representation of persons. *Infant Behavior and Development*, *17*, 83–99.

Meltzoff, A. N., & Moore, M. K. (1995). Infants' understanding of people and things: From body imitation to folk psychology. In J. Bermúdez, A. J.

Marcel, & N. Eilan (Eds.), *The body and the self* (pp. 43–69). Cambridge, MA: MIT Press.

Moore, M. K., Borton, R., & Darby, B. L. (1978). Visual tracking in young infants: Evidence for object identity or object permanence? *Journal of Experimental Child Psychology, 25,* 183–198.

Perner, J. (1991a). *Understanding the representational mind.* Cambridge, MA: MIT Press.

Perner, J. (1991b). On representing that: The asymmetry between belief and desire in children's theory of mind. In D. Frye & C. Moore (Eds.), *Children's theories of mind: Mental states and social understanding* (pp. 139–155). Hillsdale, NJ: Erlbaum.

Piaget, J. (1929). *The child's conception of the world.* New York: Harcourt, Brace.

Piaget, J. (1962). *Play, dreams and imitation in childhood.* New York: W. W. Norton.

Premack, D. (1990). The infant's theory of self-propelled objects. *Cognition, 36,* 1–16.

Searle, J. R. (1983). *Intentionality: An essay in the philosophy of mind.* New York: Cambridge University Press.

Siegel, S. (1956). *Nonparametric statistics for the behavioral sciences.* New York: McGraw-Hill.

Spelke, E. S., & Van de Walle, G. A. (1993). Perceiving and reasoning about objects: Insights from infants. In N. Eilan, R. McCarthy, & B. Brewer (Eds.), *Spatial representation: Problems in philosophy and psychology* (pp. 132–161). Cambridge, MA: Basil Blackwell.

Tomasello, M., & Barton, M. (1994). Learning words in nonostensive contexts. *Developmental Psychology, 30,* 639–650.

Wellman, H. M. (1990). *The child's theory of mind.* Cambridge, MA: MIT Press.

Wellman, H. M. (1993). Early understanding of mind: The normal case. In S. Baron-Cohen, H. Tager-Flusberg, & D. J. Cohen (Eds.), *Understanding other minds: Perspectives from autism* (pp. 10–39). New York: Oxford University Press.

Wellman, H. M., & Estes, D. (1986). Early understanding of mental entities: A reexamination of childhood realism. *Child Development, 57,* 910–923.

Wellman, H. M., & Gelman, S. A. (1988). Children's understanding of the nonobvious. In R. J. Sternberg (Ed.), *Avances in the psychology of intelligence* (pp. 99–135). Hillsdale, NJ: Erlbaum.

Wellman, H. M., & Woolley, J. D. (1990). From simple desires to ordinary beliefs: The early development of everyday psychology. *Cognition, 35,* 245–275.

TEN

Theory of Mind

Introduction

One of the most significant advances in the study of cognitive develop-ment during the last two decades is the upsurge of research on chil-dren's acquisition of a naive theory of mind (Lee & Homer, 1999). A naive theory of mind refers to people's commonsense knowledge about others' and their own mental activities. This knowledge is useful for us because it helps us to "read" another person's mind and to explain or make predictions about his or her actions. Researchers believe that adults are in fact untrained psychologists who make some basic assump-tions about the mind. Most of us believe that other minds exist even though we never have directly observed one, and that different minds have different mental activities (the existence assumption). We believe that each mind has a number of components for different functions such as perceiving, desiring, intending, knowing, and believing (the component assumption). We also believe that there are causal relations (the causality assumption) between mental activities (e.g., seeing leads to knowing, ignorance or not knowing leads to false beliefs) and between mental activities and actions (e.g., false beliefs lead to misguided actions).

While adults may share such assumptions, evidence was scanty as to their ontogeny before the 1980s. Since then, there has been an explo-sion of research on children's acquisition of these assumptions (their so-called "theory of mind"). Two issues have been the focus of much of current research: (1) children's understanding that others, and they themselves, may have a false belief about the world and hence behave accordingly and erroneously (e.g., a person thinks it is raining outside, although it is in fact sunny, and therefore goes out with an umbrella), and (2) children's understanding that either an object's or person's appearance may be different from what it really is (e.g., a food item appears to be okay to eat but may be poisonous; a friendly looking stranger may be a criminal). These two issues are respectively referred to as false-belief understanding and appearance–reality distinction, which are the focus of this classic article by Gopnik and Astington.

Reference

Lee, K., & Homer, B. (1999). Children as folk psychologists: The developing understanding of the mind. In A. Slater & D. Muir (eds), *The Blackwell reader in development psychology* (pp. 228–252). Malden, MA: Blackwell.

Further reading

Gopnik, A., & Meltzoff, A. N. (1997). *Words, thoughts, and theories.* Cambridge, MA: MIT Press.
Wellman, H. M. (1992). *The child's theory of mind.* Cambridge, MA: MIT Press.

Children's Understanding of Representational Change and Its Relation to the Understanding of False Belief and the Appearance–Reality Distinction

Alison Gopnik and Janet W. Astington

As adults we change our ideas about the world, and we also know that we change them. We see what we think is a rock, but when we pick it up it turns out to be a painted sponge. We change our beliefs about the object; now we think the object is a sponge, but we also remember our past belief. We know that we used to think the object was a rock. Moreover, we can appreciate the difference between real changes in the world and changes in our beliefs about things in the world. We know now that the object really was a sponge all along. It did not change; our ideas about it changed.

We might capture this fact by saying that as adults we have representations of objects in the world, that those representations change, and that we represent the fact that those representations change. All creatures that represent the world at all change those representations. However, human adults have the additional ability to represent their past representations of the world and to contrast them with their present representations. They can understand the process of representational change itself.

The ability to understand representational change underpins many other important abilities. Acquiring new knowledge and, perhaps more important, acquiring strategies to acquire new knowledge often depends on an understanding of representational change. We say that we learn from our mistakes, but learning from our mistakes often requires that we know we were mistaken and can recognize the conditions that led us into error. Even machine learning systems must be able to represent their past representational states and retrace the path that led them to those states in order to modify their learning strategies (Newell & Simon, 1963). Moreover, our ability to understand and benefit from many types of instruction depends on our recognition that we were wrong in the past and may turn out to be wrong again in the future. It is hard to imagine teaching someone who was unable to recognize that they had been wrong.

In addition, an understanding of representational change is deeply involved in our everyday metaphysical assumptions about the relation between the mind and the world, the assumptions that philosophers sometimes call "naive realism." As adults we make a firm distinction between the world itself and our representations of the world. One important aspect of this distinction is that we believe that our representations of the world can change, and do change all the time, even when the world itself stays the same (Forguson & Gopnik, in press).

Finally, in addition to its intrinsic interest, representational change is also interesting because it is a metarepresentational ability, an ability that requires children to construct representations of their own representations (Pylyshyn, 1984). Some metarepresentational abilities may be present from a very early age. Very young children engage in pretend play, which suggests some ability to separate representations and realities (Leslie, in press; McCune-Nicolich, 1981; Piaget, 1962). Children seem to use terms such as "think" and "know" in their spontaneous speech from age two (Bretherton & Beeghly, 1982; Shatz, Wellman, & Silber, 1983). More compellingly, Wellman and Estes (1986) have found that even three-year-old children could make some distinctions between mental events, such as dreams or images, and physical ones.

Although some metarepresentational abilities may be present at this very early age, there seems to be a particularly important change in children's understanding of representation somewhere between ages three and five. Consider, for example, the metarepresentational ability to recognize that another person may represent an object differently than you do. Although Piaget (1926) claimed that young children are egocentric, in fact, even very young children, under age three, can appreciate that under some conditions someone else might not perceive an object that they perceive (Flavell, 1978; Flavell, Everett, Croft, & Flavell, 1981). However, three-year-olds have more difficulty in a more complex situation, one in which children must recognize that someone else's perception of an object is not like their own perception of it (Flavell, 1978; Flavell et al., 1981). For example, three-year-olds have difficulty recognizing that a person who sees an object from a different angle than they do may perceive it differently. Flavell has described this as a difference between Level 1 and Level 2 perspective taking.

Similarly, although very young children may sometimes be able to appreciate that other people do not know something they themselves know, they have more difficulty understanding that another person may represent an object differently than they do (Hogrefe, Wimmer, & Perner, 1986; Wimmer & Perner, 1983). For example, in one experiment children were shown a closed box that normally contained dominoes, and then the dominoes were removed and a glove was placed in the box. Three-year-olds were likely to say that another child would immediately think that there was a glove in the box, even before they opened it; five-year-olds were more likely to say that the other child would think that there were dominoes in the box, though they themselves thought the box contained a glove. Three-year-olds are apparently unable to appreciate the fact that two people can have different representations of the same object. Five-year-olds can understand that two people could have different representations of the object.

Flavell and his associates (Flavell, 1986; Flavell, Flavell, & Green, 1983; Taylor & Flavell, 1984) have found a similar result in a different domain. Children begin to appreciate the difference between appearance and reality somewhere between three and five. A three-year-old who is given a deceptive object, such as a sponge painted to look like a rock, is likely to say either that the object looks like a sponge and really is a sponge or that it looks like a rock and really is a rock. These children are unlikely to say that the object really is a sponge but looks like a rock. This result may also indicate that three-year-olds are reluctant to apply different representations to the same object. Although they may understand the difference between a rock and a pretend rock, or an image or a dream of a rock, they are unable to understand that the same object could be represented either as a sponge or as a rock depending on one's point of view.

From these findings it appears that three-year-olds do not understand that there might be alternative representations of the same object (Flavell, 1986; Wimmer & Perner, 1983). If this is true, three-year-olds should also have difficulty understanding the fact that their own representations have changed. When we change our ideas about an object, our previous representation differs from our present representation. To understand representational change children must be able to say "I once thought this was X but now I think this is Y." This ability is similar to the ability to understand another's false belief "he thinks this is X but I think this is Y," and the appearance–reality distinction "this looks like X but really is Y."

Shatz et al. (1983) report two instances in which a child aged two to eight explicitly referred to a past mental state and contrasted this with a present mental state. There is, however, also some evidence that understanding representational change might be difficult for such young children. In an attempt to improve performance on the false-belief task, Hogrefe et al. (1986) showed children a typical container (e.g., a matchbox) that when opened turned out to have an unexpected content (e.g., chocolate), and routinely asked the children what they had originally thought was in the box. Several children answered this question incorrectly and had to be prompted to give the correct answer. Perner, Leekman, and Wimmer (1987) also reported that some children failed to answer a question about their own representational change correctly after they had been shown a candy box that turned out to contain pencils, though more children passed this control question than passed the false-belief question.

The form of the question in this experiment, however, gave the children a strong indication of what answer was expected. Children were asked, "Can you remember what's inside here?" and when they said "pencils," this question was immediately followed by the question, "But what did you think was in here?" Pragmatically, there is a strong presupposition in this question that the answer is something other than pencils. Thus it is not surprising that children did better on this question than on the false-belief question, which did not include this presupposition. Moreover, there was no control in this study to ensure that the children who did fail the task understood the representational change question itself. This experiment was, of course, not designed to investigate representational change, but these methodological problems make the results difficult to interpret. However, the results are consistent with the view that some children may have been unable to understand that they themselves had once had a different representation of an object, just as they were unable to understand that someone else had a different representation of the object. This is the possibility we explored systematically in the present study.

Empirical investigations of these issues raise particular methodological problems. The simple fact that a child fails to answer a question correctly may not necessarily indicate a cognitive deficit. The child may be unable to interpret the syntax of the question. Or the child may be unable to understand other concepts involved in the question. For example, children might be unable to answer questions about representational change if they could not understand the difference between past and present events. Or the child may be "perceptually seduced" by the present appearance of the object into giving the wrong answer (Bryant, 1974). For instance, if children see a box full of pencils in front of them, they may be tempted to answer "pencils" to any question about the contents of the box. In the present investigations, we have attempted to deal with these methodological problems. In particular, children were given a control task that was identical to the experimental task in all respects, except that it did not require the metarepresentational ability to understand representational change. Children were only included in the analysis of the results if they passed this control test.

The studies we will report were designed to accomplish three ends. First, the studies were designed to discover when children develop an ability to understand representational change. Second, we investigated the developmental relation between this problem and the appearance–reality and false-belief problems. Several different relations between these problems are possible. Children might solve all three problems at the same time, suggesting the development of a single more general metarepresentational ability at this point, or they might solve some of these problems before others. For example, we might expect that children would be able to understand representational change first and then apply this understanding to the false-belief problem; they might treat other people as if they were their own past selves. Alternatively, children might come to appreciate representational change by solving the problem of false belief; they might treat their own past selves as if they were other people. Similarly, understanding the appearance–reality distinction might be a cause or a consequence of understanding the other two problems. Finally, the study was designed to explore whether children's understanding of representational change varies in different task situations.

Experiment 1

Method

Subjects.   Subjects were 43 children attending local day-care centers. The subjects were divided into three age groups: 14 three-year-olds (mean age = 40.57 months, range = 34–48 months), 12 four-year-olds (mean age = 54.67 months, range = 50–59 months), and 17 five-year-olds (mean age = 65.88 months, range = 60–75 months).

Materials.   Materials were designed to lead the child to represent an object in one way initially and then to change that representation, without there being an actual change in the object itself. Children received variants of the Perner et al. (1987) "smarties" task and the Flavell et al. (1983) "rock" task. In the "smarties" task, children were shown a box of the candy "smarties" that had pictures of smarties on it. ("Smarties" are a popular British and Canadian candy, and "smarties" boxes are highly familiar to British and Canadian children.) When children opened the box they discovered that there were small pencils inside the box instead of smarties. We assumed that the children would initially represent the box as containing smarties and then represent it as containing pencils.

   In the "rock" task, children were shown a small sponge painted to look like a rock. (This sponge-rock deceived several adults who were shown it.) Children were initially shown the rock on the other side of a table and were then allowed to pick it up and squeeze it. We assumed that the children initially represented the object as a rock and then represented it as a sponge.

Procedure.   Children were all tested individually in a small screened-off area of the day-care center. Children were tested by two experimenters, one who administered the tasks and one who recorded the children's answers. Test sessions were audiotaped. Children were told initially, "We're going to play a game where we show you some things and ask questions about them." Children first received a control task (see below) and then received the materials described above. In each case, children were first shown the object in its deceptive form (i.e., the closed smarties box, or the rock at the other side of the table) and were told to look at it. The true nature of the object was then revealed (i.e., the children were told to open the box, and to pick up the rock and squeeze it). Then children were asked to identify the true nature of the objects. They were asked in the different tasks, "What's inside the box?" and, "What is it?" until they answered correctly. This ensured that the children did, in fact, represent the objects as containing pencils or as a sponge after the deception was revealed. The object was then returned to its previous deceptive state (i.e., the smarties box was closed, and the rock was placed away from the child). This ensured that the children were not "perceptually seduced" by seeing the pencils or by feeling the sponge. Children were then asked the test questions. At the end of the session, children were told not to talk about the tests with any other children.

Test questions.   Children were asked three sets of forced-choice questions investigating their understanding of representational change, false belief, and the appearance-reality distinction (see Appendix). The question concerning representational change for the smarties task was, "When you first saw the box, before we opened it, what did you think was inside it? Did you think there were smarties inside it or did you think there were pencils inside it?" The question was designed to be highly redundant and to stress the fact that we were asking about the child's past representation of the object.

All children received a control task that was designed to ensure that they understood the basic concepts involved in the representational change question. This task involved a real change in the world rather than a change in the child's representation of the world. In this task, children were shown a closed toy house. The roof of the house was then removed. Inside the house was an apple. The apple was then removed, a doll was put in the house, and the roof was replaced. Children were then asked what was in the house now. When they answered correctly they were asked, "When you first saw the house, before we put the man in there, what was inside it? Was there an apple inside it or was there a man inside it? The two forced-choice alternatives were counterbalanced.

To answer this question correctly, that is to say, "the apple," children had to have understood the question, understood the concept of one event occurring before another, remembered the past event, and been able to ignore the present state of the object. In short, the only conceptual difference between answering this question and answering the representational change question is the metarepresentational element. In the control question, children are asked about the past state of the object, while in the test question they are asked about their past representation of the object. Another way of putting this is that in the control question an object changes, while in the test question the object remains the same and the child's representation of the object changes. If the child answers the control question correctly but does not answer the change question correctly, it is likely that this failure is the result of an inability to understand *representational* change in particular, rather than the result of a general inability to understand change or some more general cognitive or linguistic difficulty. Children always received the control task before they received the other tasks.

To control for possible effects of order of presentation, the four test questions (representational change, false belief, and the two appearance–reality questions) were presented in eight different orders, specified by eight different lists. Half the lists presented the representational change and false-belief questions first, and half presented the appearance–reality questions first. Within each half, order of presentation of questions in each pair was alternated, and within each pair the order of presentation of the forced choices was alternated, with the constraint that the order for the first and fourth questions was the same. Half of the children were asked first about the smarties box, and the other half about the rock. For each child, the order of questions and forced choice alternatives for one set of materials was exactly the reverse of the order for the other set.

Scoring.   Children were scored as having passed the representational change question if they correctly reported their initial representation of the object. All children who passed the control task gave some response to the questions. Children were only counted as having failed if they said that they had originally known the true nature of the object, for example, if they said, "I thought there were pencils in the box." Similar procedures were used to score the false-belief question. To pass the appearance–reality question, children had to answer both parts correctly; for example, they had to say both that the object really was a sponge and that it looked like a rock. Children were given a total score of 0–2 on each question depending on whether they answered the questions correctly on neither the smarties nor the rock task, on one of the tasks, or on both.

Results

Representational change. Four of the children in the three-year-old group and one in the five-year-old group failed the control task and were excluded from further analysis. The new mean age of the three-year-olds was 41.1 months and the range was 36–48 months. Children's mean scores were subjected to a 2 (task materials) × 3 (age) × 8 (list) analysis of variance, with task materials as the within-subjects factor, and age and list the between-subjects factors. There was no effect of list, which had varied the order of task materials, questions, and forced-choice alternatives, and it did not enter into any interactions. There was a significant effect of age, with performance increasing across the three age groups, $F(2,15) = 5.38$, $p < .05$ (see fig. 1). In particular, for both tasks, less than one half of the three-year-old group answered the

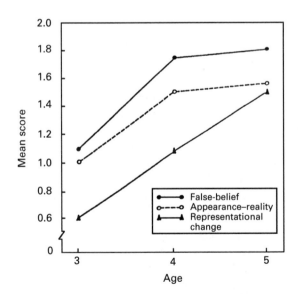

Figure 1 Mean scores on representational change, false-belief, and appearance–reality questions for three age groups in Experiment 1.

representational change question correctly, while more than two thirds of the five-year-old group answered correctly. There was also a significant effect of task materials, with the rock task appearing to be easier than the smarties task, $F(1,15) = 5.92$, $p < .05$.

It may be noted that we did not ask the children, when they first saw the box, what they thought was inside it, and thus had no way of telling for sure whether they did think there were smarties in the box or that the object was a rock. This was done intentionally because we wanted to ensure that children were not simply reporting their previous statement rather than their previous mental state. However, there were seven instances in which children did in fact spontaneously identify the objects when they first saw them, suggesting that they did make these assumptions. Moreover, it is interesting to note that in five of these instances children who did explicitly identify the objects still gave the incorrect answer on the representational change question.

Relations to other questions.   A similar ANOVA performed on the false-belief and appearance–reality scores indicated that performance on these tasks also increased with age, replicating the findings of Flavell et al. (1983) and Hogrefe et al. (1986). However, a within-subjects analysis of performance on the three types of question indicated that performance on the false-belief question was significantly better than performance on the change question, $F(1,35) = 10.43$, $p < .01$. Performance on the appearance–reality question was intermediate between the other two questions but did not differ significantly from either question (see fig. 1).

We also examined the pooled within-cell correlations between performance on the three questions for the entire sample. These correlations control for the effects of age. There were significant correlations between performance on the change question and the appearance–reality question ($r = .46$, $p < .01$) and between performance on the false-belief question and the appearance–reality question ($r = .49$, $p < .01$), although not between performance on the change question and the false-belief question ($r = .24$, $p > .05$).

It should be noted that two types of error are possible for appearance–reality; children may say that the rock both looks like a rock and really is a rock, the phenomenist error, or they may say that the rock both looks like a sponge and really is a sponge, the realist error (Flavell et al.,

1983). Children in our study, like those in Flavell's study, made the realist error more frequently, though both these errors occurred. However, there was no connection between the type of appearance–reality error a child made and performance on the other two questions. Realists and phenomenists were equally poor on the representational change and false-belief questions.

Finally, we may investigate whether children erred consistently or simply responded at chance levels. If children were responding at chance we would expect the mean score to be about 1. In fact, the three-year-olds' mean for the representational change question was considerably below this, suggesting that they were consistently making errors. Another way of investigating this question is to look at the patterns of responding across the two tasks. Only two of the ten three-year-olds performed differently on the smarties task and the rock task. Moreover, both these children passed the rock task but did not pass the smarties task. The same pattern emerged among the older children. Only five out of 28 older children performed differently on the two tasks, and only one of these children did better on the smarties task than on the rock task. Apparently most of the divergences from consistency were due to the difference in difficulty of the two tasks rather than to chance responding.

Experiment 2

Given the results of Experiment 1, three-year-olds do appear to have difficulty understanding representational change, and this difficulty is related to their difficulty in understanding false-belief and the appearance–reality distinction. Two issues deserve further investigation, however. First, we had some concerns about the linguistic form of the representational change question in Experiment 1. Some children may have had trouble understanding this complex question. Also, in the control task we had asked, "When you first looked in the house, before we put the man in there, what was inside it?" This may have indicated to the children that an answer other than "the man" was expected. Finally, in Experiment 1 there were some syntactic differences between the form of the change question and the form of the false-belief question, and such differences might have led to the difference in performance on these two questions.

Second, we wanted to see whether children would show the same difficulties across a wider range of task materials, and whether some types of materials would be more difficult than others. In the second experiment, then, we included a wider range of syntactic forms of the question and of task materials.

Method

Subjects.   Fifty-eight children from local day-care centers were tested. Again, the children were divided into three age groups: 20 three-year-olds (mean age = 44.90 months, range = 37–48 months), 21 four-year-olds (mean age = 52.91 months, range = 49–59 months), and 17 five-year-olds (mean age = 65.59, range = 60–74 months).

Materials.   Three additional sets of materials, as well as the original "smarties" and "rock" materials, were used.

The first additional set of materials, based on a task used by Chandler and Helm (1984), were used to explore children's representation of the identity of an object but did so in a rather different way than the rock task. Children were presented with a small book with pictures of animals on the cover. When children opened the book they saw a restricted view of a picture of a dog, including its ears, through a peephole. When they turned the page, the full picture of the dog was visible. Similarly, on the next page, children saw a restricted view of a rabbit, including its ears, and when they turned the page saw the full rabbit. On the following page, children again saw a restricted view of what looked like ears through the peephole, but now when they turned the page they saw that the "ears" were actually petals of a flower. The assumption was that the children would initially represent the last picture as another animal and then represent it as a flower.

The next set of materials investigated the child's understanding of properties and was adapted from a task used by Taylor and Flavell (1984). Children were shown a green cat covered by a pink transparency, which made the cat look black. Children were then told to lift the transparency, revealing that the cat was actually green. Again we assumed that the children would initially represent the cat as black and then represent it as green.

The final set of materials explored children's understanding of number. The materials consisted of two rag dolls that could be put together and covered with one dress. Children were initially shown the dressed doll, which looked like a single doll, and then the doll was undressed and the two dolls were revealed. Again the assumption was that the children would initially represent the doll as a single doll and then represent it as two dolls.

Procedure.   The procedure used was the same as that in Experiment 1. Children were given the control task first, and then the five other tasks. Children were shown the object in its deceptive form (the picture through the peephole, the cat with the transparency over it, and the dressed doll), and the true nature of the object was then revealed (the page was turned, the transparency was lifted, and the doll was undressed). Children were asked to identify the true nature of the object, and the object was then returned to its original deceptive state and the children were asked the test questions.

Questions.   The control task question was changed to avoid the pragmatic problems of the question in the first experiment. One form of this question read, "When you first saw the house, before we took the roof off, what was inside it?" All children received a representational change question and false-belief question for all tasks. Appearance–reality questions would not have been appropriate for all the new tasks, and we were slightly concerned about the naturalness of the appearance–reality question in the "smarties" task. Therefore, these questions were asked only for the "rock" task and the "cat" task, the two tasks most closely analogous to Flavell's tasks. Twenty-one of the children received questions analogous to the questions in Experiment 1, 17 children received questions of Form A, such as "When you first saw the box, all closed up like this, what did you think was inside it?," and the remaining 20 children received questions of Form B, such as "What did you think was inside the box before we opened it?" (see Appendix). In each case children received the same form of the question in the control task, the change task, and the false-belief task. In Experiment 1, many children answered the representational change and false-belief questions immediately before the forced-choice part of the question could be administered. Therefore, in this experiment, children were given an open-ended question first. If children did not respond they were asked the forced-choice question.

Tasks and questions were presented in six different orders specified by six different lists. The three tasks that did not have appearance–reality questions were presented equally often in first, third, or fifth position, and the two tasks that did have appearance–reality questions were presented equally often in second or fourth position. The representational change and false-belief questions were always asked first; within the pair, each type of question appeared first at least twice, and first not more than twice in succession, on each list. In addition, on each list the order of questions for appearance and reality was alternated for the two tasks that had appearance–reality questions.

Scoring.   Scoring procedures were generally the same as those used in the previous experiment. Children received a score of 0–5 on the representational change and false-belief questions and a score of 0–2 on the appearance–reality question, depending on how many times they answered each question correctly. To compare scores on the three questions, the appearance–reality score was transformed to a comparable scale to that used for the other two questions by multiplying each appearance–reality score by 5/2.

Results

Representational change.   Five three-year-olds failed the control task and were not included in the analysis of the results. The new mean age of the three-year-old group was 45.0 months and the range was 40–48 months. Children's mean scores were subjected to a 5 (task materials) × 3 (age) × 6 (list) × 3 (syntactic form of question) analysis of variance, with task materials as the within-subjects factor, and age, list, and syntactic form between-subjects factors. The three-way interaction and the interaction of list and syntactic form were suppressed and pooled with the within-cell variance. There were no effects of list, or syntactic form, and no interactions of either with age, suggesting that the results were not due to the order of presentation of the questions or to the particular syntactic form of the question.

There was a significant effect of age, which was similar overall to the age effect found in the first experiment, $F(2,30) = 6.39$, $p < .01$ (see fig. 2).

There was also a significant effect of task materials, $F(4,120) = 5.85$, $p < .001$. Children's performance on the "smarties" and "rock" tasks was comparable to their performance in Experiment 1. However, the "book" and "cat" tasks appeared to be somewhat easier than the other two

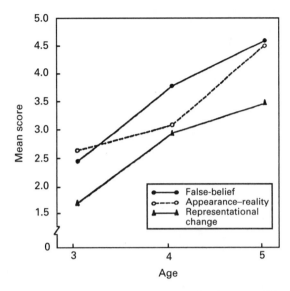

Figure 2 Mean scores on representational change, false-belief, and appearance–reality questions for three age groups in Experiment 2.

tasks, and the "doll" task appeared to be more difficult. Across all three age groups, the proportion of children who answered the representational change question correctly was .69, .66, .52, .49, and .39 for the "book," "cat," "rock," "smarties," and "doll" tasks, respectively. For the three-year-olds, the proportion of correct answers on each task ranged from .47 to .27. Thus, even the easiest of the tasks was still failed by more than half of the three-year-olds.

Relation to other questions.   As in Experiment 1, the false-belief question proved to be significantly easier than the change question, $F(1,50) = 24.02, p < .01$ (see fig. 2). Moreover, this difference was consistent across the five tasks. For each individual task, children performed better on the false-belief question than on the change question. As in the previous experiment, the results on the appearance–reality question appeared to fall between the other two results. In this experiment, however, appearance–reality performance was significantly better than change performance, $F(1,50) = 7.16, p < .01$, but was not significantly worse than false-belief performance.

The pooled within-cell correlations of performance on the three types of question were also examined. There were significant correlations between performance on all three types of question. The correlations between the change question and the appearance–reality question ($r = .49$, $p < .01$) and between the false-belief question and the appearance–reality question ($r = .44$, $p < .01$) were comparable to those in the previous experiment. In the present experiment, however, there was also a significant correlation between performance on the change and false-belief questions ($r = .62$, $p < .001$).

Again, as in the previous experiment there were 40 instances in which children spontaneously identified the objects when they first saw them. Children explicitly said "smarties," "a rock," and "a doll" and identified the flower as an animal, though they did not explicitly identify the color of the cat. As before, in 14 of these cases children who explicitly identified the objects answered the representational change question incorrectly.

Again as before, realist answers to the appearance–reality questions predominated. This was true even in the "cat" task, where Flavell et al. found a predominance of phenomenist errors. However, as in the previous experiment, there was no clear relation between the type of appearance–reality error and the results on the other two questions.

As in the previous experiment, the fact that the three-year-olds' mean score on the representational change question was less than 2.5 suggests that these children were not responding at chance. The task differences in this study made it difficult to use children's consistency across tasks to indicate whether they were guessing or choosing a particular incorrect answer. However, a reliability coefficient (Cronbach's alpha = .69) across the five tasks also suggests that children were not performing at chance.

General Discussion

Children's understanding of representational change seems to develop between ages three and five. In particular, three-year-olds are likely to behave as if their present representation of an object was always their representation of it. They are unable to appreciate that their past representation of an object was different from their present representation.

However, performance on this task may vary depending on what kinds of task materials are used. A possible, though speculative, explanation for this fact is that it is easier to construct metarepresentations of representations that are more perceptually based than those that are more abstract. For example, the Level 2 visual perspective-taking ability, which involves perceptually based claims about the appearance of objects, seems to arise somewhat earlier than the solution of the false-belief task, which involves more abstract propositions about relations between objects. It seems plausible that it is more difficult to metarepresent more abstract and sophisticated representations, such as the representations of number in the "doll" task, than more perceptually based representations, such as the representations of color in the "cat" task.

There also are interesting relations between understanding representational change and understanding false belief and the appearance–reality distinction. All three of these tasks involve the ability to consider two alternative conflicting representations of the same object. All three of these abilities seem to develop at about the same point, between three and five, and all three abilities are correlated even when age is controlled. These three abilities may reflect some more general ability to consider alternative representations of reality that develops at about this time.

However, it appears that, for each particular task, children consistently understand the false-belief question before they understand the representational change question. There are a number of possible interpretations of this finding. One possibility might be that children are less willing to attribute errors to themselves than to other people and are therefore motivated to conceal their own ignorance. According to this account, some children know about their past representation, but they lie about it to the experimenter, or somehow suppress their own knowledge of their past representation. Notice that this explanation will not work as an explanation of the change effect in general. When children are incorrect on both the false-belief question and on the change question, it seems implausible to attribute both these errors to motivational or emotional factors. To do so, we would have to assume that these children are motivated to lie to the experimenter about both their own state and the state of other children.

This explanation of the difference between these two questions seems implausible on several grounds. First, it assumes that three-year-old children have the ability to formulate metarepresentational propositions and then have the further metarepresentational ability to deceive another person (or themselves) about those propositions. Second, and most significant, this explanation fails to account for the effect of task materials. We would have to assume, on this model, that while five-year-olds were not motivated to deceive the experimenter or themselves about their representations in the other tasks, they were so motivated in the "doll" task.

An alternative, more promising explanation is that children actually learn to understand changes in their own mental states by appreciating the difference between their own mental state and that of another. Although this may at first seem counterintuitive, it might be consistent with a Vygotskyan view of cognitive development. Such a view would claim that certain concepts are learned first in a social setting and are then internalized. In particular, because children and other people use the same language, children's own states will often conflict explicitly with the states of others. Although it may be easy to ignore your own contradictions, it is less easy to ignore, say, the vociferously repeated contrary claims put forward by your older brother.

A final interesting aspect of these results is their implications for studies of children's memory. The representational change question tests one aspect of the child's memory as well as testing metacognitive skills. Apparently, three-year-old children can easily remember states of the external world, but they may have more difficulty remembering internal psychological states such as their previous representations of the world. This is consistent with some of the findings in the naturalistic investigation of early event memory (Nelson & Ross, 1980).

More generally, there is a growing consensus that there are significant and profound changes in children's concept of the mind between three and five (Astington, Harris, & Olson, in press). Developing an understanding of representational change appears to be one of these changes.

Appendix: Question Forms
Experiment 1

Control

When you first looked in the house, before we put the man in there, what was inside it? Was there an apple inside or was there a man inside?

Smarties

Representational change. When you first saw the box, before we opened it, what did you think was inside it? Did you think there were pencils inside it or did you think there were smarties inside it?

False belief. X hasn't seen inside this box. If X sees the box all closed up like this, what will [s]he think is inside it? Will [s]he think there are pencils inside it or will [s]he think there are smarties inside it? [Note: X is another child in day care, not yet tested.]

Appearance. Does it look like this box has pencils in it or does it look like it has smarties in it?

Reality. What's really inside this box? Are there really pencils inside it, or are there really smarties inside it?

Rock

Representational change. When you first saw this, before you touched it or squeezed it, what did you think it was? Did you think it was a rock or did you think it was a sponge?

False belief. X hasn't touched this, [s]he hasn't squeezed it. If X just sees it over here like this, what will [s]he think it is? Will [s]he think it's a rock or will [s]he think that it's a sponge?

Appearance. What does this look like? Does it look like a rock or does it look like a sponge?

Reality. What is this really? Is it really a rock or is it really a sponge?

Experiment 2

Form A
Control

When you first saw the house at the beginning, what was inside it?

Smarties

Representational change.   When you first saw the box, all closed up like this, what did you think was inside it?

False belief.   X hasn't seen inside this box. When [s]he first sees the box, all closed up like this, what will [s]he think is inside it?

Rock

Representational change.   When you first saw this, over here like this, what did you think it was?

False belief.   X hasn't touched this, [s]he hasn't squeezed it. When [s]he first sees it, over here like this, what will [s]he think it is?

Book

Representational change.   When you first saw the picture, through the peephole like this, what did you think it was?

False belief.   X hasn't seen these pictures. When [s]he first sees the picture, through the peephole like this, what will [s]he think it is?

Cat

Representational change.   When you first saw the cat, all covered up like this, what color did you think it was?

False belief.   X hasn't seen this. When [s]he first sees the cat, all covered up like this, what color will [s]he think it is?

Doll

Representational change.   When you first saw this, all dressed up like this, how many dolls did you think there were?

False belief.   X hasn't seen this, [s]he hasn't played with it. When [s]he first sees it, all dressed up like this, how many dolls will [s]he think there are?

Form B
Control

What was in the house before we took the roof off?

Smarties

Representational change.   What did you think was inside the box before we opened it?

False belief.   X hasn't seen inside this box. What will [s]he think is inside it before [s]he opens it?

Rock

Representational change.   What did you think this was before you touched it or squeezed it?

False belief.   X hasn't touched this, [s]he hasn't squeezed it. What will [s]he think it is before [s]he touches it or squeezes it?

Book

Representational change.   What did you think this was before we turned the page?

False belief.   X hasn't seen these pictures. What will [s]he think it is before [s]he turns the page?

Cat

Representational change.   What color did you think the cat was before we uncovered it?

False belief.   X hasn't seen this. What color will [s]he think the cat is before [s]he uncovers it?

Doll

Representational change.   How many dolls did you think there were before we took the dress off?

False belief. X hasn't seen this, [s]he hasn't played with this. How many dolls will [s]he think there are before [s]he takes the dress off?

Forms A and B (appearance–reality)
Rock

Appearance. What does this look like? Does it look like a rock or does it look like a sponge?

Reality. What is this really? Is it really a rock or is it really a sponge?

Cat

Appearance. What does this look like? Does the cat look black or green?

Reality. What is this really? Is the cat really green or really black?

References

Astington, J. W., Harris, P. L., & Olson, D. (Eds.) (in press). *Developing theories of mind.* New York: Cambridge University Press.

Bretherton, I., & Beeghly, M. (1982). Talking about internal states: The acquisition of an explicit theory of mind. *Developmental Psychology,* 18, 906–921.

Bryant, P. (1974). *Perception and understanding in young children.* London: Methuen.

Chandler, M. J., & Helm, D. (1984). Developmental changes in the contribution of shared experience to social role-taking. *International Journal of Behavioral Development,* 7, 145–156.

Flavell, J. H. (1978). The development of knowledge about visual perception. In C. B. Keasey (Ed.), *Nebraska symposium on motivation* (Vol. 25, pp. 43–76). Lincoln: University of Nebraska Press.

Flavell, J. H. (1986). The development of children's knowledge about the appearance–reality distinction. *American Psychologist,* 41, 418–425.

Flavell, J. H. Everett, B. A., Croft, K., & Flavell, E. R. (1981). Young children's knowledge about visual perception: Further evidence for the Level 1-Level 2 distinction. *Developmental Psychology,* 17, 99–103.

Flavell, J. H., Flavell, E. R., & Green, F. L. (1983). Development of the appearance–reality distinction. *Cognitive Psychology,* 15, 95–120.

Forguson, L., & Gopnik, A. (in press). The ontogeny of common sense. In J. W. Astington, P. L. Harris, & D. Olson (Eds.), *Developing theories of mind.* New York: Cambridge University Press.

Hogrefe, G.-J., Wimmer, H., & Perner, J. (1986). Ignorance versus false belief: A developmental lag in attribution of epistemic states. *Child Development,* 57, 567–582.

Leslie, A. (in press). Some implications of pretense for mechanisms underlying the child's theory of mind. In J. W. Astington, P. L. Harris, & D. Olson (Eds.), *Developing theories of mind.* New York: Cambridge University Press.

McCune-Nicolich, L. (1981). Toward symbolic functioning: Structure of early use of pretend games and potential parallels with language. *Child Development,* 52, 785–797.

Nelson, K., & Ross, G. (1980). The generalities and specifics of long-term memory in infants and young children. *New Directions for Child Development,* 10, 87–101.

Newell, A., & Simon, H. (1963). GPS, a program that simulates human thought. In E. Feigenbaum & J. Feldman (Eds.), *Computers and thought* (pp. 279–293). New York: McGraw-Hill.

Perner, J., Leekman, S., & Wimmer, H. (1987). Three-year-olds' difficulty with false belief: The case for a conceptual deficit. *British Journal of Developmental Psychology.*

Piaget, J. (1926). *The language and thought of the child.* New York: Harcourt.

Piaget, J. (1962). *Play, dreams and imitation in childhood.* London: Routledge & Kegan Paul.

Pylyshyn, Z. (1984). *Computation and cognition.* Cambridge, MA: MIT Press.

Shatz, M., Wellman, H. M., & Silber, S. (1983). The acquisition of mental verbs: A systematic investigation of the first reference to mental state. *Cognition,* 14, 301–321.

Taylor, M., & Flavell, J. (1984). Seeing and believing: Children's understanding of the distinction between appearance and reality. *Child Development,* 55, 1710–1720.

Wellman, H. M., & Estes, D. (1986). Early understanding of mental entities: A reexamination of childhood realism. *Child Development,* 57, 910–923.

Wimmer, H., & Perner, J. (1983). Beliefs about beliefs: Representation and constraining function of wrong beliefs in children's understanding of deception. *Cognition,* 13, 103–128.

ELEVEN

Memory and Suggestibility

Introduction

The suggestibility of children is a relatively new area of memory development research. It is a new extension of a century-long investigation of children's memory capacity, strategy use, and metamemory (see Kail, 1990), and arises from the upsurge in the number of children who have been called upon to testify in courts in the last two decades (100,000 children per year in the US alone, according to Gray, 1993). Research on suggestibility informs us about the vulnerability of children's memory to post-event suggestions – currently a very controversial issue. The authors of this article argue that children's memory is susceptible to post-event suggestions. Other researchers disagree (Eisen & Goodman, 1998). Controversy notwithstanding, debate and empirical research on this issue will certainly help legal professionals to make policy decisions about the use of children as eye witnesses in the court, and to develop procedures that ensure the accuracy of child eye-witness reports.

References

Eisen, M. L., & Goodman, G. S. (1998). Trauma, memory, and suggestibility in children. *Development and Psychopathology, 10,* 717–38.

Gray, E. (1993). *Unequal justice: The prosecution of child sexual abuse.* New York: Macmillan.

Kail, R. (1990). *The development of memory in children* (3rd edn). New York: W. H. Freeman.

The Suggestibility of Young Children

Maggie Bruck and Stephen J. Ceci

Since the beginning of the 1980s, there have been a number of legal cases in which young children have provided uncorroborated testimony involving sexual abuse. Although it seemed from the evidence that the children in many of these cases were subjected to a number of suggestive interviews, the primary issue in deciding guilt or innocence was the degree to which such interviews could actually bring children to make serious allegations.

Until recently, scientific data provided little insight into this forensic issue. Specifically, although there were a number of studies showing that young children are more suggestible than adults (reviewed by Ceci & Bruck, 1993), these studies were limited to examinations of the influence of single misleading suggestions on children's recall of neutral, and often uninteresting, events. In other words, the conditions of the studies were not similar to the conditions that brought children to court. This empirical vacuum forced a new conceptualization of issues related to children's suggestibility, which, in turn, resulted in an outpouring of new research in the area. In general, two features of the newer research make it more relevant to forensic issues. First, the studies are designed to examine children's suggestibility about events that are personally salient, that involve bodily touching, and that involve insinuations of sexual abuse. Second, the concept of suggestive techniques has been expanded from the traditional view of asking a misleading question or planting a piece of misinformation, so that now studies examine the larger structure and the components of suggestive interviews. In this article, we provide an overview of the results of these newer studies of children's suggestibility.

Interviewer Bias and Suggestive Interviewing Techniques

We have proposed that *interviewer bias* is the central driving force in the creation of suggestive interviews. Interviewer bias characterizes an interviewer who holds a priori beliefs about the occurrence of certain events and, as a result, molds the interview to elicit from the interviewer statements that are consistent with these prior beliefs. One hallmark of interviewer bias is the single-minded attempt to gather only confirmatory evidence and to avoid all avenues that may produce disconfirmatory evidence. Thus, a biased interviewer does not ask questions that might provide alternate explanations for the allegations (e.g., "Did your mommy tell you, or did you see it happen?"). Nor does a biased interviewer ask about events that are inconsistent with the interviewer's hypothesis (e.g., "Who else beside your teacher touched your private parts? Did your mommy touch them, too?"). And a biased interviewer does not challenge the authenticity of the child's report when it is consistent with the interviewer's hypothesis. When a child provides inconsistent or bizarre evidence, it is either ignored or interpreted within the framework of the biased interviewer's initial hypothesis.

A number of studies highlight the effects of interviewer bias on the accuracy of children's reports (reviewed in Ceci & Bruck, 1995). In some studies, children are engaged in a staged event. Later, naive interviewers, who did not witness the event, are given either accurate or false information about the event and then told to question the children. Interviewers who are given false information are unaware of this deliberate deception, which is carried out to create a "bias." In other studies, children are asked to recall a staged event by an experimenter who intentionally conveys a bias that is either consistent or inconsistent with the staged event. In both types of studies, when questioned by interviewers with false beliefs, children make inaccurate reports that are consistent with the interviewers' biases.

According to our model, interviewer bias influences the entire architecture of interviews, and it is revealed through a number of different component features that are suggestive. We briefly describe some of these in this section.

In order to obtain confirmation of their suspicions, biased interviewers may not ask children open-ended questions, such as "What happened?" but instead resort to a barrage of specific questions, many of which are repeated, and many of which are leading. This strategy is problematic because children's reponses to open-ended questions are more accurate than their responses to specific questions. This finding has been reported consistently since the beginning of the century (e.g., see Ceci & Bruck, 1995) and is highlighted in a recent study by Peterson and Bell (1996), who interviewed children after they visited an emergency room for a traumatic injury. Children were first asked open-ended questions (e.g., "Tell me what happened"), and then asked more specific questions (e.g., "Where did you hurt yourself?" or "Did you hurt your knee?"). The children were most likely to report the important details accurately in response to open-ended questions (91% accuracy); errors increased when children were asked specific questions (45% accuracy). Forced-choice questions (e.g., "Was it black or white?") also compromise the reliability of children's reports because children tend not to respond, "I don't know" (e.g., see Walker, Lunning, & Eilts, 1996), even when the question is nonsensical (Hughes & Grieve, 1980).

Not only does accuracy decrease when children are asked specific questions, but there is increased risk of taint when young children are repeatedly asked the same specific questions, either within the same interview or across different interviews (e.g., Poole & White, 1991). Under such circumstances, young children tend to change their answers, perhaps to provide the interviewer with the information that they perceive he or she wants.

Some interviewers convey their bias by asking leading questions and providing information about the alleged target events. When these techniques are repeated across multiple interviews, children's reports may become tainted. For example, in one study (Bruck, Ceci, Francoeur, & Barr, 1995), five-year-old children visited their pediatrician and received an inoculation. One year later, they were interviewed four times about salient details of that visit. Children who were repeatedly interviewed in a neutral, nonleading manner provided accurate reports about the original medical visit. In contrast, children who were repeatedly given misinformation about some of the salient details were very inaccurate; not only did they incorporate the misleading suggestions into their reports (e.g., falsely claiming that a female research assistant, rather than the male pediatrician, inoculated them), but they also reported nonsuggested but inaccurate events (e.g., falsely reporting that the female research assistant had checked their ears and nose).

Interviewers can also use subtle verbal and nonverbal cues to communicate bias. At times, these cues can set the emotional tone of the interview, and they can also convey implicit or explicit threats, bribes, and rewards for the desired answer. Children are attuned to these emotional tones and act accordingly. In one study, for example, children were asked to recall the details of a visit to a university laboratory that had occurred four years previously (Goodman, Wilson, Hazan, & Reed, 1989). At the four-year follow-up interview, the researchers deliberately created an atmosphere of accusation by telling the children that they were to be questioned about an important event and by saying, "Are you afraid to tell? You'll feel better once you've told." Although few children remembered the original event from four years earlier, a number of the children assented to suggestive questions implying abuse; some children falsely reported that they had been hugged or kissed, or that they had had their picture taken in the bathroom, or that they had been given a bath. Thus, children may give incorrect information to misleading questions about events for which they have no memory, if the interviewer creates an emotional tone of accusation.

Stereotype induction is another possible component of a suggestive interview. For example, if a child is repeatedly told that a person "does bad things," then the child may begin to incorporate this belief into his or her reports. A study of preschool children illustrates this pattern (Leichtman & Ceci, 1995). On a number of occasions, the experimenters told the children about their "clumsy" friend Sam Stone, whose exploits included accidentally breaking Barbie dolls and ripping sweaters. Later, Sam came to the children's classroom for a short, accident-free visit. The next day, the teacher showed the children a torn book and a soiled teddy bear. Several weeks later, a number of these three- to four-year-old children reported that Sam had been responsible for these acts; some even claimed that they had seen him do these things. Children who had not received the stereotype induction rarely made this type of error.

Techniques that have been especially designed for interviewing children about sexual abuse may be potentially suggestive. For example, anatomically detailed dolls are commonly used by professionals when interviewing children about suspected sexual abuse. It is thought that the use of the dolls overcomes language, memory, and motivational (e.g., embarrassment) problems. However, the existing data indicate that the dolls do not facilitate accurate reporting. In some cases, children are more inaccurate with the dolls, especially when asked to demonstrate certain events that never happened (e.g., Gordon et al., 1993). Thus, dolls may be suggestive if children have not made any allegations but are asked by an interviewer who suspects abuse to demonstrate abuse with the dolls.

Our recent studies provide evidence for this hypothesis (Bruck, Ceci, & Francoeur, 1995; Bruck, Ceci, Francoeur, & Renick, 1995). Three- and four-year-old children had a medical examination during which some of them received a routine genital examination. After the children were interviewed about the examination, they were given an anatomical doll and told, "Show me on the doll how the doctor touched your genitals." Approximately 50% of the children who had not received a genital examination falsely showed touching on the doll. Furthermore, when the children who had received a genital examination were asked the same question, a number of them incorrectly showed that the doctor had inserted a finger into their genitals; the pediatrician had never done this. Next, when the children in the study were given a stethoscope and a spoon and asked to show what the doctor did or might do with these instruments, some children incorrectly showed that he used the stethoscope to examine their genitals, and some children inserted the spoon into the genital or anal openings or hit the doll's genitals. None of these actions had occurred. We concluded that these false actions were the result of implicit suggestions that it was permissible to show sexualized behaviors. Also, because of the novelty of the dolls, children were drawn to insert fingers and other objects into their cavities.

Guided imagery is another interviewing technique that is potentially suggestive. Interviewers sometimes ask children to try to remember if or pretend that a certain event occurred and then to create a mental picture of the event and to think about its details. Because young children sometimes have difficulty distinguishing between memories of actual events and memories of imagined events (e.g., Parker, 1995; Welch-Ross, 1995), when asked to pretend about or imagine certain events, children may later come to report them as real and believe them to be so. This hypothesis is supported by studies in which young children were repeatedly asked to think about real as well as imaginary events, creating mental images each time they did so. In one of these studies (Ceci, Loftus, Leichtman, & Bruck, 1994), children increasingly assented to false events with each successive interview. When these children were told after 11 sessions that some of the imagined events had not happened, most of the children who had previously assented to false beliefs continued to hold onto their false statements. These data indicate that a number of the children had actually come to believe that they had experienced the false events.

Conclusions and Qualifications

In summary, interviewer bias is revealed by a number of suggestive techniques, each of which can compromise the accuracy of young children's reports. In this section, we qualify and elaborate on this conclusion by raising several points. First, although most developmental studies have focused on the suggestibility of preschool children, there is still reason for concern about the reliability of older children's testimony when they are subjected to suggestive interviews. There is ample evidence that children older than six years of age are suggestible about a wide range of events (e.g., Goodman et al., 1989; Poole & Lindsay, 1996; Warren & Lane, 1995) and that adults' recollections are impaired by suggestive interviewing techniques (e.g., Hyman & Pentland, 1996; Loftus & Pickrell, 1995).

Second, although there are consistent findings of age differences across studies, there are nevertheless individual differences. Some preschoolers are very resistant to interviewers' suggestions, whereas some older children will immediately fall sway to the slightest suggestion. Researchers are a long way from understanding the source of these individual differences but are beginning to assess the association between suggestibility and a number of cognitive characteristics (e.g., knowledge base, memory), psychosocial factors (e.g., compliance, self-esteem), and interviewing techniques (e.g., the use of various suggestive components).

Third, contrary to previous claims that children are suggestible only about peripheral details (e.g., Melton, 1992), the newer studies show that children are also suggestible about central events. These central events may involve bodily touching that may have sexual connotations. Thus, in some suggestibility studies, children falsely claimed that a nurse licked their knees, a scientist put something "yucky" in their mouths, a pediatrician inserted a spoon into their genitals, and a man kissed their friends on the lips and removed some of the children's clothes.

Fourth, the number of suggestive interviewing techniques (which reflects the degree of interviewer bias) can account for variations in suggestibility estimates across and within studies. If a biased interviewer uses more than one suggestive technique, there is a greater chance for taint than if he or she uses just one technique. For example, we (Bruck, Ceci, & Hembrooke, in press) constructed interviews that combined a variety of suggestive techniques (visualization, repeated questioning, repeated misinformation) to elicit children's reports of true events (helping a visitor in the school, getting punished) and false events (helping a woman find her monkey, seeing a thief taking food from the day care). After two suggestive interviews, most children in this study had assented to all events, a pattern that continued to the end of the experiment.

Fifth, the procedures used in most studies do not allow one to determine if the children's false reports reflect false belief (false memory) or merely knowing compliance to the interviewer's suggestion. There may be a time course for the emergence of these different states. Children may start out knowingly complying to suggestions, but with repeated suggestive interviews, they may come to believe the suggestions and incorporate them into their memories. There are a few studies that show that when suggestions are repeated to children over time, a number of the children do develop false beliefs (e.g., Ceci et al., 1994; Leichtman & Ceci, 1995; Poole & Lindsay, 1996). Furthermore, if the suggestive interviews cease for a period of time, these false memories fade (e.g., Huffman, Crossman, & Ceci, 1996; Poole & Lindsay, 1996).

Sixth, children who have undergone repeated suggestive interviews appear highly credible. When highly trained professionals in the fields of child development, mental health, and forensics view videotaped interviews of these subjects, they cannot reliably discriminate between children whose reports are accurate and children whose reports are inaccurate as the result of suggestive interviewing techniques (see Leichtman & Ceci, 1995). We have attempted to isolate the linguistic markers that might differentiate true narratives from false narratives that emerge as a result of repeated suggestive interviews (Bruck et al., in press). We have found that with repeated suggestive interviews, false stories quickly come to resemble true stories in terms of the number of details, the spontaneity of utterance, the number of details not previously reported (reminiscences), inconsistency across narratives, the elaborativeness of the details, and the cohesiveness of the narrative. It is only the greater consistency of narratives of true events that differentiates them from narratives of false events. Thus, suggestive interviewing procedures can result in highly credible but inaccurate witnesses.

Finally, although we have focused here on the conditions that can compromise reliable reporting, it is also important to acknowledge that a large number of studies show that children are capable of providing accurate, detailed, and useful information about actual events, including traumatic ones (for reviews, see, e.g., Fivush, 1993; Goodman, Batterman-Faunce, & Kenney, 1992). What characterizes these studies is the neutral tone of the interviewers, the limited use of leading questions (for the most part, if suggestions are used, they are limited to a single occasion), and the absence of any motive for the children to make false reports. When such conditions are present, it is a common (although not universal) finding that children are relatively immune to suggestive influences, particularly about sexual details. When such conditions are present in actual forensic or therapeutic interviews, one can have greater confidence in the reliability of children's allegations. It is these conditions that one must strive for when eliciting information from young children.

References

Bruck, M., Ceci, S. J., & Francoeur, E. (1995, March). *Anatomically detailed dolls do not facilitate preschoolers' reports of touching.* Paper presented at the biannual meeting of the Society for Research on Child Development, Indianapolis, IN.

Bruck, M., Ceci, S. J., Francoeur, E., & Barr, R. J. (1995). "I hardly cried when I got my shot!": Influencing children's reports about a visit to their pediatrician. *Child Development, 66*, 193–208.

Bruck, M., Ceci, S. J., Francoeur, E., & Renick, A. (1995). Anatomically detailed dolls do not facilitate preschoolers' reports of a pediatric examination involving genital touching. *Journal of Experimental Psychology: Applied, 1*, 95–109.

Bruck, M., Ceci, S. J., & Hembrooke, H. (in press). Children's reports of pleasant and unpleasant events. In D. Read & S. Lindsay (Eds.), *Recollections of trauma: Scientific research and clinical practice.* New York: Plenum Press.

Ceci, S. J., & Bruck, M. (1993). The suggestibility of the child witness: A historical review and synthesis. *Psychological Bulletin, 113,* 403–439.

Ceci, S. J., & Bruck, M. (1995). *Jeopardy in the courtroom: A scientific analysis of children's testimony.* Washington, DC: American Psychological Association.

Ceci, S. J., Loftus, E. W., Leichtman, M., & Bruck, M. (1994). The role of source misattributions in the creation of false beliefs among preschoolers. *International Journal of Clinical and Experimental Hypnosis, 62,* 304–320.

Fivush, R. (1993). Developmental perspectives on autobiographical recall. In G. S. Goodman & B. Bottoms (Eds.), *Child victims and child witnesses: Understanding and improving testimony* (pp. 1–24). New York: Guilford Press.

Goodman, G. S., Batterman-Faunce, J. M., & Kenney, R. (1992). Optimizing children's testimony: Research and social policy issues concerning allegations of child sexual abuse. In D. Cicchetti & S. Toth (Eds.), *Child abuse, child development, and social policy* (pp. 139–166). Norwood, NJ: Ablex.

Goodman, G. S., Wilson, M. E., Hazan, C., & Reed, R. S. (1989, April). *Children's testimony nearly four years after an event.* Paper presented at the annual meeting of the Eastern Psychological Association, Boston.

Gordon, B., Ornstein, P. A., Nida, R., Follmer, A., Creshaw, C., & Albert, G. (1993). Does the use of dolls facilitate children's memory of visits to the doctor? *Applied Cognitive Psychology, 7,* 459–474.

Huffman, M. L., Crossman, A., & Ceci, S. (1996, March). *An investigation of the long-term effects of source misattribution error: Are false memories permanent?* Poster presented at the biannual meeting of the American Psychology-Law Society, Hilton Head, SC.

Hughes, M., & Grieve, R. (1980). On asking children bizarre questions. *First Language, 1,* 149–160.

Hyman, I. E., & Pentland, J. (1996). The role of mental imagery in the creation of false childhood memories. *Journal of Memory and Language, 35,* 101–117.

Leichtman, M. D., & Ceci, S. J. (1995). The effects of stereotypes and suggestions on preschoolers' reports. *Developmental Psychology, 31,* 568–578.

Loftus, E. F., & Pickrell, J. E. (1995). The formation of false memories. *Psychiatric Annals, 25,* 720–725.

Melton, G. (1992). Children as partners for justice: Next steps for developmentalists. *Monographs of the Society for Research in Child Development, 57*(5, Serial No. 229), 153–159.

Parker, J. (1995). Age differences in source monitoring of performed and imagined actions on immediate and delayed tests. *Journal of Experimental Child Psychology, 60,* 84–101.

Peterson, C., & Bell, M. (1996). Children's memory for traumatic injury. *Child Development, 67,* 3045–3070.

Poole, D. A., & Lindsay, D. S. (1996, June). *Effects of parents' suggestions, interviewing techniques, and age on young children's event reports.* Paper presented at the NATO Advanced Study Institute, Port de Bourgenay, France.

Poole, D. A., & White, L. (1991). Effects of question repetition on the eyewitness testimony of children and adults. *Developmental Psychology, 27,* 975–986.

Walker, N., Lunning, S., & Eilts, J. (1996, June). *Do children respond accurately to forced choice questions?* Paper presented to the NATO Advanced Study Institute: Recollections of Trauma: Scientific Research and Clinical Practice, Talmont Saint Hilaire, France.

Warren, A. R., & Lane, P. (1995). The effects of timing and type of questioning on eyewitness accuracy and suggestibility. In M. Zaragoza (Ed.), *Memory and testimony in the child witness* (pp. 44–60). Thousand Oaks, CA: Sage Publications.

Welch-Ross, M. (1995). Developmental changes in preschoolers' ability to distinguish memories of performed, pretended, and imagined actions. *Cognitive Development, 10,* 421–441.

Further reading

Poole, D. A., & Lindsay, D. S. (in press). Assessing the accuracy of young children's reports: Lessons from the investigation of child sexual abuse. *Applied and Preventative Psychology.*

TWELVE

Language

Introduction

The first cognitive development research on language acquisition was perhaps a cruel experiment carried out by Psammetichus, ruler of Egypt in the seventh century BC. Psammetichus wondered whether Egyptian language was the language that children are born with or, in his words, the language of God. He ordered two newborn children to be placed in isolation and prohibited anyone from conversing with them. Psammetichus reasoned that if the children's first word was an Egyptian word, then the language of God would be Egyptian. To his dismay, his hypothesis was rejected: the children's first word was "becos," a Phrygian word for "bread."

Psammetichus's barbaric experiment does not resemble how language development research is done today! Among many modern research methods, two are commonly used. One is the Wug Task, pioneered by Berko (1958), in which children are shown a novel object or event and told that it is called a "wug," or any other nonsense word. By presenting the object or event in different ways, we can assess children's understanding of grammatical rules such as plurality (e.g., "This is one wug. Here are two _.") and past tense (e.g., "Today, they wug. Yesterday, they _."). In addition, a modified Wug Task can be used to study how children acquire the meanings of new words (e.g., referring to a novel object with a novel feature as "wug" to see whether children think the word refers to the whole object or its feature; Markman, 1991).

The second commonly used method, pioneered by Roger Brown (1973), is to record children's utterances in their natural habitat (e.g., home or day care) systematically in a longitudinal study. The recordings are then painstakingly transcribed and coded so as to characterize each child's knowledge of grammatical rules. Because such recordings are time-consuming and costly, usually they are done on a small number of children, often by the children's parents who may be linguists or psychologists. This method leads to methodological problems: for example, the unique experience of the child under investigation may contribute to the child's language development and hence may not represent the developmental course of children in general.

To circumvent this problem, MacWhinney (1995) and his colleagues have set up a database that houses transcriptions produced by a number of researchers. The database is nonproprietary; it can be accessed from anywhere in the world and downloaded by any researcher at no cost. New transcriptions can also be added to it. Most importantly, because all researchers use a standardized coding procedure, transcriptions of children's utterances are formatted in the same manner. This allows researchers to search for specific types of word and grammatical rule use to test out specific hypotheses about language development in a group of children. This article by Gary Marcus is a prime example of the use of the database for testing a half-century-old hypothesis originally proposed in 1959 by Noam Chomsky, who asked: Do children spontaneously generate grammatical rules with limited language input from the environment?

References

Berko, J. (1958). The child's learning of English morphology. *Word, 14*, 150–77.

Brown, R. (1973). *A first language: The early stages*. Cambridge, MA: Harvard University Press.

Chomsky, N. (1959). A review of B. F. Skinner's verbal behavior. *Language, 35*, 26–58.

MacWhinney, B. (1995). *The CHILDES project: Tools for analyzing talk* (2nd edn). Hillsdale, NJ: Lawrence Erlbaum.

Markman, E. M. (1991). The whole-object, taxonomic, and mutual exclusivity assumptions as initial constraints on word meanings. In S. A. Gelman, Susan A. Byrnes, & J. P. Byrnes (eds), *Perspectives on language and thought: Interrelations in development* (pp. 72–106). New York: Cambridge University Press.

Why Do Children Say "Breaked"?

Gary F. Marcus

Errors can yield special insights into learning mechanisms. In language development, perhaps the most notorious error is the past-tense over-regularization. Most English verbs form their past tense regularly, by adding the suffix -ed (e.g., *walk–walked*). About 180 verbs, though, form their past tense idiosyncratically (e.g., *sing–sang*). Overregularizations result when the regular -ed suffix is applied to an irregular verb (e.g., *singed*).

Because parents almost never overregularize, these errors demonstrate that language learning involves more than mere imitation. Instead, children must possess mechanisms that detect and extend linguistic generalizations.

Although the production of overregularizations has typically been ascribed to the application of a mental rule, the mere fact that the regular pattern has been overextended does not guarantee that overregularization errors are produced by a rule. Instead, as Rumelhart and McClelland showed, a single uniform neural network that contains no explicit rules and makes no explicit distinction between regular and irregular words can produce overregularizations.[1]

In 1988, Pinker and Prince pointed out several limitations to Rumelhart and McClelland's model.[2] Since then, characterizing the mechanisms responsible for overregularization has become a central focus of detailed empirical comparisons between symbolic, rule-based models and connectionist neural network models that explicitly forsake rules in favor of networks of connections between nodes.

The Rule-and-Memory Model

A model of overregularization that my colleagues and I have proposed depends on the existence of mental rules. According to this model, children's grammars and adults' grammars are structured as similarly as possible. The model has three simple components.

First, speakers have access to a symbolic, default rule that says roughly, "To form the past tense, and -*ed* to any word carrying the symbol [verb]." What makes this a rule is that it can apply to any verb, regardless of its resemblance to stored examples. What makes it a default is that it applies any time access to the lexicon fails, that is, to any word that lacks a stored past-tense form, including low-frequency words (*snarfed*), unusual sounding words (*ploamphed*), and complex words that are not treated as roots, such as verbs derived from nouns (*The soldiers ringed the city*). Children readily generalize the -*ed* inflection to nonsense words like *wug* and to novel verbs derived from nouns (e.g., *ring*, meaning to put a ring on a finger).[3]

Second, past-tense forms of irregular roots are stored in memory. Because all memory is fallible, memory for irregular verbs is imperfect.

Third, a stored irregular form always takes precedence over the rule; hence, *sang* blocks *singed*. The default applies if and only if no irregular inflected form can be found.

When memory for irregular verbs is taxed, even adults may overregularize. For instance, many adults overregularize *strive* as *strived*, because the irregular form *strove* is rare and hence difficult to retrieve. Upon retrieval failure, the default rule steps into the breach, yielding an overregularization.

The rule-and-memory model holds that children's grammars are structured similarly to adults'. But because children have had less exposure than adults to correct forms, their memories for irregular forms are weaker. Whenever access to an irregular past-tense form fails, the child adds -*ed*, producing an overregularization.

To test this model, using data from a publicly available archive of children's spontaneous speech, CHILDES,[4] my colleagues and I conducted a systematic, quantitative analysis of children's overregularizations, extracting and analyzing 11,521 past-tense utterances from the spontaneous speech of 83 children.[5]

Several observations support the rule-and-memory model. First – contrary to popular opinion reported everywhere from *Newsweek* to the primary literature – there is no stage in which children completely replace correct forms with overregularizations. Instead, we discovered that children overregularize in only about 4% of their opportunities, demonstrating a systematic preference for correct irregular forms. Thus, errors appear to be a consequence of performance limitations rather than a qualitatively inaccurate grammar. The representative longitudinal plots of three children in figure 1 show that low rates of overregularization are not artifacts of averaging over time; our data also show that these low rates are consistent across children and hold for most individual verbs.

Second, if overregularizations are the consequence of retrieval failure, verbs that are more difficult to remember should be more likely to be overregularized. To test this hypothesis, we used frequencies of parents' use of irregular verbs as an index of retrievability. As predicted, the more often a parent used a verb, the less likely the child was to overregularize it. The correlation was in the predicted direction for 18 of 19 children, with a mean of −.34.[6]

Third, irregular forms that are reinforced by similar-sounding irregular forms should be easier to remember than irregular forms that lack such reinforcement. Thus, *sing*'s past tense *sang* should be easier to remember because of the presence of similar-sounding verbs that follow similar patterns, such as *ring–rang* and *drink–drank*. Indeed, we found that verbs with greater irregular-cluster strength (as measured by the number and frequency of use of similar forms) were less prone to overregularization. The correlation was in the predicted direction for 16 of 19 children's overregularization rates, with a mean of −.08. This correlation holds even if we statistically factor out the effects of the verb's frequency.

Fourth, if overregularization errors disappear as a consequence of improving facility at retrieving correct forms, rather than qualitative grammatical change, then they should disappear gradually. Indeed, the sample of preschoolers that we studied overregularized at a rate of 4.2%; rates for first graders and fourth graders were 2.5% and 1%, respectively, and even adults overregularize occasionally, about once in every 25,000 opportunities.

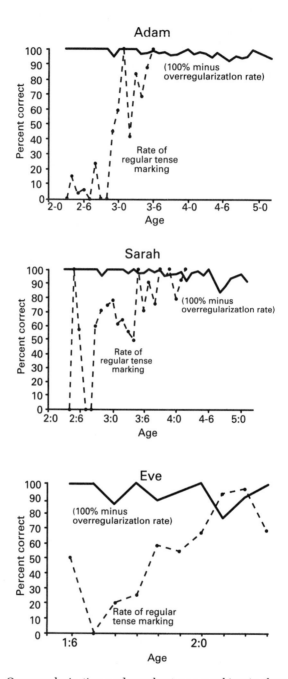

Figure 1 Overregularization and regular tense marking in three children as a function of age. In each panel, the heavy line plots the percentage of overregularization subtracted from 100%, and the dashed line plots the percentage of regular past-tense contexts in which the child has successfully supplied the regular past tense.

Finally, the "add -*ed*" rule, because it is English-specific, cannot be innate. Before it is learned, retrieval failures should be left unmarked (e.g., *I sing yesterday*). These errors should be replaced by overregularizations only after the English-specific default -*ed* is acquired. As the rule-and-memory model predicts, before children reliably inflect regular verbs for past tense in contexts that require it (e.g., *I walked yesterday*), they go through an initial period in which irregular verbs are used correctly or left unmarked, but never overregularized. Figure 1 shows that the onset of overregularization appears to coincide with the development of reliable regular past-tense marking in contexts that demand past-tense inflection. Rates of regular tense marking are significantly greater during the period of overregularization than before (Adam: 73% vs. 8%; Sarah: 85% vs. 44%; Eve: 66% vs. 11%), suggesting that overregularization is tied to the acquisition of a rule.[5]

Parallel Distributed Processing

Consider now the connectionist alternative. In single uniform networks such as those proposed by Rumelhart and McClelland and by Plunkett and Marchman, words are represented as distributed patterns of activation over a network of nodes and connections. In a simplified version of such a network, *sing* would be represented as a set of units representing the initial consonant, the vowel nucleus, and the final consonant. An external teacher presents a network with pairs of stem and past-tense forms. Learning the mapping from *sing* to *sang* involves strengthening connections that run from the input nodes that represent the sound *ing* to the output nodes that represent the sound *ang*. Similar-sounding words overlap in their representations, yielding an explanation for why adults sometimes inflect the novel word *spling* as *splang*.[7]

Regular inflection is treated identically: Exposure to *walk–walked* strengthens the connections between input nodes representing *alk* and output nodes representing *alked*, generalizing to similar words like *talk–talked*.

Overregularizations are produced when regular patterns exert too strong an attraction on irregular verbs. For instance, *grow* might be overregularized to *growed* because pairs like *glow–glowed* increase the strength of the connection between nodes representing the input *ow* and the output *owed*. As the network is exposed to more such pairs, the chance of overregularization increases. Thus, "the level of generalizations . . . [is] closely related to the total number [and proportion] of regular verbs in the vocabulary."[8] This relationship might be dubbed the *regular-attraction hypothesis*, and it is central to most connectionist models of inflection.[9]

But although the network's overregularization is driven primarily by attraction to stored pairs in which stems are linked to regular past-tense forms, four types of evidence suggest that children's overregularizations may not be.

Longitudinal test

In typical network models, overregularization occurs during sudden shifts in the proportion of vocabulary that is regular.[10] Children's overregularization, however, appears to be independent of changes in the composition of vocabulary. Quantitatively, there is no positive correlation between increases in the number or proportion of regular verbs acquired (whether measured in *types*, the number of different verbs used, or *tokens*, the number of times each word has been used) by a child and the child's rate of overregularization. Instead, as figure 2 shows, the proportion of regular verbs in Adam's and Sarah's vocabulary increases less rapidly during the period of overregularization than before – precisely the opposite of the regular-attraction hypothesis.[11] Thus, the onset of overregularization does not depend on dramatic increases in the proportion of vocabulary that is regular.

Lexical test

The regular-attraction hypothesis predicts that irregular verbs will be more frequently overregularized if they are similar to regular verbs; thus, *feel* should be drawn to *feeled* by similar neighbors such as *heal–healed* and *peel–peeled*. To test this hypothesis, we calculated a verb-wise measure of regular-cluster strength, based on the number (and frequency of use) of each verb's similar-sounding regular neighbors. There was no correlation between regular-cluster strength and overregularization: Verbs with many regular neighbors were no more likely to be overregularized than verbs with few regular neighbors, suggesting that overregularizations are not the result of an attraction to regular verbs.

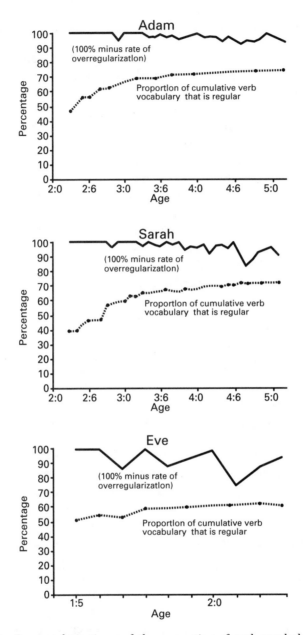

Figure 2 Overregularization and the proportion of verb vocabulary that is regular in three children as a function of age. In each panel, the upper line plots the percentage of overregularization subtracted from 100%, and the lower line plots the proportion of the child's cumulative verb vocabulary that is regular.

Comparison between noun plurals and verbs

In English, the system for noun plurals contains a greater proportion of regular words (excluding learned Latinate plurals like *bacterium-bacteria*, more than 98% of noun plural types are regular) than does the system for the past tense (only 86% of the 1,000 most frequent types are regular). But like *-ed*, the *-s* plural is generalized whenever no irregular root can be found in the lexicon, including cases of memory failure in which existing roots cannot be accessed, but also including cases in which there is no irregular root, such as regular words (*cat*), plurals derived from names (*We had a fabulous meal at the Childs*), onomatopoeia (*The cartoon climax had seven POWs*), and unusual-sounding words (*kiosks*). Further evidence that regular inflection is generalized independently of type frequency comes from the fact that individual children's rates of overregularizing the plural do not differ significantly from their rates of overregularizing the past tense.[12]

Cross-linguistic test

If generalization of regular inflection is truly independent of type frequency, speakers should generalize regular inflection even when there are far fewer regular words than in the English systems for noun plurals and past tense. One test case is the German *-s* plural, which applies to fewer than 10% of German nouns (whether measured by types or tokens) and is just one of five different plural suffixes, ø, *-e*, *-er*, *-(e)n*, *s*. Despite its infrequency, the *-s* plural behaves as the default. Just as the English plural *-s* applies when no irregular form is available, as with names, borrowings, and onomatopoeia, so too does the German *-s* plural apply to names (*Thomas Manns*), borrowings (*Kiosks*), and onomatopoetic words (*Wau-waus*).[9]

German-speaking children often overregularize with *-s*, more often than might be predicted by a frequency-based approach,[13] and children are more likely to generalize the *-s* pattern than other patterns to novel words that are unusual sounding or presented as names.[14] These facts strengthen the conclusion that generalization of the default does not require that the regular pattern be highly frequent.

Conclusions

Overregularization errors do not correspond with increases in the proportion of vocabulary that is regular, are not more common for irregular words that resemble other regular words than for irregular words that do not, are not more common in inflectional systems that have a higher proportion of regular words, and occur even in languages in which the regular pattern is infrequent. Rather than generalizing default inflection by analogy to stored exemplars, children generalize default inflection by a rule that applies whenever access to irregular forms fails.

Default inflection seems to be a natural property of many linguistic systems and to be readily learned by children. Although the input to children varies widely, English- and German-speaking children, for example, rapidly converge on the same sorts of inflectional systems. The English past tense, English noun plural (almost entirely regular), and German noun plural (almost entirely irregular) appear to develop similarly. Because single uniform neural networks tend to be closely tied to the input, they have difficulty explaining why children develop similar linguistic systems despite differing input conditions. Instead, generalization of regular inflection seems to be best explained in terms of a rule.

The key property of a rule appears to be its ability to treat all instances of a class equally, regardless of their degree of resemblance to stored forms. Rules do not generalize in a gradient of similarity, but rather apply in an all-or-none fashion depending on whether an item carries the appropriate symbol. For example, the "add *-ed*" rule applies equally readily to any novel word carrying the symbol [verb]. This mode of generalization, which is driven not by resemblance but by the presence of a symbol, may be central to other domains of cognition.

For example, this ability to suppress resemblance and treat all tokens of a class equally is crucial for word recognition. A speech segment such as /ba/ can be uttered in many different ways, varying in pitch, amplitude, accent, and other characteristics. But the output of the speech perception system remains the same, regardless of whether a given utterance of /ba/ is more or less similar to previously heard examples.

Similarly, people can identify someone as a grandmother regardless of whether she has gray hair or cooks chicken soup; likewise, they can override perceptual similarity to identify a raccoon as a raccoon, even if it has been surgically transformed to look like a skunk.[15] There is little doubt that the mind can track information about similarity and resemblance (and calculate that Priscilla Presley is not a typical grandmother), but the ability to override information about resemblance and treat all members of a class identically – precisely the work done by rules that manipulate symbols – also appears to be an essential property of cognition.

A simple model that depends on the existence of such symbolic rules explains a wide range of data: Irregular forms are retrieved from memory and block the application of the default regular rule (add -*ed*); if a child fails to retrieve the past tense of an irregular form, the regular rule applies by default, and the child produces an overregularization.

Notes

1 D. Rumelhart and J. McClelland, On learning the past tenses of English verbs: Implicit rules or parallel distributed processing?, in *Parallel distributed processing: Explorations in the microstructure of cognition*, J. McClelland, D. Rumelhart, and the PDP research group, Eds. (MIT Press, Cambridge, MA, 1986); for a more recent model, see K. Plunkett and V. Marchman, From rote learning to system building: Acquiring verb morphology in children and connectionist nets, *Cognition*, *48*, 21–69 (1993).

2 S. Pinker and A. Prince, On language and connectionism: Analysis of a Parallel Distributed Processing model of language acquisition, *Cognition*, *28*, 73–193 (1988).

3 J. Berko, The child's learning of English morphology, *Word*, *14*, 150–177 (1958); J. J. Kim, G. F. Marcus, S. Pinker, M. Hollander, and M. Coppola, Sensitivity of children's inflection to grammatical structure, *Journal of Child Language*, *21*, 173–209 (1994); S. Pinker, Rules of language, *Science*, *253*, 530–555 (1991).

4 B. MacWhinney and C. Snow, The Child Language Data Exchange System, *Journal of Child Language*, *12*, 271–296 (1985).

5 G. F. Marcus, S. Pinker, M. Ullman, M. Hollander, T. J. Rosen, and F. Xu, Overregularization in language acquisition, *Monographs of the Society for Research in Child Development*, *57*(4, Serial No. 228) (1992).

6 Lexical correlations could be tested for only 19 children because for the remainder we lacked individual databases or found no overregularizations in our samples.

7   S. Prasada and S. Pinker, Similarity-based and rule-based generalizations in inflectional morphology, *Language and Cognitive Processes*, 8, 1–56 (1993).

8   Plunkett and Marchman, note 1, p. 55.

9   G. F. Marcus, U. Brinkmann, H. Clahsen, R. Wiese, and S. Pinker, German inflection: The exception that proves the rule, *Cognitive Psychology*, 29, 189–256 (1995).

10 The model of Plunkett and Marchman (note 1) displays a similar, abrupt external change, in which the onset of overregularization coincides with a sudden shift in training regime from a slow pace that allows the network to learn each irregular verb individually to a rapid pace that forces the network to generalize. See G. F. Marcus, The acquisition of inflection in children and multilayered connectionist networks, *Cognition*, 56, 271–279 (1995).

11 Using novel sampling techniques from biostatistics, my colleagues and I (Marcus et al., note 5, chap. V) have shown that this finding is not an artifact of a cumulative vocabulary measure that necessarily decelerates over time.

12 G. F. Marcus, Children's overregularization of English plurals: A quantitative analysis, *Journal of Child Language*, 22, 447–459 (1995).

13 The only systematic study of how input frequency affects network generalization is a series of simulations conducted by Plunkett and Marchman (note 1). In this study, when the initial proportion of regular vocabulary was less than 50%, their simulation failed to generalize the regular pattern to "novel indeterminate stems" (i.e., novel words).

14 S. Bartke, G. F. Marcus, and H. Clahsen, Acquiring German noun plurals, in *Proceedings of the 19th Annual Boston University Conference on Language Development*, D. MacLaughlin and S. McEwen, Eds. (Cascadilla Press, Boston, 1995).

15 F. C. Keil, *Concepts, Kinds, and Cognitive Development* (Bradford Books, Cambridge, MA, 1989); G. F. Marcus, Children's overregularization and its implications for cognition, in *Models of language acquisition: Inductive and deductive approaches*, P. Broeder and J. M. J. Murre, Eds. (MIT Press, Cambridge, MA, 1996).

THIRTEEN

Symbolic Development

Introduction

Symbols are omnipresent in our daily lives. We see symbols in our homes (such as a painting on the wall), on the road (traffic lights and signs), when reading a book (written scripts), and when we visit a museum (a dinosaur model). An intriguing characteristic of symbols is that they have dual qualities. On one hand, symbols are things in their own right. For example, paintings are two-dimensional objects containing colors and shapes; traffic lights are colored lights; written words are patterned graphic designs; and a dinosaur model is a physical structure made of certain materials. On the other hand, symbols stand for or represent something else. Pictures depict things in the real or imagined world; red, green, and orange traffic lights signal "stop," "go," and "caution"; written words are visual representations of spoken language; and a dinosaur model stands for the now extinct animal.

Fundamental questions in symbolic development research include: When do children understand this duality of symbols? When children's understanding of dual meanings for symbols emerges, does it occur slowly over time, or does it appear rather suddenly? Finally, how do children's use and production of symbols reflect their understanding of symbolic representation? These questions are addressed by a field of developmental research called "notational development" (Lee & Karmiloff-Smith, 1996).

DeLoache's article focuses on the emergence of children's understanding of scale models, one of the many symbol systems used by humans. Generally, symbol-referent relations are purely arbitrary in that the symbol bears little physical resemblance to the object to which it refers (e.g., traffic signs, letters, numbers, and words). Scale models, however, are special because they are the only symbol system in which the symbol (the scale model) closely resembles the object that it stands for, and both are three-dimensional. Thus, it is of particular interest to determine when young children begin to use three-dimensional objects (the scale models) to represent the spatial arrangement of other three-dimensional objects (e.g., real objects in a real room). The question becomes: In the young child's mind, what does the symbol actually stand for? Will they be confused by the dual nature of a scale model? And will it take many years for children to learn to use scale models properly as a symbol system? This article presents surprising answers.

Reference

Lee, K., & Karmiloff-Smith, A. (1996). The development of external symbol systems: The child as a notator. In R. Gelman & T. Au (eds). *Perceptual and cognitive development: Handbook of perception and cognition* (2nd edn) (pp. 185–211). San Diego, CA: Academic Press.

Further reading

DeLoache, J. S. (1995). Early understanding and use of symbols: The model. *Current Directions in Psychological Science*, 4, 109–13.

Rapid Change in the Symbolic Functioning of Very Young Children

Judy S. DeLoache

The results of the research described here reveal the sudden achievement, in a group of children between two and a half and three years of age, of an important developmental milestone: the realization that an object can be understood both as a thing itself and as a symbol of something else. Symbolization is a hallmark of human cognition, and the development of symbolic functioning has been assigned a prominent role in many major theories of cognitive development.[1] The specific symbolic relation examined here is that between a scale model and the larger space it represents. It is argued that understanding the representational role of a symbolic object requires thinking about one thing in two different ways at the same time – a crucial aspect of mature, flexible thought.

Previous research has established that very young children are extremely competent at remembering the location of a hidden object.[2] For the research reported here, a young child watched as an attractive toy was hidden within a scale model of a room. (For example, a miniature dog was hidden behind the small couch in the model.) The child was then asked to find an analogous toy that had been concealed in the corresponding place in the room itself (for example, a larger stuffed dog hidden behind the full-sized couch). To succeed, the child had to realize that the model represented the room and that, by remembering the location of the object hidden in the model, he or she could determine the location of the object concealed in the room.

Each experimental session began with an extensive orientation phase highlighting the correspondence between the room (4.80 m by 3.88 m by 2.54 m) and its scale model (71 cm by 65 cm by 33 cm), which was located in an adjoining room. The experimenter explicitly described and demonstrated the correspondence between the two toys to be hidden, between the room and the model, and between the individual items of furniture (the hiding places) within the two spaces.

Immediately after the orientation phase, each child was given four trials, each of which involved three parts. (i) Hiding event – the subject watched as the miniature toy was hidden under or behind an item of furniture in the model. (The toy was hidden in a different place for each trial.) (ii) Retrieval 1 – the child was asked to retrieve the larger toy from the room. On each trial, the child was reminded that the larger toy was hidden in the "same place" as the miniature one. (iii) Retrieval 2 – as a memory check, the child was returned to the model and asked to retrieve the toy that he or she had observed being hidden at the beginning of the trial.[3] Thus, retrieval 2 tapped the child's memory for the original hiding event, and retrieval 1 assessed transfer of that memory to a new context.

The subjects for experiment 1 were 32 children, 16 in a younger group (30 to 32 months; mean age, 31 months) and 16 in an older group (36 to 39 months; mean age, 38 months). The hiding space was counterbalanced with age: half the subjects in each age group watched as the miniature toy was hidden in the model, as described above, and half saw the larger toy being hidden in the room.

The results were dramatic. Figure 1 shows the mean number of error-less retrievals of the analogous toy (retrieval 1) and of the original memory object (retrieval 2). The mean level of performance of the older children (old) was better than that of the younger children (young) (old − young = 1.34, SE = 0.17), and overall performance on retrieval 2 (R2) was higher than overall performance on retrieval 1 (R1) (R2 − R1 = 1.59, SE = 0.23). More importantly, the pattern of performance differed for the two age groups. The difference between performance on retrievals 1 and 2 for the older subjects was only 0.27, whereas for the younger children it was 2.69 (SE = 0.32).[4] This difference in the performance of the younger and older children is highly replicable.[5] The results were unaffected by whether the toy was originally hidden in the room or in the model.

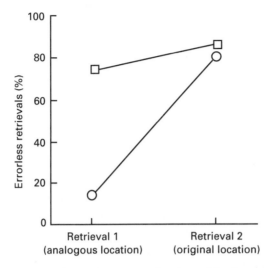

Figure 1 Percentage of errorless retrievals achieved by the two age groups in experiment 1 ($n = 16$ in each age group). The trials of the older children are represented by □ and those of the younger children by ○.

For retrieval 2, the younger and older children showed little difference in memory for the original hiding event; their equivalently, high performance on the memory check was expected in light of previous memory research.[2] However, the large difference between the two age groups on retrieval 1 – retrieving the analogous object – indicated that they differed dramatically in the use of their memory of one event to reason about another. The older children drew on their knowledge of the location of one hidden object to infer the location of a different object. They were highly adept at making this inference; there was no significant difference between their success as a group in finding the object they had seen and finding the one they had not seen being hidden.

In contrast, the younger children did not use what they knew about the original hiding event to figure out where the other toy had to be. The absence of any systematic pattern to their searching (that is, few correct responses and no identifiable error patterns) suggests that they were unaware that they had any basis for knowing where the toy was without looking for it. Indeed, they gave no evidence, either in their search or in other behavior, that they realized that the two spaces had anything to do with each other.

Why did the younger children in experiment 1 fail to understand the correspondence between the model and the room, to realize that the model represented the room? Experiment 2 evaluated the hypothesis that the problem had to do with a limitation on the symbolic capabilities of the younger children. Success in a model task such as this one requires a dual orientation to the model. On the one hand, it is a real, three-dimensional object (actually, a set of objects) that the child manipulates. On the other hand, the child must realize that the model also stands for or represents something else, in this case, that it is a symbol for the room. Perhaps the younger children think of the model in only one way; the fact that it is a real, three-dimensional object may preclude their realizing that it also stands for something else.

If it is the three-dimensional nature of the model that interferes with the younger children's appreciation of it as a symbol, performance should be better with a purely symbolic medium. A photograph, unlike a real object, typically has no role other than as a symbolic representation of something else[6] and, hence, does not require a dual orientation. Therefore, in experiment 2, the information about where the object was hidden in the room was provided through photographs, rather than through the model, and it was predicted that performance would be better with the photographs than with the model. This prediction is directly contrary to the standard view of the efficacy of pictures versus real objects. Two-dimensional stimuli are generally thought of as less salient and less informative relative to three-dimensional objects. Developmental and cross-cultural studies have repeatedly shown better learning and memory result with real objects than with pictures.[7]

Sixteen children of about the same ages as the younger subjects in experiment 1 (30 to 33 months; mean age, 31.6 months) were observed twice, once in the standard task with the model and once with photographs used in place of the model. Half the children participated in the photograph task first and half in the model task first. For each of the four trials of the photograph task, the child was shown an array of four color photographs (20.3 cm by 25.4 cm), each of which pictured one or more of the hiding places (items of furniture) in the room. On each trial, the experimenter pointed to a different one of the photographs and said, "He's hiding back [under] here." Then the child was taken into the room and encouraged to find the toy.

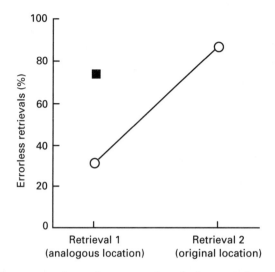

Figure 2   Percentage of errorless retrievals with photographs and with model, experiment 3 ($n = 16$). The trials using a model room are designated by ○ and those using photographs by ∎.

Figure 2 shows the results of experiment 2. Just like the comparable age group in experiment 1, these children were unable to find the toy after seeing it hidden in the model; they were, however, able to find it after seeing a photograph of its hiding place. Performance in the photograph task (photo) was significantly better than performance on retrieval 1 in the model task (model) (photo – model = 1.56, SE = 0.44).[8] Although performance on retrieval 1 was slightly higher for those children who had had the photograph task first, the order effect did not approach significance.

The results of experiment 2 support the hypothesis that the source of two-and-a-half-year-old children's difficulty with the model task was the necessity of maintaining a dual orientation to the model.[9] Although a photograph is a less rich and less salient stimulus than a model, its only function is as a symbol, and even very young children have had substantial experience with pictorial representation. The younger children in this research understood that the photographs represented the room, and they were thus able to apply the pictured information to the room. When faced with a model, they treated it only as a real object. Hence, their knowledge about the location of the hidden object remained specific to that particular toy and that particular space.

One would expect the pattern of developmental change reported here only in domains in which the symbol to be understood is a real object, in line with recent claims that different symbol systems show divergent patterns of development.[10] The current research does not establish the generalizability of these findings; we need to know, for example, to what extent young children's understanding of the relation between a model and a larger space is affected by the degree of difference in scale between the two spaces, the extent of physical similarity between them, and the congruence of the spatial relations among the objects in the spaces.

In conclusion, the failure of two-and-a-half-year-old children to think about a symbolic object both as an object and as a symbol prevented them from generalizing their experience; in other words, it limited their knowledge to the particular instance, rather than the general rule. Understanding the dual role of symbolic objects is thus a crucial developmental step.[11] The possibility of a strongly maturational underpinning for this step is raised by the abrupt nature of the developmental change displayed by the children in these experiments – from failure to nearly universal success in the space of a few months.

Notes

1 H. Werner and B. Kaplan, Eds., *Symbol formation* (Wiley, New York, 1963); L. S. Vygotsky, Ed., *Mind in society* (Harvard University Press, Cambridge, 1978).

2 J. S. DeLoache and A. L. Brown, *Child Development*, 54, 888 (1983); *Developmental Psychology*, 20, 37 (1984); J. S. DeLoache et al., *Child Development*, 56, 125 (1985).

3 Retrieval 2 also provided a motivation check; high performance here would rule out low motivation as an explanation of poor performance on retrieval 1.

4 According to an age by hiding space by sex by retrieval mixed analysis of variance (ANOVA) of the number of correct responses, there were statistically significant main effects for age [$F(1,24) = 62.33$, $P < 0.00001$] and retrieval, [$F(1,24) = 49.70$, $P < 0.00001$], but no statistically significant effects for sex or for hiding space. The primary result of the analysis was the significant interaction of age by retrieval [$F(1,24) = 23.41$, $P < 0.0001$].

5   The results of experiment 1 have been replicated several times with the same model and room, as well as with different spaces and with substantial variations in the instructions and orientation procedures. The results are not attributable to differences in verbal skills: the younger children clearly understood every aspect of the instructions except the correspondence between the spaces, and this was in spite of the fact that they did understand the meaning of "the same," as shown in independent comprehension checks.

6   M. C. Potter, in *Symbolic functioning in childhood*, N. R. Smith and M. B. Franklin, Eds. (Erlbaum, Hillsdale, NJ, 1979), pp. 41–65.

7   M. Cole and S. Scribner, *Culture and thought* (Wiley, New York, 1974); J. S. DeLoache, *Cognitive Development*, *1*, 123 (1986); D. G. Hartley, *Developmental Psychology*, *12*, 218 (1976).

8   There was a significant main effect for task in a task (photograph versus model, retrieval 1) by order by sex ANOVA [$F(1,12) = 12.42$, $P < 0.005$].

9   Further support has been provided in subsequent studies. Retrieval 1 performance is the same when a wide-angle photograph or line drawing of the room is used in place of the individual photographs used here. Also, pointing to the correct place in the model produces the same low level of performance that hiding the object in the model does.

10 D. Wolf and H. Gardner, in *Early language acquisition and intervention*, R. Schiefelbusch and D. Bricker, Eds. (University Park Press, Baltimore, MD, 1981), pp. 286–327.

11 This step may be related to other developmental phenomena involving the appreciation that a single reality can be understood in different and even conflicting ways by one person or by different people, for example, the appearane–reality distinction [J. H. Flavell et al., *Cognitive Psychology*, *15*, 95 (1983)]; level 2 perspective taking [J. H. Flavell et al., *Developmental Psychology*, *17*, 99 (1981)]; and understanding false belief [H. Wimmer and J. Perner, *Cognition 13*, 103 (1983)].

FOURTEEN

Spatial Knowledge and Gender Differences

Introduction

"Men are from Mars; women are from Venus." This metaphor is used by a popular writer to illustrate how differently men and women think, talk, and feel. Is there any empirical evidence to support this assertion? So far, research on this issue does suggest that men and women process information differently in the domain of cognitive functioning. Using a simple Piagetian task (asking children and adults to draw a titled half-empty glass of milk), Vasta and Liben discover the intriguing origin of gender differences in spatial representation. Their findings illustrate that if men and women do not grow up in different spaces, they at least process spatial information differently.

Further reading

Baenninger, M., & Newcombe, N. (1989). The role of experience in spatial test performance: A meta-analysis. *Sex Roles, 20*, 327–44.

Liben, L. S. (1991). The Piagetian water-level task: Looking beneath the surface. In R. Vasta, Ross (ed.), *Annals of child development*, Vol. 8 (pp. 81–143). London, UK: Jessica Kingsley.

Vasta, R., Belongia, C., & Ribble, C. (1994). Investigating the orientation effect on the water-level task: Who? When? and Why? *Developmental Psychology, 30*, 893–904.

The Water-Level Task: An Intriguing Puzzle

Ross Vasta and Lynn S. Liben

Take a moment to look at figure 1. It presents one of several variations of an intriguing problem known as the water-level task (WLT). The correct response to the problem is to draw a horizontal line across the bottle, reflecting the general principle that the surface of a liquid is invariantly horizontal regardless of the orientation of its container. Variations of the task have included presenting the tilted bottle alone, using real containers rather than drawings, and asking subjects whether a waterline in a tilted container looks "correct" (rather than having them draw a line).[1]

The WLT might appear to be a simple problem. In reality, researchers have found that a surprisingly large proportion of adolescents and adults draw slanting lines in the tilted bottles (often with considerable confidence!), and are unable to articulate or identify the physical principle underlying the task. Determining which subjects are most likely to make errors, and why they do so, has been a 30-year scientific puzzle that continues to challenge investigators.

In this article, we begin by tracing the WLT to its source and original purpose – Piaget's work on children's spatial development. We then examine how the task provided an inadvertent battleground for the theoretical debate surrounding gender differences that emerged during the 1970s. Finally, we consider current attempts to explain the fascinating data that continue to be generated by the WLT, and we suggest some directions future research might take.

Figure A shows a bottle with some water in it.

In figure B the bottle has been tilted.
Draw a line to show how the waterline would look.

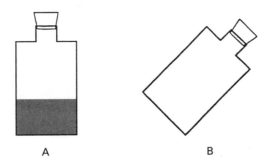

A   B

Figure 1   The water-level task.

Origins of the Problem

The WLT was developed by Piaget and Inhelder (1948/1956) as part of their investigation of children's emerging spatial concepts. Piaget and Inhelder proposed that children gradually come to construct a euclidean (three-dimensional) conceptual system of horizontal and vertical axes with which to represent space. This reference system functions as an abstract geometric container and is independent of the objects found within it. However, because the physical environment itself contains horizontals (e.g., the horizon, tabletops) and verticals (e.g., flagpoles, intersections of walls), a true test of "whether the child has any real understanding of these notions . . . [requires determining how the child] discovers real physical laws . . . such as the constancy of the surface of a liquid whatever the angle of the container" (Piaget & Inhelder, 1948/1956, p. 380). Piaget and Inhelder thus viewed the ability to perform accurately on the WLT as a key indicator that the child has developed a mature euclidean reference system.

Based on their study of children at various ages, Piaget and Inhelder charted the developmental sequence illustrated in figure 2. They reported that the drawings of very young children (under age four) do not even portray the planar surface of the water (Stage IA). Slightly older children typically represent the waterline as fixed relative to the sides of the container by drawing the waterline parallel to the

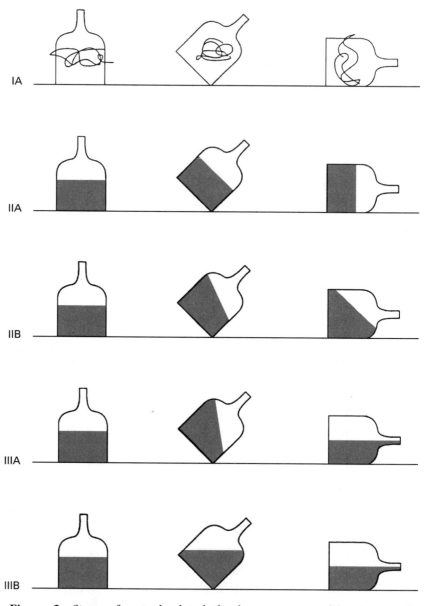

Figure 2 Stages of water-level task development proposed by Piaget and Inhelder (1948/1956).

Source: From Downs & Liben (1991).

container's base (Stage IIA). Children next begin to indicate that the water's position changes relative to the sides of the container, first mistakenly showing the water as tilted in all but upright containers (Stage IIB), and later erring only when one axis of the container is not horizontal (Stage IIIA). Finally, by about age nine, children consistently produce horizontal lines (Stage IIIB). From these original reports, it seemed a given that adolescents and adults would have little trouble with the WLT.

In 1964, however, Rebelsky reported that some of her graduate and undergraduate students at Boston University had considerable difficulty with the task. And since that time, many other investigators have confirmed that many college-educated adults do not respond correctly on the task. In addition, Rebelsky reported that females were less accurate than males, a finding that has been replicated by virtually all subsequent researchers.

Modern Study of the Task

Since Piaget's early developmental work on the WLT, most studies have involved older subjects, whose failure to perform accurately poses the major puzzle. The research also is no longer exclusively Piagetian, but now invokes biological, information processing, and other theoretical models and mechanisms to explain the findings.

Gender differences

The 1970s witnessed an explosion of psychological research concerned with gender differences and their origins. Correspondingly, in the era immediately following Rebelsky's (1964) empirical revelations, much of the work on the WLT focused on the observed gender differences. Meta-analyses of spatial abilities research have found these differences to be significant and meaningful, as indicated by statistical effect sizes[2] on the WLT and related tasks that range from .44 for all subjects to around .60 for adults (Linn & Petersen, 1985; Voyer, Voyer, & Bryden, 1995). It is difficult to pinpoint the proportions of males and females who have difficulty with the task, as these vary with methodological factors such as the version of the task that is used. Nevertheless, a recent report of three WLT experiments with undergraduate subjects is probably representative: Results for males showed that about 50% performed very well and about 20% performed poorly, whereas results for females showed that about 25% performed very well and about 35% performed poorly (Sholl & Liben, 1995).

Note, then, that although the differences are robust, not all males perform well and not all females perform poorly. Thus, any explanation that ties WLT performance exclusively to the subject's biological sex is untenable. In fact, Thomas and Lohaus (1993) have gone so far as to assert that there are no differences between the males and females who do well on the task or between the males and females who do poorly; the only gender difference is in the proportions of people who perform well and who perform poorly. This conclusion grows out of the researchers' application of a mathematical model to the performance of subjects ranging from young children to adults. Although provocative, the conclusion is preliminary and needs additional support because, in at least some studies, performance differences between males and females have been detected even within low- and high-scoring groups (Sholl & Liben, 1995) and within groups defined by whether or not they know the principle (Vasta, Lightfoot, & Cox, 1993).

Some explanations of the gender differences have involved biological mechanisms. For example, researchers have proposed that (a) a recessive gene on the X chromosome both facilitates acquisition of the horizontality principle and is more frequently expressed in men than in women (Thomas & Jamison, 1981), (b) different levels of exposure to sex-related hormones, such as androgen and estrogen, during the prenatal period cause the brains of males and females, including those areas that involve spatial ability, to develop differently (Collaer & Hines, 1995), and (c) gender differences in the effectiveness of the vestibular system of the brain may influence the perception of gravitational upright, and thus the perpendicular horizontal (Liben & Stern, 1996; Sholl, 1989). Although each of these explanations has supporting evidence, none can account for all of the findings.

Socialization models, too, have been proposed to explain the gender differences on the task. Most such models are based on the assumption that in our culture, boys are more strongly encouraged than girls to participate in activities that promote the development of spatial skills (e.g., block play, carpentry, math and science courses). Some correlational evidence does relate good WLT performance to self-reports of early participation in spatial activities, but methodological and cause–effect issues cloud firm conclusions (Baenninger & Newcombe, 1995). Similarly, there is evidence that performance on the WLT is related to subjects' vocational choices, although gender differences persist within occupations and the cause–effect relations therefore remain unclear (Robert & Harel, 1996; Vasta, Rosenberg, Knott, & Gaze, in press).

Another method of investigating possible socialization influences is through the use of a training paradigm. To the extent that gender differences result from differential experience with certain spatial activities, a training regimen designed to provide such experiences could improve the performance of females on the task and thereby reduce or even eliminate the gender differences. Of course, any salutary effects of a training program could result from females' learning to use a strategy that, although effective, is different from the one used by males or from the "natural" path of learning. Even in this case, however, the results would indicate that, at the very least, the gender differences in task performance are not inevitable, as might be predicted by a strong biological model. Some training studies, in fact, have reported success at improving the WLT performance of women, even to the point of bringing it to the level of males' performance (Baenninger & Newcombe, 1995; Liben & Golbeck, 1984; Vasta, Knott, & Gaze, 1996).

Interactional models probably hold the greatest likelihood of explaining the gender differences. Such models include variations on the "bent-twig" idea that males begin with stronger biologically based spatial interests and abilities. These characteristics presumably lead them to seek out more spatial activities and experiences, thereby promoting their spatial skills even further (Sherman, 1978). Recent data reported by Casey (1996), for example, extend this model to differences in spatial abilities among women. Casey's research was based on a theory of brain lateralization which posits that right-handed females with left-handed or ambidextrous relatives are more likely to be genetically endowed with strong spatial abilities than are women who display other handedness patterns (Annett, 1994). Casey hypothesized that only women who possessed this particular biological spatial advantage would benefit from experiences that have the potential to promote spatial skills. And indeed, her research demonstrated that among women who had taken many math and science courses, those with the stipulated pattern of familial handedness performed best on a spatial task requiring them to rotate a three-dimensional figure in their minds. A specific combination of biological potential and prior experiences thus appears necessary to produce in women a high level of the spatial ability assessed by this task. It is conceivable, then, that a similar model accounts for the finding that many women perform poorly on the WLT, whereas a minority perform very well.

Individual differences: Perceptual factors

Much of the recent study of the WLT has subsumed the gender differences under the more general search for variables that separate good from poor performers. One such set of variables operates at the sensory-perceptual level.

The WLT is an example of a spatial task involving spatial perception ability. Such tasks require subjects to locate the horizontal or vertical axis in the face of competing perceptual cues (Linn & Petersen, 1985; Voyer et al., 1995). Spatial perception may be related to the concept of field dependence/independence (FD/I), developed by Witkin (Witkin & Goodenough, 1981). In his analysis of cognitive style, Witkin contended that individuals who are field independent are able to focus on a task or problem independent of its context, whereas those who are field dependent have more difficulty doing so. If spatial perception is indeed linked to FD/I, individuals who are field dependent would be expected to err in determining the horizontal axis (i.e., waterline) when it is located within a tilted frame. A number of studies, in fact, have reported significant positive correlations between subjects' scores on the WLT and on Witkin's principal task for assessing FD/I, the rod-and-frame test, in which subjects attempt to place a movable rod at vertical within a tilted frame (Liben, 1978; Sholl, 1989).

Spatial perception ability plays a role in WLT performance because the oblique sides of a tilted container provide cues that compete with subjects' ability to locate the horizontal axis. Indeed, the WLT may be thought of as similar to a visual illusion in which the tilted frame induces subjects to perceive internal horizontal or vertical lines as displaced in the direction opposite the frame's tilt (fig. 3; Coren & Hoy, 1986).

Support for the role of this perceptual process has come from studies showing that accuracy on the WLT improves when the container has rounded sides that interfere less with drawing a waterline that is horizontal (Vasta et al., 1993), and from studies showing that subjects have

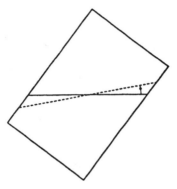

Figure 3 The visual frame illusion. When viewing a tilted frame, most subjects perceive the horizontal (solid line) as displaced in the direction opposite the frame tilt (dashed line).
Source: From Sholl & Liben (1995).

difficulty even when water is removed from the problem entirely – for example, when subjects are asked simply to draw horizontal lines within tilted rectangles (Liben & Golbeck, 1986; Vasta et al., 1993), or when they are asked to draw a horizontal bar pivoted on a tilted rod surrounded by a tilted frame (Liben, 1991).

But perceptual processes alone cannot explain the differences between successful and unsuccessful performers on the WLT. Even among subjects who understand the behavior of water and who perform well on the task, illusory tilt promotes the perception of a horizontal line appearing nonhorizontal. Thus, some other variable or variables must separate these groups (Sholl & Liben, 1995).

Individual differences: Cognitive factors

It may be clear, by this point, why most theoretical models of the WLT have viewed it as a task involving a number of different skills and competencies. These competencies include the categories of motor skills, sensory-perception abilities, graphic skills, and cognitive processes. In recent years, some especially exciting research on the WLT has focused on the last of these areas, as researchers have begun to identify the cognitive mechanisms that are active during the task and that are instrumental in determining a subject's success or failure.

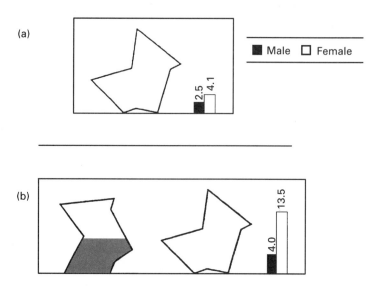

Figure 4 Tasks and results from a study of water-level task performance using containers of various shapes, and presented in a one-bottle (a) or two-bottle (b) format. The bars represent the average degrees of deviation from horizontal for the waterlines drawn by male and female subjects.

The variable that most clearly predicts performance on the WLT is subjects' knowledge of the physical principle that the surface of a liquid remains invariantly horizontal. As would be expected, those who can articulate or identify the principle are considerably more accurate on the task than those who cannot (Liben & Golbeck, 1984; Vasta et al., 1993). Nevertheless, this measure does not predict performance perfectly; some subjects who know the principle perform poorly, and others who do not know it perform well.

Some subjects, after drawing their waterlines in the tilted containers, report they imagined the water was in motion, rather than at rest. These subjects tend to produce larger errors on the task. And, perhaps not surprisingly, more females than males have been found to fall into this category (Robert & Morin, 1993).

Research that currently holds great promise for understanding the WLT involves the cognitive strategies subjects bring to bear on the task. Consider, for example, figure 4a. When subjects are told the object is a glass container and that they should draw a line to show how the container would look if half full of water, virtually every subject draws a near-horizontal line. Yet, when instead shown figure 4b and asked to

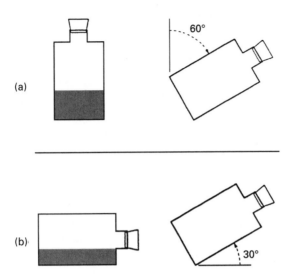

(a)

(b)

Figure 5 Two tasks used in a study investigating the potential role of mental rotation in the water-level task. The reference lines have been added for illustration and were not present in the original task.
Source: From Vasta, Belongia, & Ribble (1994).

draw the waterline in precisely the same empty container, many subjects draw markedly nonhorizontal lines (Vasta, 1994). Because the containers are identical in the two tasks, the errors by the latter subjects cannot result from, for example, perceptual characteristics (oblique lines) inherent in the shape of the container. Rather, before drawing their waterlines in the empty container, these subjects must perform some sort of cognitive operation that apparently is induced by the presence of the partially filled upright container.

Research has shown further that the particular relation between the two containers also affects subjects' drawings. For example, one study compared the lines subjects drew in the empty containers in figures 5a and 5b, which differ in the degree to which the empty containers appear to have been rotated from the partially filled containers. Even though the empty containers are identical, subjects' lines deviated more from horizontal in figure 5a, in which the empty container appears to have been rotated 60°, than in figure 5b, in which the empty container appears to have been rotated 30°.

One cognitive mechanism proposed to account for these findings is mental rotation. According to this hypothesis, subjects who encounter a tilted container mentally rotate it from its original position before drawing their waterlines, and the amount of required mental rotation is positively related to the size of subjects' errors (Vasta, Belongia, & Ribble, 1994).

The potential role of cognitive strategies was also demonstrated in research comparing subjects who scored poorly on the WLT with subjects who scored well. The task involved determining whether lines drawn in tilted rectangles were horizontal or slightly tilted. In one condition, subjects simply made their responses, whereas in a second condition, they were instructed to first superimpose an imaginary grid on the page to assist in locating the horizontal and vertical axes. The results showed that subjects who were low scorers performed worse in the first condition than when using the grid strategy. Subjects who were high scorers performed the same in both conditions (Sholl & Liben, 1995). These data suggest that adults who perform well on the WLT spontaneously activate cognitive strategies to assist them on the task, whereas those who perform poorly do not – even though they apparently could if so instructed.

Future Directions

Evidence from a number of different areas is now beginning to reveal why the WLT proves difficult even for adolescents and adults, and why some individuals are especially prone to having difficulty. But the puzzle is far from solved, and a number of important questions and issues remain. Fortunately, several directions of inquiry appear to offer considerable promise for addressing these questions.

One fundamental issue involves the developmental origins of the skills needed for success on the task. One approach to determining which biological factors and early experiences contribute to success on the WLT later in life would be to identify the factors that appear to affect performance in adults, and then study these factors prospectively in children using longitudinal research designs. Thus, data from the same individuals would be available from childhood, adolescence, and adulthood, and the various pathways to success and failure could be examined more directly. This approach not only would shed light on why many adults do poorly on the task, but also might go a long way toward explaining the observed gender differences. Although a longitudinal approach requires considerable patience, it promises to provide important information about the developmental course that separates successful from unsuccessful subjects.

Another potential focus of future work is studying the WLT in its larger scientific context. The growing literature on adults' misunderstanding of everyday physical principles suggests that ignorance of the physical behavior of water is hardly an isolated problem. Adults have been shown to hold naive beliefs regarding many aspects of physics and often err, for example, when asked to draw the correct trajectory of a car driving off a cliff or a ball emerging from a spiral tube (McCloskey 1983). From this perspective, it seems important to continue to explore the correlates of good and poor WLT performance, correlates that might transcend the laboratory to include learning tasks posed by educators in the classroom and supervisors in the workplace.

The finding that so many adults perform poorly on a task designed originally for children represents a particular challenge to developmentalists, especially those who endorse a universalist perspective regarding the processes and end states of cognitive development. It is important to recognize, however, that adults and children may have difficulty with the task for very different reasons. For example, children's errors may indeed reflect the absence of a euclidean spatial system, as argued by Piaget and Inhelder half a century ago, but it is doubtful that adults' errors signify the same deficit. Rather, it is more likely that most normal adults have developed a mature spatial system (probably, as predicted, by about age nine), but that a considerable proportion fail to apply it when necessary. However, to whatever extent some adults have truly failed to establish a euclidean reference system, it will be necessary to identify the alternative spatial concepts they apply in the WLT and why these, in particular, have developed.

The WLT remains an enigma, despite being one of the most widely investigated spatial problems. But as psychologists continue to identify mechanisms that contribute to task mastery, they will move ever closer to solving this intriguing puzzle.

Notes

1   For more variations on the task, see the Further Reading.
2   Effect size is a statistic used to calculate the influence of the independent variable on the dependent variable. When we report that scores from two

levels of an independent variable are significantly different, we mean that the difference between their mean scores is not likely to result from chance. But in order to say something about the size of this effect, we must consider more than just the difference between the mean scores; we must also consider the variability within each group. For example, one way to calculate effect size is to divide the difference between the two means by the standard deviation of the groups being compared (Cohen, 1977). Effect size thus reveals more than whether the group differences are statistically significant; it can tell us whether the effect is large or small.

References

Annett, M. (1994). Handedness as a continuous variable with dextral shift: Sex, generation and family handedness in subgroups of left and right handers. *Behavioral Genetics, 24,* 51–63.

Baenninger, M., & Newcombe, N. (1995). Environmental input to the development of sex-related differences in spatial and mathematical ability. *Learning and Individual Differences, 7,* 363–379.

Casey, M. B. (1996). Understanding individual differences in spatial ability within females: A nature/nurture interactionist framework. *Developmental Review, 16,* 240–261.

Cohen, J. (1977). *Statistical power analysis for the behavioral sciences.* New York: Academic Press.

Collaer, M. L., & Hines, M. (1995). Human behavioral sex differences: A role for gonadal hormones during early development? *Psychological Bulletin, 118,* 55–107.

Coren, S., & Hoy, V. S. (1986). An orientation illusion analog to the rod and frame: Relational effects in the magnitude of distortion. *Perception and Psychophysics, 39,* 159–163.

Downs, R. M., & Liben, L. S. (1991). The development of expertise in geography: A cognitive-developmental approach to geographic education. *Annals of the Association of American Geographers, 81,* 304–327.

Liben, L. S. (1978). Performance on Piagetian spatial tasks as a function of sex, field dependence, and training. *Merrill-Palmer Quarterly, 24,* 97–110.

Liben, L. S. (1991). Adults' performance on horizontally tasks: Conflicting frames of reference. *Developmental Psychology, 27,* 285–294.

Liben, L. S., & Golbeck, S. L. (1984). Performance on Piagetian horizontality and verticality tasks: Sex-related differences in knowledge of relevant physical phenomena. *Developmental Psychology, 20,* 595–606.

Liben, L. S., & Golbeck, S. L. (1986). Adults' demonstration of underlying Euclidean concepts in relation to task context. *Developmental Psychology, 22,* 487–490.

Liben, L. S., & Stern, R. M. (1996, November). *Water-level task performance and susceptibility to visually-induced motion sickness.* Paper presented at the meeting of the Psychonomic Society. Chicago.

Linn, M. C., & Petersen, A. C. (1985). Emergence and characterization of sex differences in spatial ability: A meta-analysis. *Child Development, 56,* 1479–1498.

McCloskey, M. (1983). Intuitive physics. *Scientific American, 248,* 122–130.

Piaget, J., & Inhelder, B. (1956). *The child's conception of space* (F. J. Langdon & J. L. Lunzer, Trans.). London: Routledge & Kegan Paul. (Original work published 1984)

Rebelsky, F. (1964). Adult perception of the horizontal. *Perceptual and Motor Skills, 19,* 371–374.

Robert, M., & Harel, F. (1996). The gender difference in orienting liquid surfaces and plumb lines: Its robustness, its correlates, and the associated knowledge of simple physics. *Canadian Journal of Experimental Psychology, 50,* 280–314.

Robert, M., & Morin, P. (1993). Gender differences in horizontality and verticality representation in relation to initial position of the stimuli. *Canadian Journal of Experimental Psychology, 47,* 507–522.

Sherman, J. (1987). *Sex-related cognitive differences.* Springfield, IL: Charles C. Thomas.

Sholl, M. J. (1989). The relation between horizontality and rod-and-frame and vestibular navigational performance. *Journal of Experimental Psychology: Learning, Memory, and Cognition, 15,* 110–125.

Sholl, M. J., & Liben, L. S. (1995). Illusory tilt and euclidean schemes as factors in performance on the water-level task. *Journal of Experimental Psychology: Learning, Memory, and Cognition, 21,* 1624–1638.

Thomas, H., & Jamison, W. (1981). A test of the X-linked genetic hypothesis for sex differences on Piaget's water-level task. *Developmental Review, 1,* 274–283.

Thomas, H., & Lohaus, A. (1993). Modeling growth and individual differences in spatial tasks. *Monographs of the Society for Research in Child Development, 58*(9, Serial No. 237).

Vasta, R. (1994, June). *Do adults perceive tilted bottles on the water-level task as rotated?* Paper presented at the annual meeting of the American Psychological Society, Washington, DC.

Vasta, R., Belongia, C., & Ribble, C. (1994). Investigating the orientation effect on the water-level task: Who? When? and Why? *Developmental Psychology, 30,* 893–904.

Vasta, R., Knott, J. A., & Gaze, C. E. (1996). Can spatial training erase the gender differences on the water-level task? *Psychology of Women Quarterly, 20,* 549–567.

Vasta, R., Lightfoot, C., & Cox, B. D. (1993). Understanding gender differences on the water-level problem: The role of spatial perception. *Merrill-Palmer Quarterly, 39*, 391–414.

Vasta, R., Rosenberg, D., Knott, J. A., & Gaze, C. E. (in press). Experience and the water-level task revisited: Does expertise exact a price? *Psychological Science.*

Voyer, D., Voyer, S., & Bryden, M. P. (1995), Magnitude of sex differences in spatial abilities: A meta-analysis and consideration of critical variables. *Psychological Bulletin, 117*, 250–270.

Witkin, H. A., & Goodenough, D. R. (1981). *Cognitive styles: Essence and origins.* New York: International Universities Press.

Further reading

Kalichman, S. C. (1988). Individual differences in water-level performance: A component skills analysis. *Developmental Review, 8*, 273–295.

Liben, L. S. (1991). The Piagetian water-level task: Looking beneath the surface. In R. Vasta (Ed.), *Annals of child development: Vol. 8* (pp. 81–144). London: Kingsley.

Pascual-Leone, J., & Morra, S. (1991). Horizontality of water level: A neo-Piagetian developmental review. In H. W. Reese (Ed.), *Advances in child development and behavior: Vol. 23* (pp. 231–276). San Diego: Academic Press.

FIFTEEN

Mathematical Knowledge

Introduction

What is the relationship between thought and language? This question has intrigued philosophers, linguists, psychologists, and even politicians for many years. In the late 1940s and early 1950s when Russian psychologists addressed this question, the Russian dictator Joseph Stalin joined the debate. Stalin even wrote a book to proclaim that thinking must be carried out with a spoken language; he suggested that those without the capability to speak a language (e.g., deaf and mute individuals) do not think! Furthermore, living up to his reputation, Stalin made his conclusion a Politburo resolution that virtually silenced any dissenting views, and opponents were persecuted.

In the West, debating about the relationship between language and thought, far from being life-threatening, has been lively, diverse, and open to any opinion. A self-taught linguist, Benjamin Whorf (1956), challenged the dominant view of his time that thinking determines language. He proposed that language shapes the way that people think (ironically, this bears some resemblance to Stalin's view). This hypothesis has intrigued many researchers in the last four decades, but direct empirical proof has been elusive to this day. The data reported in this article, though far from proving the hypothesis, suggest that language at least may facilitate or hinder children's thinking about numbers.

Reference

Whorf, B. L. (1956). *Language, thought, and reality*. Cambridge, MA: MIT Press.

Further reading

Geary, D. C. (1996). International differences in mathematical achievement: Their nature, causes, and consequences. *Current Directions in Psychological Science*, 5, 133–7.

Preschool Origins of Cross-National Differences in Mathematical Competence: The Role of Number-Naming Systems

Kevin F. Miller, Catherine M. Smith,
Jianjun Zhu, and Houcan Zhang

Because mathematics is fundamental to scientific discourse, cross-national differences in mathematical development constitute an issue of considerable importance. Dramatic differences in mathematical achievement between US and Asian schoolchildren have been documented (Husen, 1967; Stevenson, Lee, & Stigler, 1986; Travers et al., 1987). These differences in achievement have been attributed to differences in basic abilities (Lynn & Dziobon, 1980), in cultural values and emphases (Stevenson et al., 1986), and in the content and contexts of instruction (Stevenson & Stigler, 1992; Stigler, Lee, Lucker, & Stevenson, 1982). Looking more closely at when such differences emerge in development and which mathematical abilities they involve may lead to a more refined understanding of the sources of the mathematical shortcomings American students exhibit. Cross-language data will also contribute to understanding how cultural and general developmental factors interact in developing mathematical competence. The research reported here demonstrates that (*a*) differences in mathematical competence appear well before school entry, by age four years, and (*b*) these early differences reflect variations in number-naming systems that make accessing some mathematical relations more difficult in English than in Chinese.

Early counting is an ideal domain for studying effects of language on cognitive development, because it is at the same time a universal cognitive accomplishment and one that utilizes specific cultural systems (i.e., for representing number). Although the base-ten Arabic numerals are used throughout the world, names for numbers in different languages reflect older, often more complex systems (Hurford, 1975, 1987; Menninger, 1969). The specific pattern of similarities and differences between Chinese and English suggests specific points in acquisition at which differences in structure might be reflected in different patterns of acquisition. Four portions of the number-naming sequence are particularly relevant. First, counting to ten in either Chinese or English requires mastering an unordered set of names (i.e., one cannot predict that *nine* follows *eight* or that *jiǔ* follows *bā*). Second, after ten, the languages diverge. English names for 11 and 12 bear only a historical relation to *one* and *two*, and names for numbers in the teens are formed by a different rule than are higher number names, with the unit value named before the decade value. Chinese number names above ten follow a consistent base-10 rule (e.g., a literal translation of the Chinese name for 11 is "ten one"). Third, in the range from 20 to 99, both systems converge on roughly isomorphic rules: A decade unit (e.g., *six*) is followed by –*ty* or *ten* and then a unit value, if any, in the range from one to nine. The only morphological difference between Chinese and English names for numbers from 20 to 99 is that Chinese uses unit values for decade names (instead of modifying them as in English *twen*– or *thir*–) and uses the unmodified name for ten to designate decades (instead of the English –*ty*). Finally, above 100, both Chinese and English form hundred names by using unit values from one to nine plus a term for the unit (*hundred/bǎi*). With one exception, names for the last two digits of numbers above 100 (e.g., the 12 of 112) are not affected by being incorporated into a larger number. The single exception is that Chinese number names from 100 to 109 (and 200 to 209, etc.) interpose a term (*líng*) to represent the absent tens value. In general, however, both languages converge after 20 on a regular base-10 system for forming number names.

A previous comparison of early mathematical development in the United States and China reported some differences favoring Chinese children exist in the year prior to school entry (Miller & Stigler, 1987), suggesting that American children enter school with a mathematical disadvantage. If the source of this disadvantage is the complexity of

English number names, stronger predictions can be made: First, differences in counting ability between US and Chinese children should emerge only after children begin to learn the teens, where differences in the number-naming sequence first appear. Second, differences in counting ability should focus on areas in which the languages differ; specifically, American children should have greater trouble learning teens names and the base-10 structure of number names than do Chinese children. Third, cross-language differences in counting competence should generally be limited to the symbolic system of number names, and not involve other aspects of counting, such as understanding the mathematical basis of counting or using counting in problem solving (Gelman, 1991; Gelman & Gallistel, 1978). To test these predictions, data on a series of counting tasks were collected from preschoolers in the United States and China.

Method

Subjects

Subjects were recruited from preschools and through advertising in university communities in Champaign-Urbana, Illinois, and Beijing, China. Chinese subjects (total = 99) were 29 three-year-olds (3.2 to 3.95 years; mean age = 3.6 years), 35 four-year-olds (4.0 to 4.9 years; mean age = 4.5 years), and 35 five-year-olds (5.0 to 5.97 years; mean age = 5.5 years). US subjects (total = 98) were 30 three-year-olds (3.0 to 3.9 years; mean age = 3.5 years), 32 four-year-olds (4.0 to 4.8 years; mean age = 4.5 years), and 36 five-year-olds (5.0 to 5.98 years; mean age = 5.5 years).

Procedure

Children took part in a series of counting-related tasks.

In the abstract counting task, children were asked to count as high as possible and, if necessary, were prompted ("like one, two, three, . . . ?"). Whenever they stopped, they were encouraged to continue with two prompts. First, they were asked, "What comes after N?" (where N was the last number counted). If this did not elicit continued counting, the experimenter repeated the last three numbers counted, ending on a rising, expectant tone (e.g., "27, 28, 29, . . . ?"). This task was presented at the beginning and end of the session. For analyses reported here, data from the best performance were used.

In the object-counting task, children counted objects (small stones used in Chinese chess) arranged in random configurations. Three set sizes were used: small (three to six items), middle (seven to ten items), and large (14 to 17 items).

In the problem-solving (Panda) task, children were asked to help a Panda bear mother make sure her child had just the right number of candies to eat. They were asked to produce sets of two, four, seven, and 12 items (Chinese chess stones) taken from a pot containing about 100 stones. When children appeared to be done, they were routinely queried in a neutral tone ("Is that N candies?"), and the task stopped when they responded affirmatively.

Children's performance was videotaped, and these data were coded in a two-step process. Native speakers of the child's language performed a first-level coding in which the counting sequences children produced were written down and any counting errors were identified. Then secondary coding of error types was performed on these transcripts without regard to child's language. To assess reliability of secondary coding, independent coders recoded one boy and one girl for each language at each age, with 97% agreement between codings.

Results

Abstract counting

Median levels of abstract counting are presented in figure 1. An Age (3: three, four, and five years) × Language (2: English vs. Chinese) analysis of variance of counting level revealed significant effects of age ($F[2, 191] = 68.28$, $p < .01$) and language ($F[1, 191] = 14.94$, $p < .01$), and an Age × Language interaction ($F[2, 191] = 3.35$, $p < .05$). Bonferroni-adjusted language contrasts within age group showed significant differences favoring Chinese children at ages four and five. These data show that significant differences in counting do not emerge until fairly late in the preschool period. The median levels of performance in figure 1 suggest indirectly that these differences occur because English-speaking children require substantially longer than Chinese-speaking children to master names for numbers in the teens.

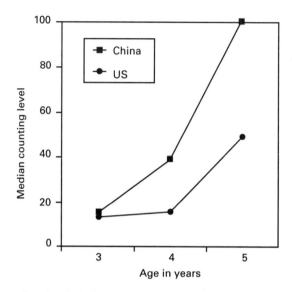

Figure 1   Median level of abstract counting (highest number reached) by age and language. Significant differences favoring Chinese-speaking subjects were found at ages four and five years, but not at age three.

Analysis of both stopping points and errors indicates that US children's difficulty with teens accounts for language differences in abstract counting. Figure 2 presents the percentage of children by language (pooled over age) who reached each number. In order to assess whether specific portions of the number-naming sequence present special stumbling blocks for children learning the Chinese and English number-naming systems, these profiles of counting "mortality" were analyzed using survival analysis techniques (McCullagh & Nelder, 1991). Survival analyses revealed no significant language differences in percentage of counts terminating before ten. Significant language differences were found for the teens decade (shaded region of fig. 2); 94% of American children and 92% of Chinese children could count to ten; 74% of Chinese children but only 48% of Americans could count to 20. From 20 to 99, there were no significant language differences in counting survival: both US and Chinese samples showed a scalloped profile featuring mistakes at decade boundaries. Finally, after 100, Chinese subjects showed a large drop that was significantly greater than the drop for US children. This larger drop corresponds to the greater complexity

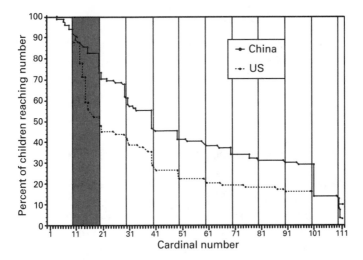

Figure 2 Percentage of children reaching each number in the abstract counting task. The difficulty US children have in mastering the teens structure is shown by their rapid drop-off in performance during this range (shaded region).

of Chinese compared with English number names from 100 to 109 (described earlier). The counting mortality profiles presented in figure 2 map closely onto the linguistic analysis of the two number-naming systems.

Error data confirm that US children have particular trouble learning teens names and inducing the base-10 structure of number names. When first counting above 20, American preschoolers often produce idiosyncratic number names, indicating that they fail to understand the base-10 structure underlying larger number names. For example, they may count, "Twenty-eight, twenty-nine, twenty-ten, twenty-eleven, twenty-twelve." Overall, this type of mistake was produced by 14 children, two Chinese subjects (both three-year-olds) and 12 Americans (three three-year-olds, seven four-year-olds, and two five-year-olds). Reflecting the simpler nature of decade names in Chinese, Chinese children were somewhat more likely than US children to mistakenly count by tens. Most commonly, this took the form of counting, ". . . shí-bā, shí-jiǔ, èr-shí, sān-shí, sì-shí" (literally, "ten-eight, ten-nine, two-ten, three-ten, four-ten"). This mistake was made by 12 Chinese subjects but by only five US children.

The most common error in both countries was to skip a number name, with 61% of US children and 39% of Chinese children skipping at least one number name. English-speaking children were much more likely than Chinese speakers to omit one or more teen number names (41% of US subjects vs. 10% of Chinese subjects), providing yet another indication that learning teens names is more difficult in the English than in the Chinese system.

Object counting and problem solving

Despite large language effects on abstract counting, no language differences were found in children's ability to solve simple mathematical problems or to count arrays of ten or fewer objects. Both tasks are difficult for young children, but neither revealed language differences.

Data on children's object-counting errors are presented in table 1. These errors were categorized into three types:

- principle errors (violating the rule that exactly one number name should be said each time an object is counted),
- attention errors (skipping or recounting objects), and
- sequence errors (deviations from conventional number naming).

Because both successful performance and errors are categorical variables, logistic regression analyses were conducted for each error category and for success on the object-counting and Panda tasks. Significant language differences were found, favoring Chinese children, only with the large sets (14–17 items): for success, $G^2(1, N = 197) = 5.39, p < .05$, and for sequence errors, $G^2(1, N = 197) = 21.29, p < .01$. This was the only set size for which the greater difficulty English-speakers have in learning teens names might affect object counting, and it did so. US and Chinese children showed similar developmental patterns in preserving one-to-one correspondence between objects and names in counting and in their ability to keep track of counted items. Logistic regression analyses of problem-solving (Panda task) data found significant age effects, but no language differences for any set size (two, four, seven, and 12 items).

Object-counting and problem-solving results extend the pattern shown on the abstract counting task. US children do not demonstrate any disadvantage in the attentional and conceptual aspects of counting

Table 1   Object-counting errors by country and age

Counting pattern	Three-year-olds			Four-year-olds			Five-year-olds		
	Small set	Middle set	Large set	Small set	Middle set	Large set	Small set	Middle set	Large set
US children									
Correct	73.3	33.3	.0	96.9	68.8	18.8	100	83.3	33.3
Principle error	6.7	23.3	36.7	.0	15.6	21.9	.0	.0	8.3
Attention error	20.0	56.7	90.0	3.1	25.0	65.6	.0	16.7	38.9
Sequence error	.0	10.0	53.3	.0	3.1	43.8	.0	.0	38.9
Chinese children									
Correct	82.8	37.9	3.4	97.1	71.4	25.7	94.3	85.7	60.0
Principle error	3.4	20.7	37.9	.0	5.7	8.6	.0	.0	2.9
Attention error	6.9	44.8	96.6	2.9	22.9	74.3	5.7	14.3	40.0
Sequence error	6.9	17.2	37.9	.0	.0	8.6	.0	.0	.0

The numbers in the table show the percentage of children showing each counting pattern. Principle errors involve a violation of the principle that there should be one and only one number name spoken each time an object is counted. Attention errors involve skipping or recounting objects. Sequence errors are any violations of the conventional number-naming sequence. For US children, n = 30 three-year-olds, 32 four-year-olds, and 36 five-year-olds. For Chinese children, n = 29 three-year-olds, 35 four-year-olds, and 35 five-year-olds. Small sets contained three to six items, middle sets contained seven to ten items, and large sets contained 14 to 17 items.

involved in successfully counting or producing small sets of objects. Compared with their Chinese peers, however, they have a substantially greater difficulty mastering the system of number names that their native language employs.

Discussion

Although language differences were confined to tasks involving number-naming systems, later mathematical development largely involves learning relations and operations represented symbolically. The English number-naming system appears to present obstacles to children's understanding of the base-10 principle of number representation, and to acquiring arithmetical carrying and borrowing strategies (Fuson & Kwon, 1992; Miura, 1987; Miura, Kim, Chang, & Okamoto, 1988). Furthermore, research on the development of addition points to the importance of counting in children's early addition strategies

(Hitch, Cundick, Haughey, Pugh, & Wright, 1987; Siegler, 1987), and the accuracy of children's counting strategies for particular problems shows up as a strong predictor of adult performance on those problems. Even with single-digit numbers, the sophistication of addition strategies of US and Chinese children have been shown to differ significantly at the time of school entry (Geary, Fan, & Bow-Thomas, 1992).

Arabic numerals provide a consistent base-10 representation for numbers; use of these numerals may partly compensate for the complexity for English number names. American adults show a greater decrement in performing numerical manipulations with words instead of numerals than do Chinese subjects with characters versus numerals (Miller, 1990; Miller & Zhu, 1991). Familiarizing American children with Arabic numerals at an earlier age than at present might help compensate for the complexity of English number names. That very complexity, however, constitutes a stumbling block to using Arabic numerals. Fuson, Fraivillig, and Burghardt (1992) found that explicit instruction using multiunit blocks was a necessary prerequisite to teaching American children the tens-structured addition methods taught in East Asian countries.

Finding large cross-national differences in mathematical competence before school entry implies that the US educational system does not bear all the responsibility for differences in older children. Nonetheless, shortcomings in US education have been well documented (Stevenson & Stigler, 1992). Such shortcomings would exacerbate disadvantages English-speaking children show at school entry. The finding that US – Chinese differences center on verbal systems for representing number does call into question claims that such differences reflect variations in general intelligence of innate mathematical competence. These results suggest further that efforts at improving early mathematical development in the United States should include efforts aimed at making the base-10 structure of number names more accessible to young children.

References

Fuson, K. C., Fraivillig, J. D., & Burghardt, B. H. (1992). Relationships children construct among English number words, multiunit base-ten blocks, and written multidigit addition. In J. I. D. Campbell (Ed.), *The nature and origins of mathematical skills* (pp. 39–112). New York: North-Holland.

Fuson, K. C., & Kwon, Y. (1992). Effects of the system of number words and other cultural tools on children's addition and subtraction. In J. Bideaud & C. Meljac (Eds.), *Pathways to number: Children's developing numerical abilities* (pp. 127–149). Hillsdale, NJ: Erlbaum.

Geary, D. C., Fan, L., & Bow-Thomas, C. C. (1992). Numerical cognition: Locus of ability differences comparing children from China and the United States. *Psychological Science, 3,* 180–185.

Gelman, R. (1991). Epigenetic foundations of knowledge structures: Initial and transcendent constructions. In S. Carey & R. Gelman (Eds.), *The epigenesis of mind: Essays on biology and cognition* (pp. 293–322). Hillsdale. NJ: Erlbaum.

Gelman, R., & Gallistel, C. R. (1978). *The child's understanding of number.* Cambridge, MA: Harvard University Press.

Hitch, G., Cundick, J., Haughey, M., Pugh, R., & Wright, H. (1987). Aspects of counting in children's arithmetic. In J. A. Sloboda & D. Rogers (Eds.), *Cognitive processes in mathematics* (pp. 26–41). Oxford: Clarendon Press.

Hurford, J. R. (1975). *The linguistic theory of numerals.* Cambridge, UK: Cambridge University Press.

Hurford, J. R. (1987). *Language and number.* Cambridge, UK: Cambridge University Press.

Husen, T. (1967). *International study of achievement in mathematics.* New York: Wiley.

Lynn, R., & Dziobon, J. (1980). On the intelligence of Japanese and other Mongoloid peoples. *Personality and Individual Differences, 1,* 95–96.

McCullagh, P., & Nelder, J. A. (1991). *Generalized linear models.* New York: Chapman & Hall.

Menninger, K. (1969). *Number words and number symbols.* Cambridge, MA: MIT Press.

Miller, K. F. (1990, November). *Language, orthography, and number: When surface structure matters.* Paper presented at the annual meeting of the Psychonomic Society, New Orleans.

Miller, K. F., & Stigler, J. (1987). Counting in Chinese: Cultural variation in a basic cognitive skill. *Cognitive Development, 2,* 279–305.

Miller, K. F., & Zhu, J. (1991). The trouble with teens: Accessing the structure of number names. *Journal of Memory and Language, 30,* 48–68.

Miura, I. T. (1987). Mathematics achievement as a function of language. *Journal of Educational Psychology, 79,* 79–82.

Miura, I. T., Kim, C. C., Chang, C.-M., & Okamoto, Y. (1988). Effects of language characteristics on children's cognitive representation of number: Cross-national comparisons. *Child Development, 59,* 1445–1450.

Siegler, R. S. (1987). The perils of averaging data over strategies: An example from children's addition. *Journal of Experimental Psychology: General, 116,* 250–264.

Stevenson, H. W., Lee, S.-Y., & Stigler, J. W. (1986). Mathematics achievement of Chinese, Japanese, and American children. *Science, 233,* 693–699.

Stevenson, H. W., & Stigler, J. W. (1992). *The learning gap.* New York: Summit.

Stigler, J. W., Lee, S. Y., Lucker, G. W., & Stevenson, H. W. (1982). Curriculum and achievement in mathematics: A study of elementary school children in Japan, Taiwan and the United States. *Journal of Educational Psychology, 74,* 315–322.

Travers, K. J., Crosswhite, F. J., Dossey, J. A., Swafford, J. O., McKnight, C. C., & Cooney, T. J. (1987). *Second international mathematics study summary report for the United States.* Champaign, IL: Stipes.

SIXTEEN

Scientific Reasoning

Introduction

Are children scientists in the making? At which age do they begin to think and carry out investigations in the same manner as scientists? How do they acquire the knowledge and skills of scientific inquiry? These fundamental questions have driven the field of cognitive development for nearly a century and inspired Piaget to study the mind of children for almost his entire career. To answer them, one must consider whether children use a theoretical framework to provide causal explanations about an event, whether they use theories to make predictions about future events, and whether they can plan and perform tests to confirm or disconfirm their theories.

While Piaget and his colleagues (Inhelder & Piaget, 1958) concluded that children begin thinking like scientists only in their teens, more recently researchers have discovered that certain scientific thinking begins at an earlier age. Very young children appear to make theory-like assumptions about the world around them as they operate in their environment, using different "theories" to deal with physical, biological, and psychological events. As Karmiloff-Smith (1992) puts it, children are naive physicists, biologists, psychologists, and linguists. In this article, Wellman, Hickling, and Schult focus on how children explain events of different ontological natures. With evidence from a number of studies, they illustrate that children as young as two years of age use three basic reasoning systems to make causal explanations about everyday physical, biological, and psychological events.

References

Inhelder, B., & Piaget, J. (1958). *The growth of logical thinking from childhood to adolescence*. New York: Basic Books.

Karmiloff-Smith, A. (1992). *Beyond modularity: A developmental perspective on cognitive science*. Cambridge, MA: MIT Press.

Further reading

Shauble, L. (1996). The development of scientific reasoning in knowledge-rich contexts. *Developmental Psychology, 32*, 102–19.

Sodian, B., Zaitchik, D., & Carey, S. (1991). Young children's differentiation of hypothetical beliefs from evidence. *Child Development, 62*, 753–66.

Young Children's Psychological, Physical, and Biological Explanations

Henry M. Wellman, Anne K. Hickling, and Carolyn A. Schult

When we explain something, we make sense of it within some framework or another. Beyond such general descriptions, defining what we mean by an explanation is not a simple matter. Understanding complex psychological constructs of this sort requires more a theory than a straightforward definition. But, minimally, explanations capture our search for and beliefs about what connects with what and what accounts for what. Moreover, explanations range over many phenomena and partake of many reasoning systems. Imagine someone whose body is shaking all over. Adults in our society might believe that the person is shaking with fear (a psychological reason), shivering with a fever (a biological cause), or even shaking from an earthquake tremor (a physical explanation). In this chapter we claim that early in life children develop three distinctive causal-explanatory reasoning systems:

1   a naive psychology (a theory of mind) that involves construing human action in terms of actors' internal mental states;
2   a naive physics – an early understanding of mechanical or material phenomena, such as objects colliding, falling, or having mass;
3   a naive biology – an early understanding of everyday physiological states and processes, such as illness, birth, growth, and death.

A variety of research already supports such a claim (Wellman and Gelman, 1992, forthcoming). Three- and four-year-olds understand that animals and plants but not inanimate objects grow and heal (Backscheider, Shatz, and Gelman, 1993; Inagaki and Hatano, 1996; Rosengren, Gelman, Kalish, and McCormick, 1991); that natural phenomena such as clouds, stars, and animals have natural causes rather than artificial ones (Gelman and Kremer, 1991); that persons but not dolls or rocks can think, remember, feel happy, and see (Gelman, Spelke, and Meck, 1983; Johnson and Wellman, 1982); and that thoughts are mental and nonmaterial whereas physical entities such as balls and dogs are tangible and material (Wellman and Estes, 1986). Some of these distinctions may constrain conceptual understandings from a very early age indeed; even infants appropriately distinguish between animate and inanimate entities and their movements (Legerstee, 1992; Spelke, Phillips, and Woodward, 1995). Piaget (1929), among others, claimed that children initially confuse together these forms of reasoning, which are fundamentally distinct in adults' thoughts, resulting in childhood animism, artificialism, and realism. But many current studies (such as those just cited) argue that even quite young children may reason about psychological, biological, and physical phenomena differently and appropriately.

This emerging research is incomplete, however. Rarely have investigators looked at children's reasoning comparatively, across these three topics or domains of thinking. If naive psychology, physics, and biology constitute contrasting reasoning systems, then children must come to differentiate and coordinate them in revealing fashions. Furthermore, contemporary research has typically examined children's judgments and predictions – whether rabbits can heal or grow, what actions will stem from a character's beliefs and desires. Much less is known about children's explanations. Yet, writers have often called these three reasoning systems naive theories (for example, see Wellman and Gelman, 1992), thereby emphasizing their presumed status as *explanatory* knowledge systems. If naive psychology, physics, and biology constitute developing causal-explanatory reasoning systems, then this should be especially important for, and be especially revealed by, children's explanations.

For the last few years, therefore, we have been researching children's explanations of psychological, biological, and physical phenomena. We have examined a range of topics and events, but in this chapter we concentrate on children's explanation of human movements and actions.

Explanations of Human Behavior

Both theoretical and methodological reasons make children's explanations of human movements an important and revealing topic. Methodologically, if the aim is to compare children's psychological, physical, and biological reasoning, human beings and human movement are the primary phenomena where all three explanations appropriately apply. Recall the example of the person who is shaking all over. Humans are not only psychological entities motivated by mental processes, they are also physical bodies subject to objectlike movements and biological organisms subject to physiological forces and movements. Thus, studying children's explanations of human movements provides a focus for comparing their reasoning across a variety of explanatory systems.

Theoretically, assume for the moment that young children do possess several different explanatory reasoning systems – say, psychological, physical, and biological ones. Then how do children coordinate the different sorts of entities to be explained with the distinctive principles or constructs that may be used to explain them? One obvious possibility is that children apply each reasoning system to every sort of entity. This possibility provides a plausible core to Piaget's varied claims about animism, realism, and artificialism. Children might very well use physical, biological, or psychological explanations indiscriminately for a very wide range of phenomena, at least at some early point in their cognitive development. The opposite possibility is also plausible. That is, each reasoning system could have its own proprietary entities, at least early in a child's development. Thus, for young children mental-psychological explanations might apply always and solely to people, mechanical-physical explanations always and solely to inanimate physical objects, and biological explanations always and solely to nonhuman living things. Carey and Spelke (1994), among others, argue for this entity-based possibility – entities and explanations go together, to begin with, in certain tightly woven ways. Targeting human beings and human movements provides a way to test these alternative proposals.

We know from some earlier work of our own that when asked to explain simple human actions (for example, "Jane is looking for her kitten under the piano; why is she doing that?") or simple human reactions ("Joe went to school today and saw they were having grape juice for a snack. Boy was he surprised. Why is Joe so surprised?"), three- and four-year-olds, like adults, typically provide psychological explanations (Bartsch and Wellman, 1989; Wellman and Banerjee, 1991). Predominantly, children and adults explain these actions and reactions in terms of the actors' beliefs and desires ("She wants to find her kitten" or "He thought they'd have orange juice, not grape juice, for snack"). But these studies focused on a limited range of human acts; biological movements or reactions (feverish shaking) and physical, objectlike movements were not included. A few prior studies have included these sorts of human movements, and they suggest that young children might make some telling errors in applying different reasoning systems to human behavior. Shultz, Wells, and Sardo (1980) asked preschool children to judge reflex and intended behaviors. Until five years of age children judged *both* these types of behaviors to be "on purpose." Relatedly, Smith (1978) showed four-, five-, and six-year-olds videotapes of an actor engaging in voluntary acts (such as chewing something, doing arm exercises) *or* undergoing reflex reactions (yawning, saying "Ow" when poked with a stick in the ribs) *or* experiencing objectlike movement (having an arm snagged and raised by the hook of an umbrella, being pushed across the room like a large box). Children were asked whether the actor had been "trying" to do what she did, whether she had been "surprised" at what she did, and whether she had "wanted" to do what she did. Not until five years did children distinguish reflexes and objectlike movements from intentional (that is, psychologically based) behavior: "Four-year-olds tended to regard all acts/movements and their effects as intentional. Object-like movements and involuntary acts as well as voluntary acts were generally judged intentional" (p. 741).

Our Recent Studies of Children's Explanations

For several reasons we felt that earlier research might not have captured children's understandings adequately. Therefore, in a series of studies (Schult and Wellman, forthcoming) we solicited explanations from three- and four-year-olds of a variety of human actions and movements with a psychological, biological, or physical impetus. Exhibit 1 presents some of the situations we used. Voluntary actions that actors perform because they want to are prototypical psychologically caused movements (for example, a person pours milk on his cereal). Psychological explanations of such acts often stress the subject's beliefs or desires – "he wanted milk on his cereal" or "he thinks cereal is better with milk than dry." Mistakes; physical, objectlike movements; and biological movements contrast with such intended actions. For example, mistakes are unintended – something happens that is not a result or fulfillment of the subject's desires. Although unintended, mistakes require psychological explanations just as intended actions do. For adults, at least, mistakes are explained by an appeal to psychological causes such as beliefs and desires – "he didn't know the pitcher had orange juice," or "he thought it had milk." Biological human behaviors, such as reflexes, or physical, objectlike movements, such as being blown along by the wind, are like mistakes in their being unintended and also in that they often go counter to a person's desires. Yet, for adults these sorts of behaviors require *non*psychological construal and explanation; their explanations lie in the domains of physical and biological forces and processes.

In several studies three- and four-year-olds each heard four to six stories of the sort in exhibit 1, presented with the aid of several line drawings. A critical comparison to be made in these studies concerned children's responses to mistakes versus their responses to physical and biological movements. As in exhibit 1, in those three types of stories the protagonist's desire was similarly thwarted; nevertheless, for adults at least the explanations for these three actions or movements should be quite different. The stories were presented, the outcomes were noted, and the children were asked to explain what had happened. "Why did [that outcome] happen? Why did [the protagonist] do that?" For example, "Why did Jimmy pour orange juice on his cereal?"

Children's explanations ranged over a variety of topics and processes, but they were easily and reliably coded into the following categories:

- *Psychological explanations:* statements that referred to the character's mental states, such as his or her desires, preferences, beliefs, and emotions. "He wanted to get down." "She just didn't know it was ketchup." "He thought it was milk."
- *Physical explanations:* statements that appealed to or implied physical forces, such as gravity or the wind, or statements declaring the need for some other mechanism for the action to be carried out. "He's too heavy to float in the sky." "Gravity pulls him down." "Planes can fly and people can't 'cause they don't have wings."

Exhibit 1   Sample items for eliciting explanations from preschoolers

Intended action

It's time for breakfast, so Jimmy gets the cereal out of the cupboard. Now Jimmy has an idea. He wants to pour
  milk on his cereal. Jimmy takes a pitcher out of the refrigerator and pours it on his cereal. He pours milk on
  his cereal.

Mistake

It's time for breakfast, so Jimmy gets the cereal out of the cupboard. Now Jimmy has an idea. He wants to pour
  milk on his cereal. Jimmy takes a pitcher out of the refrigerator and pours it on his cereal. He pours orange
  juice on his cereal.

Biological

Robin is climbing a tree in her backyard. She's hanging from a branch, not touching the ground. Now she has an
  idea. She wants to hang on that branch forever and never let go. Robin drops to the ground.

Physical

Bobby is playing in his bedroom. He climbs on top of his stool. Now he has an idea. He wants to step off the
  stool and float in the air, up off the floor. Bobby steps off the stool and comes right down to the floor.

Source: Adpated from Schult and Wellman, forthcoming.

- *Biological explanations:* statements that referred to states of the
  body, such as fatigue or pain, or to biological processes, such as
  growth, health, blood, and germs. "He gets tired and has to sleep
  again." "His arms got hurting." "You have to grow bigger."
- *Other:* statements that reiterated the story, said "don't know," or
  were uninterpretable.

Figure 1 shows how children in a study comparing three- and four-
year-olds explained each story type. As the figure makes clear, far from
regarding all these human movements and actions as being due to the
actors' desires, beliefs, and intentions, young children were appropriately selective as to the kinds of actions that deserved a psychological
explanation. For four-year-olds, mistakes, like voluntary acts, received
psychological explanations, although these acts differed in whether the
characters' desires were achieved. Yet, in contrast to mistakes, physical,
objectlike movements received largely physical explanations, and
organic or biologically based movements received largely biological

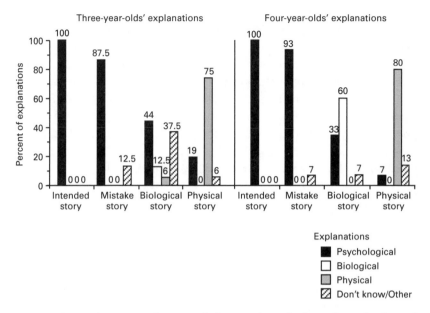

Figure 1 Explanations for intended, mistaken, biological, and physical movements or events.

Source: Adapted from Schult and Wellman, forthcoming.

explanations. Even three-hear-olds mostly fit this pattern, at least in comparing psychologically caused versus physically caused movements or events.

Note how flexible and appropriate the children's explanations were. Although not shown in exhibit 1, each physical and biological item was typically paired with an intended item focusing on the same behavioral occurrence. For example, coming down from a stool because of gravity was paired with coming down because the character wanted to. Children explained the same surface acts differently and appropriately. Moreover, items were carefully constructed so that surface features of the movements and situations to be explained could not simply elicit correct explanations. For example, the "mistake" scenario in exhibit 1 actually focuses on eating breakfast, a potentially biological activity. Children explained this scenario appropriately, in psychological terms, and not simply by recruiting various associated "biological' terms such as hunger, food, or energy. Similarly, both the biological and the physical items in exhibit 1 involved coming down to the ground from a height, but children explained these movements differently. Overall, children's explanations gave no evidence that they might simply be matching associated terms to the surface phenomena described in the scenarios (for example, eating inspiring mention of growth or nutrition, and dropping or falling inspiring mention of gravity or weight). Instead, children's explanations appropriately targeted the deeper causal event – the everyday psychological, biological, and physical forces that adults also believe are at play in such scenarios.

In an additional study we wished to explore children's reasoning about a larger array of items. Here we began by asking children to determine whether some desired action could occur. Three different types of desired actions were contrasted, as shown in exhibit 2. In the case of simple, voluntary actions like lying down or jumping, the desire or intention generally results in the action, in a straightforward manner – if you want to perform the action, you can do it. For physically or biologically impossible actions, however, like floating in the air without support or never experiencing pain, psychological motivation simply cannot bring about the desired action or result, because other forces – physical and biological constraints – are also at work. In this study three-year-olds and four-year-olds were presented with nine scenarios of the sort shown in exhibit 2. After each scenario was described, the child was asked if the character could do the desired action: "Can he do that?" Then the children were asked to explain their judgments: "Why?" or "Why not?"

There were only small and insignificant differences between the three- and four-year-olds in their judgments. When asked about the voluntary items, the four-year-olds judged 93% of the time that, yes, the character could do that (the three-year-olds did so 82% of the time). When asked about the physically impossible items, the four-year-olds judged 90% of the time that, no, the character could *not* do that (the three-year-olds judged so 83% of the time). And with the biologically impossible items, the four-year-olds judged 89% of the time that, no, the character could not do that (the three-year-olds judged so 78% of the time). Obviously, even the three-year-olds appropriately judged the biologically and physically impossible acts as impossible most of the time.

Many of the children's explanations essentially, but appropriately, reiterated their judgments – for example, "It's easy; you just do it" or

Exhibit 2   Explanations for intended, mistaken, biological, and physical movements or events

Voluntary actions, possible

Fred is in his room standing with his feet on the floor. He's been standing up a long time. Now he wants to have it different, and that's OK with his mom. He wants to stop standing up and lie down on his bed.

Cathy has been sitting outside on a bench for a long time. She's been sitting quietly watching the trees. Now she wants something different, and it's OK with her mom. She wants to stop sitting and start jumping up and down.

Physically impossible

Every time Judy jumps up she always comes back down. She jumps off the floor into the air, but then she comes right back down to the floor every time. Now she wants it different, and that's OK with her mom. She wants to jump up and just float in the air, not touching anything. She doesn't ever want to come down.

On the way to the playground there is a really big brick wall. To get to the playground Josh has to walk way over to the side to get around this wall. Every day Josh has to walk all the way around it. Now he wants it different, and that's OK with his mom. He wants to walk right through the wall. The wall would still be there, but he would ooze right through it.

Biologically impossible

Every time Henry gets poked with a needle it really hurts. The needle pokes him and ouch, does it hurt. Now he wants to have it different, and that's OK with him mom. He wants it so that when he gets poked it *won't* hurt. He'd still get poked with the needle, but it would never hurt.

Karen is three (or four) like you. Every year she gets bigger. She keeps growing and growing. Now she wants to have it different, and that's OK with her mom. She doesn't ever want to grow again. She wants to stay the same size forever.

Source : Adapted from Schult and Wellman, forthcoming.

"You can't; it's impossible." However, at times children spontaneously went beyond these simple but acceptable explanations to mention something of the underlying forces or processes at work. These extended explanations could be coded into the categories listed previously – essentially psychological, biological, and physical explanations and a residual category of "other." In this case, both the three- and the four-year-olds produced predominantly appropriate explanations for biological as well as physical items. Specifically, 86% of the time that four-year-olds gave extended explanations for the physically impossible items, they gave physical explanations for them (for the three-year-olds it was 75% of the time); 57% of the time that four-year-olds gave extended explanations to the biologically impossible items, they gave biological explanations for them (for the three-year-olds it was 55% of the time).

Natural Language Analyses

These results concerning young children's use of psychological, physical, and biological explanations are informative yet incomplete. For example, even in the study just described, we could only ask children about a limited set of phenomena – people falling, muscles fatiguing, bodies oozing through walls. Perhaps our examples represent only a few compelling islands of clarity amid a vast sea of childhood confusion. We intentionally chose target phenomena that we hoped would be particularly clear to young children. Moreover, in testing situations such as these we directly solicited children's explanations about occurrences we made very salient. Thus it remains possible that flexible use of these distinctive explanatory reasoning systems might be limited to only special items, situations, or questions. However, if young children really do acquire several complementary explanatory theories, then that ought to be abundantly clear in a variety of everyday attempts to understand and explain their world.

To supplement our experimental investigations, we examined children's everyday explanations, captured in their conversations with their parents, siblings, and peers about ordinary events in the home (Hickling, 1996; Hickling and Wellman, 1997). These conversations provide an intriguing picture of what sort of phenomena children explain and want explained and what explanations they offer for them.

It is distinctly possible that in everyday situations very young children focus on only one type of phenomena or provide only one type of explanation. In fact, in an examination of two-year-olds' explanations, Hood and Bloom (1979) concluded that children's first causal explanations were exclusively psychological, rather than physical or biological, and exclusively about people: "The children in this study simply did not talk about causal events that occurred between physical objects in the world. . . . The children did talk about intentions and motivations" (pp. 29–30). However, by some age children must evidence a range of explanatory topics and explanations. So again we were interested in which reasoning systems children apply to which topics. That is, do they indiscriminately link various sorts of explanations to any old entity (à la Piagetian animism, realism, and artificialism), or do they strictly tie each reasoning system to proprietary objects (in an entity-based fashion)? Or, indeed, are they more appropriate than the former and more flexible than the latter?

Recently we have been examining the longitudinal transcripts of English-speaking children that are available for study through the Child Language Data Exchange System (CHILDES) (MacWhinney and Snow, 1985, 1990). This natural language database now includes systematically recorded transcripts of more than ten English-speaking children. On the basis of earlier analyses (see Bartsch and Wellman, 1995), we know that four individuals among these ten represent and provide a good view of the larger group, so we began our analyses by focusing on them. These four children – Adam, Abe, Sarah, and Ross – include one girl and three boys, two children of language researchers, one child from a professional-class family, three European Americans, and one African American. The transcripts provide extensive longitudinal language samples, collected weekly or biweekly from roughly age two to age five and including more than one hundred thousand conversations recorded at home between these young children and their parents, their siblings, and occasional visitors.

In our analyses of these transcripts we were interested in any talk centering on causes or explanations of events. We focused initially on instances in which children explicitly signaled an explanation by using identifiable causal-explanatory terms, such as *why, because, cause, how, so, if,* and *then.* Often when a child uses such terms his or her intent to express a causal explanation is especially clear, and the terms just listed include many that are used by children from an early age.

For each target utterance we considered several dimensions: syntactic form, pragmatic function, temporal reference, and so on. We focus here, however, on one conceptual distinction that we consider pivotal, the distinction between the "explained topic" versus the "explanation mode." The explanation topic identifies the phenomena to be explained, the *explanandum.* The reasoning used to explain that topic is offered in the explanation mode – the *explanans.* In the utterance "The balloon will pop because you stand on it," the topic is the balloon's popping, and the mode is someone's standing on it. Here the topic comes first, followed by the explanation for the topic, or the mode. In other sentences that order can be reversed, as in "The animals didn't like the zoo, so they went

---

Exhibit 3   Categories for topics and modes in children's explanations

Explanation topics

person: "*We* have to play on the bars because I want to show you some tricks." (age 2 years, 9 months)
animal: "*The snake* bit me because he's naughty." (age 2 years, 7 months)
physical object: "*The bench* wiggles because these are loose." (age 2 years, 11 months)
plant
natural object
food
event/state

Explanation modes

psychological (internal states, dispositions): "I'm going to get the door *because I want to.*" (age 2 years, 7 months)
physical (mechanical force, changes of material state): "It [a nail] broke *because it got bent.*" (age 3 years, 1 month)
biological (physiological or biochemical states, processes, mechanisms): "Good that . . . I didn't cough in Mommy's face *'cause then she might get the germs.*" (age 4 years, 8 months)
social/conventional (social rules, prescriptions, cultural practices or conventions): "I got this candy *because it's a prize.*" (age 2 years, 11 months)
behavioral: "My hands are dirty *because I ate blueberries.*" (age 2 years, 9 months)

---

home." Here the topic is the animals' going home, and the explanation cites their not liking the zoo.

Both conversation topics and explanation modes come in different varieties; exhibit 3 shows the categories we have identified. These categories are based in part on ideas we had in advance, such as the expectation that children might talk about such topics as people versus physical objects and might offer reasons that are distinctly physical rather than biological. The categories also partly emerged from children's conversations as we scrutinized their explained topics and explanation modes. For example, we distinguished talk about foods as a separate category of explained topics after we became acquainted with children's talk about food and the impossibility of deciding whether it mostly concerned *people's* eating, foods as *animal or plant* products, both, or neither. Explanation topics were identified primarily in terms of the type of object involved. Often these objects underwent some sort of motion, action, or other occurrence. (The example for persons in exhibit 3 involves playing, the example for animals involves biting, and the example for physical objects involves wiggling.) As we noted in describing our experimental studies, however, motions can crosscut many entities and types; thus we concentrated on identifying the object types involved (for example, persons, animals, and physical objects).

Explanation modes, or *explanans*, come in many forms too. Our subcategories here were attempts to capture a general level of description rather than detailed explanatory arguments. Thus we coded for psychological explanations generally (which included appeals to desires, to beliefs, or to emotional states, specifically) and also for physical explanations generally (which included mentions of gravity, physical contact, or bending, specifically). We termed these categories *explanation modes* to denote this more general level of categorization. Besides the psychological, physical, and biological explanation modes, children also use social-conventional explanations, magical-fantastical explanations, and so on. In addition, we carefully identified a category of what we termed *behavioral explanations*. As in the last item on exhibit 3, most of these utterances explained an overt action or activity (hands getting dirty) in terms of another action or behavior (eating blueberries). Utterances representing this explanation mode (for example, "eating blueberries") did not clearly refer to one domain (such as, say, biological aspects of eating) or another (such as physical contact from hands to berries), or they may have referred to a sort of "logic of action" at the behavioral but not clearly at the psychological level. To be conservative, we simply classified all such instances as behavioral.

The example utterances in exhibit 3 are exact instances of children's speech. Each represents a type of utterance we have termed an *explanation offer*, meaning a causal statement providing an explanation in terms of both topic and mode. Explanation offers are crucial because they provide the most complete and direct opportunity to explore the relationships among children's conversational subject matter and their domains of reasoning. Other causal expressions, like *explanation requests*, by which children seek explanations, often give only a topic and so are less informative. Almost 2,500 explanation offers were provided by the four children. They also made almost 1,500 explanation requests, and they used the target causal-explanatory connectives in about 1,000 other utterances that we called *simple uses* (such as "Why?" or "Just because").

Explanation offers, explanation requests, and simple uses were provided by children at all ages, even in the earliest transcripts.

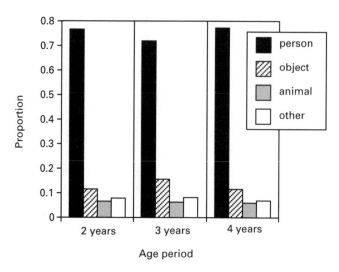

Figure 2   Explanation topics, by age group.
Source: Adapted from Hickling and Wellman, 1997.

Explanation offers – the more complete utterances in which children include both a topic and a mode – increased with age relative to explanation requests and simple uses. Consider children's explanations at three rough, successive age periods: two years (beginning at the first data collections, which ranged from two years and three months until two years and eleven months), three years (ranging from exactly three years to three years and eleven months) and four years (covering the entire fourth year). Explanation offers increased from about one third of the utterances using the target terms at two years to more than 60% of them at four years. But more important than this increase is the fact that many explanation offers appeared even in the earliest period, when the children were barely two years old. Individually, each of the four children had frequent explanation offers as two-year-olds.

Both explanation offers and explanation requests allow us to address the question of what children think is worth explaining – the *topics* of their explanations and requests for explanation. From figure 2 it is clear that children take great interest in people as topics for conversation and explanation. However, they also explain or request explanations for a variety of other topics, especially the nature and movements of physical objects and animals. This is true even in the earliest age period.

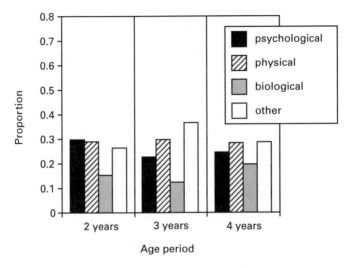

Figure 3 Explanation modes, by age group.
Source: Adapted from Hickling and Wellman, 1997.

Animals and objects thus account for more than 25% of all explanation offers and requests at all ages. Explanation of all other sorts of topics – plants, food, events such as thunderstorms, and so on – are relatively infrequent and so are collapsed together as "other" in figure 2.

Of equal interest is what sorts of reasoning – explanation modes – the children recruited to try to explain things. As shown in figure 3, children used a variety of causal explanations from early on. The sizable number of "other" modes in that figure are composed mostly of social-conventional explanations, as well as the residual category of behavioral explanations outlined earlier. However, taken together, psychological plus physical plus biological explanation modes account for about 70% of children's explanations, suggesting that these are indeed core modes of explanation for young children.

These initial analyses make it clear that these young children comment on a variety of topics and use several sorts of reasoning, and they do so from the start of our data, early in the third year of life. But how do children fit together topics and modes, entities and reasoning systems" Here is where a focused consideration of explanation of human movements and actions again becomes important. Fortunately, of the almost 2,500 explanation offers provided by the four children, nearly 1,000 distinct instances focused on persons.

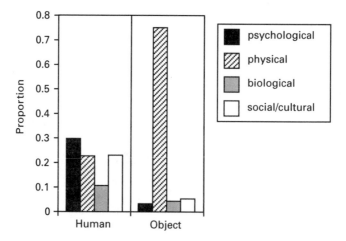

Figure 4 Explanations of human versus object behavior.
Source: Adapted from Hickling and Wellman, 1997.

To reiterate, for adults at least, human behavior can be explained in
terms of physical forces or physiological states, in addition to psychological causes. Thus if children only applied psychological explanation
to persons in these conversations, that would provide evidence for the
entity-based view, which claims that each explanatory reasoning
system at first has its own proprietary objects. Suppose, however, that
we find that children use several explanatory modes to account for
human movements and acts. That could be due either to an appropriate and flexible multimodal understanding of persons or to a profound
confusion about which sorts of reasoning applies to which sorts of
phenomena – something along the lines of Piagetian animism, realism,
and artificialism. Thus it is important to contrast explanation of persons
with explanation of some other topic. Persons versus objects is an especially informative contrast, because although for adults it is appropriate
to reason about human acts via a variety of these explanatory systems,
physical objects should receive essentially one sort of explanation – an
explanation in terms of physical systems, forces, and events.

Figure 4 shows children's reasoning about persons versus objects in
these conversations. The figure combines the data for all three age
periods, but the same pattern is readily apparent at two, three, and four
years as well. What is clear from figure 4 is that explanations of persons
and objects differ radically. Naturally enough, children often construe

---

Exhibit 4   Explanations of human acts

Psychological

"I talking very quiet because I don't want somebody to wake up." (Adam, age 3 years, 4 months)
"He never eats spinach 'cause he don't like the taste." (Ross, age 3 years, 2 months)

Biological

"He'll eat his food, because to be alive." (Ross, age 4 years, 8 months)
"I got medicine because it makes my fever go away." (Abe, age 2 years, 11 months)
"I will [be a tiny seed] because people are seeds then they grow big and then they get old." (Abe, age 3 years, 2 months)

Physical

"I pushed it because I got knocked down." (Adam, age 3 years, 3 months)
"He got a bad tooth because he fell off his bike on his face." (Ross, age 4 years, 3 months)
"The black toe hurts because Marky dropped a pan on it." (Ross, age 3 years, 8 months)

---

people's behaviors in psychological terms – in terms of their beliefs, desires, emotions, and other psychological states. But, more generally, they also explain human action in terms of physical and even biological causes. However, children's explanations for physical objects are quite different from their explanations of human actions. Essentially there is only one sort of explanation provided for objects: *physical* explanations.

The data in figure 4 can be fleshed out in two ways. First, exhibit 4 gives several examples of children's explanations of human behavior. As is evident in that exhibit, these children not only applied physical, biological, and psychological reasoning to persons, they generally did so in sensible yet flexible ways. Children's exact explanations may be only vague or even incorrect (for example, "people are seeds"), but they are sensible – they sensibly apply physical and biological explanations to only some aspects of human activities, not others. Second, the fact that in figure 4 the children *ever* applied psychological or biological thinking to physical objects, albeit infrequently, might raise suspicions that they do engage in animistic or artificialistic thinking. We certainly do not want to claim that children (or adults) never make such mistakes or speculations (see also Woolley, forthcoming). But, again, children's explanations are largely sensible. For example, the vast majority of the uses of psychological explanation to reason about physical objects tallied in figure 4 involved conversations about representational objects such as toys or dolls. For example, at age two years and ten months, Ross said, "My Snoopy [doll] is growling 'cause he wants to."

Conclusions

We conclude primarily that children evidence at least three basic everyday reasoning systems as early as two years of age – physical and psychological reasoning surely, and even biological reasoning in a rudimentary form. These reasoning systems are prevalent and important in children's everyday lives and conversational interactions. Moreover, they can be readily accessed by children to explain contrived phenomena in the laboratory, including situations they may never have directly thought about before, such as bodies potentially oozing through walls. We think that even young children, two- and three-year-olds, both differentiate and coordinate these three reasoning systems in several appropriately flexible ways. By the time they are two years old, children are neither rigidly entity-based in their explanations (restricting each reasoning system to only some special, proprietary entities) nor widely confused or fantastical (applying all sorts of explanations to all sorts of indiscriminate objects). Either or both of these patterns may characterize still earlier periods of development, but at the least our findings show that children overcome such difficulties and limitations by a very young age. Young children's frequent and largely sensible explanations in our data add support to recent claims that rather than being a culminating achievement of later cognitive development, a concern with causes and explanations may be a very early contributor to cognitive development (for example, see Gelman and Kalish, 1993; Keil, 1992; Wellman and Gelman, 1992).

Our results also reveal intriguing aspects of children's naive theories of psychology, physics, and biology. For example, burgeoning research on "theory of mind" has shown that children readily apply belief- and desire-based psychological reasoning to explain voluntary human actions. This has been taken to mean that children engage in relatively appropriate psychological reasoning by at least age three or four. However, this research has not investigated an important potential error in such psychological reasoning – possible overapplication of it to any and all sorts of human movements and acts. Our data show that young children not only apply psychological reasoning to human affairs but also limit this sort of reasoning appropriately, frequently distinguishing psychologically caused human acts from physically caused and biologically caused human movements.

Physical explanations also appear quite early in children's development, as might have been expected from contemporary studies revealing that even infants understand various physical principles as applied to the movements and states of physical objects (for example, see Baillargeon, Kotovsky, and Needham, 1995; Spelke, 1994). However, our findings do contrast with earlier claims that very young children's first verbal explanations focus only on psychological causes and explanations (for example, Hood and Bloom, 1979; Piaget, 1928). Moreover, even if infants implicitly recognize various physical principles as constraining physical objects, in order to provide the sorts of explanations we have documented, young children must also convert such recognition into explicit understandings and both articulate their physical reasoning in appropriate language and differentiate it from other potential explanations that use the same language (such as psychological explanations). At the very least, therefore, our data show an impressive early consolidation and articulation of infant physical causal understandings.

Our data are least complete with regard to biological understandings. There is currently great debate as to what might constitute an early but genuinely biological form of reasoning, distinctively independent from psychological or physical form of reasoning, distinctively independent from psychological or physical reasonings At the very least our data show that young children identify certain terms, processes, and phenomena as being outside the scope of psychological and physical reasoning – and these terms, processes, and phenomena are distinctively biological to adults. For example, consider the biological item in exhibit 1. This item does not mention any biological terms; instead it mentions a psychological construct (the character's desire) and an action or movement (coming down to the ground). We know from other carefully matched items that the children in our study could and did explain this exact same action or movement in psychological and physical ways – the character "wanted to come down," or "gravity pulled her down." Yet in explaining the biological item, four-year-old children rarely offered these easily accessed psychological or physical explanations and instead spontaneously recruited such processes as fatigue and pain to explain the scenario's outcome. Overall our data suggest that at the least, young children are often reluctant to use psychological and physical reasoning to explain certain salient "biological" phenomena of everyday life.

Finally, we believe that researching young children's explanations is both easier and more revealing than is often thought. Naturally enough, perhaps, researchers examining the thinking of young children have tended to avoid eliciting explanations in favor of presenting children with simpler judgment tasks. In reaction to Piaget's classic interview studies it has been thought that articulating verbal explanations is an especially demanding task for young children and hence one that distorts rather than reveals their basic modes of thought (see Bullock, Gelman, and Baillargeon, 1982). In fact we agree with this analysis, in part; but we propose that the richness and ease of expression of children's explanations depend on the phenomena to be explained. In these three domains – everyday psychological, physical, and biological occurrences – children are early and frequently involved in using their knowledge to explain. Part of the point, the cognitive function, of these reasoning systems is to make understandable – to explain – everyday phenomena and occurrences. In *these* domains, therefore, eliciting and analyzing children's explanations proves to be an especially revealing research method. In these domains, children's knowledge is intimately tied to the task of making sense of their world, and this is essentially the task of explanation.

References

Atran, S. "Causal constraints on categories and categorical constraints on biological reasoning across cultures." In D. Sperber, D. Premack, and A. J. Premack (eds.), *Causal cognition: A multi-disciplinary debate*. New York: Oxford University Press, 1995.

Backscheider, A. G., Shatz, M., and Gelman, S. A. "Preschoolers' ability to distinguish living kinds as a function of regrowth." *Child Development*, 1993, *64*, 1242–1257.

Baillargeon, R., Kotovsky, L., and Needham, A. "The acquisition of physical knowledge in infancy." In D. Sperber, D. Premack, and A. Premack (eds.), *Causal cognition: A multi-disciplinary debate*. New York: Oxford University Press, 1995.

Bartsch, K., and Wellman, H. M. "Young children's attribution of action to beliefs and desires." *Child Development*, 1989, *60*, 946–964.

Bartsch, K., and Wellman, H. M. *Children talk about the mind.* New York: Oxford University Press, 1995.

Bullock, M., Gelman, R., and Baillargeon, R. "The development of causal reasoning." In W. J. Friedman (ed.), *The developmental psychology of time.* Orlando: Academic Press, 1982.

Carey, S. "On the origin of causal understanding." In D. Sperber, D. Premack, and A. J. Premack (eds.), *Causal cognition: A multi-disciplinary debate.* New York: Oxford University Press, 1995.

Carey, S., and Spelke, E. S. "Domain-specific knowledge and conceptual change." In L. A. Hirschfeld and S. A. Gelman (eds.), *Mapping the mind: Domain specificity in cognition and culture.* Cambridge, UK: Cambridge University Press, 1994.

Gelman, R, Spelke, E. S., and Meck, E. "What preschoolers know about animate and inanimate objects." In D. Rogers and J. A. Sloboda (eds.), *The acquisition of symbolic skills.* New York: Plenum, 1983.

Gelman, S. A., and Kalish, C. W. "Categories and causality." In R. Pasnak and M. L. Howe (eds.), *Emerging themes in cognitive development.* New York: Springer-Verlag, 1993.

Gelman, S. A., and Kremer, K. E. "Understanding natural cause: Children's explanations of how objects and their properties originate." *Child Development*, 1991, *62*, 396–414.

Hickling, A. K. "The emergence of causal explanation in everyday thought: Evidence from ordinary conversation." Unpublished doctoral dissertation, Department of Psychology, University of Michigan, 1996.

Hickling, A. K., and Wellman, H. M. "Everyday explanation in very young children." Unpublished manuscript, 1997.

Hood, L., & Bloom, L. *What, when, and how about why: A longitudinal study of early expressions of causality.* Monographs of the Society for Research in Child Development, no. 181. Chicago: University of Chicago Press, 1979.

Inagaki, K., and Hatano, G. "Young children's recognition of commonalities between animals and plants." *Child Development*, 1996, *67*, 2823–2840.

Johnson, C. N., and Wellman, H. M. "Children's developing conceptions of the mind and brain." *Child Development*, 1982, *53*, 222–234.

Keil, F. C. "The origins of an autonomous biology." In M. Gunnar and M. Maratsos (eds.), *Minnesota symposia on child psychology: Vol. 25. Modularity and constraints in language and cognition.* Hillsdale, N.J.: Erlbaum, 1992.

Legerstee, M. "A review of the animate–inanimate distinction in infancy. *Early Development and Parenting*, 1992, *1*, 59–67.

MacWhinney, B., and Snow, C. "The Child Language Data Exchange System." *Journal of Child Language*, 1985, *12*, 271–296.

MacWhinney, B., and Snow, C. "The Child Language Data Exchange System: An update." *Journal of Child Language*, 1990, *17*, 457–472.

Piaget, J. *Judgment and reasoning in the child*. London: Paul Trench and Trubner, 1928.

Piaget, J. *The child's conception of the world*. New York: Routledge, 1929.

Rosengren, K. S., Gelman, S. A., Kalish, C. W., and McCormick, M. "As time goes by: Children's early understanding of growth in animals." *Child Development*, 1991, *62*, 1302–1320.

Schult, C. A., and Wellman, H. M. "Explaining human movements and actions: Children's understanding of the limits of psychological explanation." *Cognition*, forthcoming.

Shultz, T. R., Wells, D., and Sardo, M. Development of the ability to distinguish intended actions from mistakes, reflexes, and passive movements." *British Journal of Social and Clinical Psychology*, 1980, *19*, 301–310.

Smith, M. C. "Cognizing the behavior stream: The recognition of intentional action." *Child Development*, 1978, *49*, 736–743.

Spelke, E. S. "Initial knowledge: Six suggestions." *Cognition*, 1994, *50*, 431–455.

Spelke, E. S., Phillips, A. T., and Woodward, A. L. "Infants' knowledge of object motion and human action." In A. Premack (ed.), *Causal understanding in cognition and culture*. Oxford, UK: Clarendon Press, 1995.

Wellman, H. M., and Banerjee, M. "Mind and emotion: Children's understanding of the emotional consequences of beliefs and desires." *British Journal of Developmental Psychology*, 1991, *9*, 191–24.

Wellman, H. M., and Estes, D. "Early understanding of mental entities: A reexamination of childhood realism." *Child Development*, 1986, *57*, 910–923.

Wellman, H. M., and Gelman, S. A. "Cognitive development: Foundational theories of core domains." *Annual Review of Psychology*, 1992, *43*, 337–375.

Wellman H. M., and Gelman, S. A. "Knowledge acquisition in foundational domains." In W. Damon (ed.), *Handbook of child psychology* (5th ed.), Vol. 2 (D. Kuhn and R. Siegler, eds.): *Cognition, perception and language*. New York: Wiley, forthcoming.

Woolley, J. D. "Thinking about fantasy: Are children fundamentally different thinkers and believers from adults?" *Child Development*, forthcoming.

SEVENTEEN

Physical Knowledge

Introduction

Suppose that you were a judge in a true court case in New York. A high school dropout and petty criminal pushed a rock over the edge of the roof of a building. A policeman who was standing on the street, next to the building, was killed. The prosecution claimed that the accused had a premeditated intent to murder the policeman, while the defense suggested that it was an accident. Now, the question is: should the court allow one of the authors of this article, McCloskey, to give an expert testimony that the accused in fact did not have the cognitive understanding to carry out such murder? The judge who presided in the true case did not admit this testimony, but would you? Does this article persuade you to ask the judge to give McCloskey his day in court?

Further reading

Kaiser, M. K., McCloskey, M., & Proffitt, D. R. (1986). Development of intuitive theories of motion: Curvilinear motion in the absence of external forces. *Developmental Psychology, 22,* 67–71.

McCloskey, M. (1983). Intuitive physics. *Scientific American, 248,* 122–30.

Winer, G. A., & Cottrell, J. E. (1996). Does anything leave the eye when we see? Extramission beliefs of children and adults. *Current Directions in Psychological Science, 5,* 137–42.

The Development of Beliefs about Falling Objects

Mary Kister Kaiser, Dennis R. Proffitt, and Michael McCloskey

Recent studies indicate that many people hold striking misconceptions about the natural motions of objects in seemingly simple situations (e.g., Champagne, Klopfer, & Anderson, 1980; Clement, 1982; McCloskey, 1983a; Viennot, 1979). Figure 1 depicts two situations in which such erroneous beliefs are expressed. On the left is shown a curved tube lying flat on a horizontal surface. When asked to predict the trajectory that a ball would take after being propelled through the tube, many adults report a curved path similar to that drawn with the dotted line (McCloskey, Caramazza, & Green, 1980). To the right, a plane is shown carrying a capsule. When asked to predict the path that the capsule would take after it had been dropped, many adults report the straight down trajectory illustrated by the dotted line. In this situation, some people even predict that the capsule would fall backward along the path shown by the dashed line (McCloskey, Washburn, & Felch, 1983). Where do such erroneous beliefs come from, and what role does perception play in their development?

In investigating these questions, we have found that some beliefs reflect biases inherent to perceptual processing, whereas others do not. In particular, the misconceptions seen in the C-shaped-tube problem do not seem to stem from perceptual influences, whereas the erroneous predictions involving falling objects reflect a bias introduced in the perceptual processing of the ongoing event. Our supposition, investigated in the following studies, is that beliefs that reflect perceptual

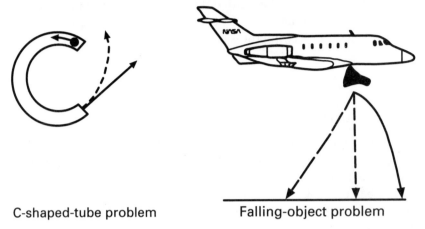

C-shaped-tube problem   **Falling-object problem**

Figure 1   Motion problems with correct solutions (solid lines) and common
incorrect responses (dashed lines).

influences follow developmental courses that are different from those
that do not.

The C-Shaped-Tube Problem

When asked to predict the path that a rolling ball will take upon exiting
a C-shaped tube, many adults report that the ball will continue to move
along a curved path. When shown contrived video sequences of balls
rolling through the C-shaped tube and then following a variety of
straight and curved paths upon exit, almost all of these adults state that
a ball following the correct straight path looks more natural than balls
following curved paths (Kaiser, Proffitt, & Anderson, 1985). Thus, when
viewing the ongoing event, people perceive as natural the correct
motion path and not the erroneous trajectories that they predict in
representational contexts.

That the misconceptions observed in the C-shaped-tube problem are
not primarily due to perceptual biases is also supported by the U-shaped
developmental course that adherence to this erroneous belief follows.
When asked to predict the path of a ball exiting a C-shaped tube, most
children of preschool and kindergarten age predict a straight path, and
in this respect perform as well as college students. Correct performance

falls off with age until the third and fourth grade, an age at which a large majority of children predict curvilinear motion paths. From fifth grade on, performance improves with age (Kaiser, McCloskey, & Proffitt, in press).

The Falling-Object Problem

Previous studies on this problem have revealed an interesting mixture of accurate knowledge and misconceptions. Most adults know that an object that moves along an elevated surface and then goes over the edge (e.g., a ball that rolls off a table, a car that runs over the edge of a cliff) continues to move forward as it falls. However, many adults fail to realize that an object that is carried by a moving body and then dropped (e.g., a ball dropped by a walking person, a bomb dropped from an airplane) continues to move forward while falling (McCloskey, 1983a, 1983b; McCloskey et al., 1983). Many adults erroneously predict that the released object will fall straight down. This finding is surprising since, in terms of the relevant physics, the situation involving a carried object and that involving a rolling object are identical. In both cases, the forward and downward motions combine to produce a trajectory that is nearly parabolic. Thus, the path of a carried object that is dropped will be identical to that of an object that rolls off an elevated surface, as long as the two objects are initially moving at the same speed and fall from the same height.

Why, then, do many adults know that objects rolled off elevated surfaces continue forward while falling, but at the same time believe that carried objects fall straight down when dropped? McCloskey et al. (1983) suggested that this misconception was due to a visual illusion in which objects that are dropped are often perceived as falling straight down. McCloskey et al. argued as follows: When people observe carried objects that are dropped (for example, a book dropped by a walking person), the moving carrier (e.g., the walking person) often acts as a frame of reference against which the falling object is viewed. Studies of motion perception (e.g., Hochberg & Fallon, 1976; Johansson, 1950; Wallach, 1959, 1976) have shown that when an object is viewed against a moving frame of reference, the object's motion relative to the reference frame may be misperceived as its absolute motion (i.e., motion relative to the stationary environment). Ignoring effects of air resistance, an object dropped from a moving carrier falls straight down relative to the carrier, and so may be perceived as falling in a straight vertical path. Experiments show that an illusion of this sort does in fact occur when people observe carried objects that are dropped (McCloskey et al., 1983).

Given that adults hold erroneous beliefs concerning falling objects due to misleading perceptual experiences, one could hypothesize several patterns of development for children's conceptions in this domain. The hypothesis we advance is that young children initially formulate an omnibus belief about falling: "All unsupported objects fall straight down." In most situations that confront a young child, this naive theory would work pretty well, as it captures the most salient aspect of the falling event. Perceptual experience would provide grounds for modifying this belief in the case of rolling objects that fall. However, due to the effects of the moving reference frame illusion discussed above, perceptual experience would be in accord with the child's naive theory in the case of carried objects. Formal training, of course, should force a modification of the omnibus belief in both cases. Empirical support for this hypothesis would include the finding that young children hold to an "all objects fall straight down" belief for both rolling and carried objects. Over the course of development, this belief about falling would change more rapidly for rolling, as opposed to carried, objects.

A reasonable alternative to this hypothesis asserts that children initially formulate an accurate belief about the motion of falling objects. Shepard (1981, 1984) has proposed that, due to the selective pressures of biological evolution, significant dynamic constraints in the physical world are inherent in human motion processing mechanisms. This proposal leads to the hypothesis that accurate naive beliefs might be present early in development, as is observed in C-shaped-tube problems. Misconceptions about the trajectories of carried objects would arise from repeated perceptual experience with the moving reference frame illusion. Empirical support for this hypothesis would include the finding that young children initially hold accurate beliefs about all falling objects and that misconceptions about carried objects develop with age, at least up to the time of formal training.

With respect to either hypothesis, we propose that beliefs that reflect perceptual influences follow different developmental courses from those that do not. Thus, both hypotheses suggest that the developmental course for beliefs about the motions of falling objects will diverge for carried as opposed to rolling objects. With respect to the first hypothesis, perceptual experience should motivate a reformulation of the omnibus "things fall straight down" belief only for the case of rolling objects. With respect to the second hypothesis, perceptual experience should influence the initial accurate belief only in the case of carried objects. Thus, whether early conceptions are accurate or not, beliefs about rolling and carried objects should diverge over development due to the perceptual bias introduced by the moving reference frame illusion.

Experiment 1

In this experiment, children and adults were asked to predict the trajectory of a ball rolled off the edge of a table and that of a ball dropped from a moving model train.

Method

Subjects. The subjects were 100 middle-class children, four and a half to twelve years of age, and 20 college students. The children were placed into four age groups according to the last grade of school completed. There were 23 preschool and kindergarten children (P&K; 14 boys, 9 girls). 19 first and second graders (1&2; 11 boys, 8 girls), 30 third and fourth graders (3&4; 12 boys, 18 girls), and 28 fifth and sixth graders (5&6; 14 boys, 14 girls). Nine additional children (five from the P&K group, four from the 1&2 group) failed to understand the task and were excluded from the study. The college sample (COL) consisted of ten men and ten women, 16 of whom had taken high school or college physics.

Apparatus. An HO-scale model train traveled around an oval track mounted on a table 1 m above the ground, as shown in figure 2. A steel ball, 1 cm in diameter, rode on a flatcar behind the engine. The flatcar was constructed so that the ball could automatically be dropped from the car when it reached a particular point on the track. A section of the table adjacent to the track in this area had been cut out so that the ball, when released, would fall to the floor.

Also mounted on the table, parallel to the train track, was a clear plastic tube that ran to the edge of the cut-out area of the table (see

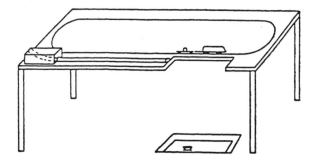

Figure 2   Schematic of experimental layout employed in Experiment 1.

figure 2). One end of the tube was elevated so that when the 1 cm steel ball was placed in this end, it would roll to the other end of the tube and fall to the floor. The speed of the ball when it emerged from the tube was the same as the speed of the train. A scale-model building hid the elevated end of the tube from the subject's view.

A 28 × 38-cm piece of paper was placed on the floor beneath the cut-out area of the table. An outline of the cutout was drawn on the paper to help the subject align points on the table with points on the paper.

Procedure.   The subjects were asked to predict the behavior of the ball under three conditions. In the Stationary condition, the subjects were to predict where on the ground the ball would land if it were dropped by a stationary figure standing at the left edge of the cutout. In the Rolled condition, the subjects were to observe the ball moving through the plastic tube and predict where it would land if it rolled out of the tube and fell to the floor. The end of the tube was blocked so that the ball did not actually emerge and fall. Finally, in the Carried condition, the subjects were to watch the train moving around the track and predict where the ball would land if it were dropped from the train when it reached the left edge of the cutout. The ball was not actually dropped.

The subjects made their predictions by placing a cup, 4 cm in diameter, on the floor where they thought it would catch the falling ball. Subjects' predictions were classified as straight down if the cup was placed less than 3.5 cm from the edge of the cutout. The subjects were then asked to explain their predictions. After each subject gave responses for all three conditions, the actual motions were shown, and the subject was questioned about any discrepancies between predictions and actual outcomes.

In all three conditions, the point at which the ball left the table was the same. In the Stationary condition, the ball had no forward motion and so, of course, fell straight down. In the Rolled and Carried conditions, the ball had a forward velocity of 45 cm/sec when it left the table, so that in both conditions it traveled forward a distance of 20 cm before striking the ground.

The Stationary condition, which was included as a pretest to ensure that the subjects understood the task, was always administered first. Since all subjects responded correctly in this condition, it will not be considered further. The order of presentation of the Rolled and Carried conditions was counterbalanced across subjects.

Results

The results for the college-age subjects replicated previous findings (e.g., McCloskey et al., 1983). All of the college students knew that the ball rolled through the tube would continue moving forward as it fell. However, seven of the students (35%) thought that the ball dropped from the moving train would fall straight down. All of the adults who gave correct responses in the Carried condition had taken physics in high school or college.

The children's data present an interesting pattern, as shown in figure 3. Almost all of the preschool and kindergarten children thought that the ball would fall straight down in both the Carried and the Rolled conditions. For the Rolled condition, with age, the children showed a steady increase in awareness that the ball would continue to move forward while falling. The percentage of subjects indicating that the ball rolled through the tube would continue forward increased from 9% for the preschoolers and kindergartners to 50% for the fifth and sixth graders. Grade level was significantly related to proportion of correct responses $[\chi^2(3) = 10.59, p < .02]$. For the Carried condition, however, there was no significant improvement with age $[\chi^2(3) = 2.13, p > .50]$. Only 21% of the fifth and sixth graders indicated that the ball dropped from the train would move forward while it fell. No effects of gender or order of condition presentation were found for either condition.

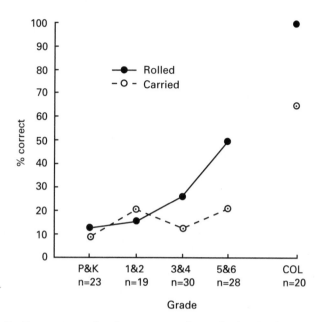

Figure 3 Proportion of subjects at each grade level who gave correct responses in the Rolled and the Carried conditions in Experiment 1.

Subjects' predictions in the Rolled condition indicated that even those children and adults who realized the ball would continue forward as it fell tended to underestimate the distance the ball would travel before striking the ground. The mean estimate of 12.9 cm was significantly less than the actual distance of 20 cm [$t(48) = 12.9$, $p < .01$]. Among these subjects, there was no significant difference between the adults' and children's mean predictions [14.8 and 11.6 cm, respectively; $t(47) = 1.27$].

Experiment 2

We were concerned that the young children's failure to realize that the ball rolled through the tube would continue to move forward as it fell might reflect the specific conditions of our experiment (e.g., the relatively slow velocity of the ball, the use of a passive and hidden mechanism to start the ball moving), and not a general failure to realize that an object rolling from an elevated surface continues to move forward while falling. Hence, before attempting to interpret the findings of Experiment 1, we decided to test a limited number of children under conditions in which the rolled ball's initial forward motion was more salient in order to ensure that the children's straight down responses were not artifactual.

In this experiment we varied the speed of the rolling ball and the means by which it was set in motion. As in Experiment 1, children and adults predicted where the ball would land if it rolled through a tube and fell to the floor.

Method

Subjects. Eleven preschool through second-grade children (P-2; six boys and five girls), 11 third through sixth graders (3–6; five boys and six girls), and 17 college students (COL; nine men and eight women) participated in the study. The children were from middle-class families who responded to a solicitation in the university newspaper.

Apparatus and procedure. Two launching mechanisms and three speeds of the ball were used. The passive-launch condition involved three clear plastic tubes with one end elevated to initiate the ball's motion. Three different elevations (4.5, 10.5, and 19 cm) were used to produce velocities approximately equal to, twice as great as, and three times as great as the velocity of the ball in Experiment 1. Thus, for the three velocities, the ball traveled 23, 43, and 58 cm forward while falling. In the active-launch condition, a pinball-type spring-loaded piston was used to start the ball moving through the tube. Three different settings of the launcher were used to produce three velocities approximately equal to those in the passive-launch condition. In both conditions, the tubes were 85 cm in length and were mounted on a 1-m-high table with the tubes ending at the edge of the table.

The heights of the tubes and the tension of the spring launcher were always visible to the subject. For each launch type by speed combination, the subject viewed the launch of the ball and its movement to the edge of the table twice. On each occasion, the experimenter stopped the ball before it began to fall. After viewing the ball's motion, the subject predicted where the ball would have landed if it had been allowed to fall. The subjects indicated their predictions by marking the floor at the point where they thought the ball would hit.

Any prediction less than 3.5 cm from the point of launch (horizontally) was classified as straight down. The subjects were also asked to draw the trajectory of the ball on a 100 × 70 cm drawing pad mounted perpendicular to the floor.

The subjects made predictions for all three velocities in each of the two launch mechanism conditions. The order of presentation of the two launching conditions was counterbalanced across subjects. Within each launching condition, the three speeds were presented in order from slow to fast.

Results

As in Experiment 1, a substantial proportion of the younger children thought that the ball would fall straight down after leaving the table. Table 1 presents for the three age groups the percentage of subjects predicting a straight-down path for the slow, medium, and fast speeds in the passive- and active-launch conditions. It can be seen from the table that, as in the first experiment, the percentage of straight-down predictions decreased as the age of the children increased $[\chi^2(1) = 6.14, p < .05]$. The passive- versus active-launch manipulation had virtually no effect on the percentage of straight-down predictions $[\chi^2(1) = 2.00, p > .10]$. The speed of the ball had a marginal effect in the passive-launch condition $[\chi^2(2) = 5.21, p < .10]$, but no significant effect in the active-launch condition $[\chi^2(2) = 2.36]$.

Table 1   Percent of subjects predicting straight-down trajectories for passive- and active-launch mechanisms in Experiment 2

| | *Velocity* | | | | | |
| | *Slow* | | *Medium* | | *Fast* | |
Group	*Passive launch*	*Active launch*	*Passive launch*	*Active launch*	*Passive launch*	*Active launch*
P–2	88%	55%	66%	55%	66%	44%
3–6	66%	44%	33%	33%	22%	22%
COL	0%	0%	0%	0%	0%	0%

Among those children who did not give straight-down responses, all but two predicted either a parabolic path or an inverted-L path (i.e., the ball continues horizontally for some distance, then falls straight down). To be classified as parabolic, a subject's drawing needed to indicate that the ball began to fall as soon as it left the support surface and fell at an increasingly greater speed. Predictions were classified as inverted-L if the ball traveled some distance before beginning to fall and the transition from horizontal to vertical motion occurred abruptly. A comparison of these path forms indicates that, across ages, children who predicted parabolic paths were more accurate in judging the horizontal distance the ball travels before striking the ground. Figure 4 shows the actual distance, the average distance predicted by children employing inverted-L paths, and the average distance predicted by children's parabolic paths for the slow, medium, and fast velocities in the passive-

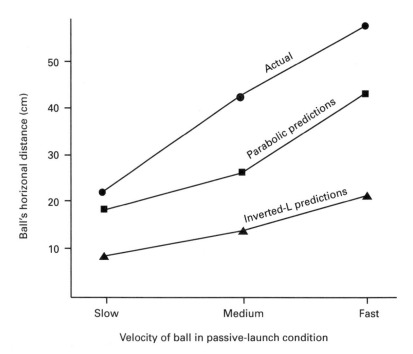

Figure 4 Average horizontal distance predicted by children employing parabolic versus inverted-L paths compared with the actual distances in Experiment 2.

launch condition. Across velocities, children using parabolic paths were closer to correct [$t(10) = 2.38$, $p < .05$]. Furthermore, at all three velocities, children predicting inverted-L paths significantly underestimated the horizontal distance of the ball [$t(4) = 5.71$, $p < .01$, for slow; $t(4) = 11.98$, $p < .005$, for medium; and $t(4) = 17.68$, $p < .005$, for fast]. Although children employing parabolic paths still tended to underestimate the horizontal distance, the underestimation is not significant [$t(6) = .06$ for slow; $t(6) = 2.09$ for medium; $t(6) = 1.56$ for fast].

Lastly, we examined whether subjects recognized the monotonic relationship between the ball's velocity and the horizontal distance it travels before striking the ground. As shown in table 2, older subjects were far more likely to recognize this relationship, in both the passive-launch [$\chi^2(2) = 21.09$, $p < .01$] and active-launch [$\chi^2(2) = 11.31$, $p < .01$] conditions.

Discussion

The results of Experiment 2 demonstrate that the straight-down responses of the younger children in all conditions in Experiment 1 cannot be attributed to artifacts such as the low velocity of the ball or the passive nature of the launch mechanism. Many young children continued to demonstrate the belief that the ball would fall straight down

Table 2 Number of subjects who recognized the monotonic relation between velocity and horizontal distance in Experiment 2

| | Launch condition | | | |
| | Passive | | Active | |
Group	Monotonic	Other	Monotonic	Other
P–2	2	9 (6)*	5	6 (4)
3–6	8	3 (2)	8	3 (2)
COL	17	0	17	0

*( ) indicates number who gave straight-down predictions for all three velocities.

when rolled off the edge of the table, despite our efforts to increase the salience of the ball's horizontal momentum. Furthermore, even those children who understood that such objects continue to move forward as they fall often held misconceptions concerning the trajectories, as well as the relationship between the horizontal velocity of the object and the distance it will travel before striking the ground.

Children's inability to think abstractly about the two determinants of the falling ball's motion (the ball's forward velocity, and gravity) may be linked to a general inability to perform mental combinations. Young children may focus their attention on the most salient vector operating on the object at any given time, much as they concentrate on the most salient dimension in physical conservation problems (Flavell, 1977). Thus, when the rolling ball reaches the edge of the table, the gravitational vector becomes very salient to the child, who realizes that in the absence of support objects invariably fall down. Even when children come to recognize that the gravitational vector does not immediately negate the ball's horizontal momentum, they tend to give responses that still fail to integrate the two vectors. Hence, they predict that the ball will continue horizontally for some distance, then fall straight down (i.e., the inverted-L path). Only those subjects who give responses that we have classified as parabolic understand that the ball will move *both* forward and downward at the same time, and integrate the two vectors successfully. Once such an integration is achieved, the consequence of increasing the magnitude of one vector (e.g., the ball's horizontal momentum) is much easier to comprehend. To develop an accurate understanding of the motion of an object in a particular type of situation, one must have not only the cognitive capabilities needed to understand the object's motion, but also appropriate perceptual experience with the motion. In the case of carried objects that are dropped, however, perceptual experience may be misleading rather than informative. The motion of an object's carrier becomes a moving reference frame when the object's fall is observed, thereby producing the perception of a "straight-down" fall.

Thus, our results show that children maintain the belief in a straight-down motion for a carried object even when they are cognitively capable of integrating an object's horizontal and vertical motions in the case of a rolling object. Understanding of the motion of objects dropped from a moving carrier, when it is achieved, appears to result primarily from formal instruction in physics.

One question that arises from the current findings is what young children perceive when viewing these events. We attempted to show the subjects in both experiments the actual outcomes of the events they predicted, and their reactions lend some insight. When the ball was released from the train, both the children and the adults who had given erroneous predictions were surprised that the ball did not fall straight down. Many concluded that the ball must have been released later than the experimenter had indicated; some suggested that the flatcar must have pushed the ball as it released it. A few did conclude that the ball kept moving forward as it fell, but their comments indicated that they could not explain the ball's motion.

Similarly, when shown the ball rolled off the table, some of the young children denied that it had moved forward as it fell and indicated a point beneath the table's edge as "where the ball really hit." Repeated demonstrations did convince some of these subjects that the ball continued to move forward as it fell. When these children were then asked to draw the trajectory of the ball, many gave inverted-L responses (the ball rolled out, then fell straight down), but a few did draw correct parabolic paths. Regardless of the path they drew, the children were unable to explain why the ball had fallen as it did, except to suggest that it was "going faster than I thought."

Clearly, it would be of interest to examine whether children who give straight-down predictions perceive straight-down trajectories as natural (and parabolic trajectories as anomalous) when viewing such events. Previous research suggests that people are often better at judging the natural outcome of events than at predicting what that outcome will be. For example, Shanon (1976) found that while many adults described free-falling objects as maintaining a constant velocity, most recognized an accelerating free fall as dynamically correct. Similarly, Kaiser and Proffitt (1984) demonstrated that children as young as five were sensitive to whether or not momentum is conserved in simple collision events only when they could observe the ongoing situation.

Conclusion

People's incorrect predictions concerning the outcome of simple mechanical events arise from several sources. First, as was found in research on the C-shaped-tube problem (Kaiser et al., in press), errors can result from the application of an erroneous belief about natural motions. In such situations, younger children who have not yet acquired this belief may actually perform better than older children. A second cause of error is to draw upon perceptual experiences which support erroneous beliefs. This is the case with the trajectory of objects dropped from moving bodies. Here, the moving reference frame illusion reinforces subjects' erroneous straight-down belief. Finally, when subjects are asked to solve motion problems in a representational context, cognitive limitations may constrain the subject's ability to integrate all relevant factors in the problem.

As previously demonstrated (Kaiser & Proffitt, 1984; Shanon, 1976), a person's ability to judge the appropriateness of dynamics in ongoing visual displays may greatly outstrip his or her ability to reason abstractly about such situations. Although it may be inappropriate to suggest an autonomous relationship between "perceptual" and "conceptual" understandings, it does seem wise to recognize that a person may possess a perceptual appreciation of the natural dynamics of physical events, yet be unable to draw upon this knowledge when asked to conceptualize an event's outcome in a representational context.

References

Champagne, A. B., Klopfer, L. E., & Anderson, J. H. (1980). Factors influencing the learning of classical mechanisms. *American Journal of Physics, 48,* 1074–1079.

Clement, J. (1982). Students' preconceptions in introductory mechanics. *American Journal of Physics, 50,* 66–71.

Flavell, J. H. (1977). *Cognitive development.* Englewood Cliffs. NJ: Prentice-Hall.

Hochberg, J., & Fallon, P. (1976). Perceptual analysis of moving patterns. *Science, 194,* 1081–1083.

Johansson, G. (1950). *Configuration in event perception.* Uppsala, Sweden: Almquist and Wiksell.

Kaiser, M. K., McCloskey, M., & Proffitt, D. R. (in press). Development of intuitive theories of motion: Curvilinear motion in the absence of external forces. *Developmental Psychology.*

Kaiser, M. K., & Proffitt, D. R. (1984). The development of sensitivity to causally-relevant dynamic information. *Child Development, 55,* 1614–1624.

Kaiser, M. K., Proffitt, D. R., & Anderson, K. (1985). Judgments of natural and anomalous trajectories in the presence and absence of motion. *Journal of Experimental Psychology: Learning, Memory, and Cognition, 11,* 795–803.

McCloskey, M. (1983a). Intuitive physics. *Scientific American, 248*(4), 122–130.

McCloskey, M. (1983b). Naive theories of motion. In D. Gentner & A. L. Stevens (Eds.), *Mental models.* Hillsdale, NJ: Erlbaum.

McCloskey, M., Caramazza, A., & Green, B. (1980). Curvilinear motion in the absence of external forces: Naive beliefs about the motion of objects. *Science, 210,* 1139–1141.

McCloskey, M., Washburn, A., & Felch, L. (1983). Intuitive physics: The straight-down belief and its origin. *Journal of Experimental Psychology: Learning, Memory, and Cognition, 9,* 636–649.

Shanon, B. (1976). Aristotelianism, Newtonianism and the physics of the layman. *Perception, 5,* 241–243.

Shepard, R. N. (1981). Psychophysical complementarity. In M. Kubovy, & J. R. Pomerantz (Eds.), *Perceptual organization.* Hillsdale, NJ: Erlbaum.

Shepard, R. N. (1984). Ecological constraints on internal representations: Resonant kinematic of perceiving, imagining, thinking, and dreaming. *Psychological Review, 91,* 417–447.

Viennot, L. (1979). Spontaneous reasoning in elementary dynamics. *European Journal of Science Education, 1,* 205–221.

Wallach, H. (1959). The perception of motion. *Scientific American, 201,* 56–60.

Wallach, H. (1976). *On perception.* New York: Quadrangle/The New York Times Book Company.

EIGHTEEN

Moral Understanding

Introduction

Bussey's article is an excellent example of research on the development of social cognition. In this area, psychologists study children's understanding of social entities (e.g., gender, race), social values (e.g., morality), social events (e.g., emotional interactions), and social institutions (e.g., family, religion). Knowing what a lie is and whether it is right or wrong to tell a lie are conceptual and moral issues central to children's acquisition of moral understanding. Acquiring a mature understanding of lying and its moral value are not as simple as they may seem.

This article shows that a number of factors affect children's conceptual and moral understanding of lying, including whether a statement is factually true, whether the speaker has an intent to deceive, whether a lie is believed by the lie-recipient, and whether a lie is punished. Additional studies have shown that children's definitions and moral judgments of lying also depend on whether the speaker believes a statement is false, whether the speaker makes a false statement with a general intention to help or harm a listener, and, last but not least, whether a lie is told in a particular culture for a particular cultural purpose.

Given the complexity of this issue, it is no wonder that lying and its moral value have attracted the attention of many philosophers, linguists, sociologists, anthropologists, and psychologists. While, to date, we are far from fully comprehending the developmental trajectory of children's understanding of lying, Bussey's article (edited for this reader) tells an interesting story about when and how such an understanding may begin.

Further reading

Lee, K., Cameron, C. A., Xu, F., Fu, G., & Board, J. (1997). Chinese and Canadian children's evaluations of lying and truth telling: Similarities and differences in the context of pro- and antisocial behaviors. *Child Development*, *68*, 924–34.

Lee, K., & Ross, H. J. (1997). The concept of lying in adolescents and young adults: Testing Sweetser's folkloristic model. *Merrill Palmer Quarterly*, *43*, 255–70.

Siegal, M., & Peterson, C. C. (1998). Preschoolers' understanding of lies and innocent and negligent mistakes. *Developmental Psychology*, *34*, 332–41.

Wimmer, H., Gruber, S., & Perner, J. (1984). Young children's conception of lying: Lexical realism – moral subjectivism. *Journal of Experimental Child Psychology*, *37*, 1–30.

Lying and Truthfulness: Children's Definitions, Standards, and Evaluative Reactions

Kay Bussey

Despite the centrality of lying and truthfulness to all major theories of morality (Bandura, 1986, 1991; Freud, 1940/1964; Piaget, 1932/1965) this aspect of morality has largely been neglected by developmental psychologists. The complexity of the topic may well have contributed to this neglect; moral philosophers concede that lying and truthfulness are problematic concepts (Bok, 1978). Nonetheless, children do make judgments about these concepts almost daily. What judgments do they make about lies and truthful statements and what factors guide their judgments?

Previous research on children's lying and truthfulness (Peterson, Peterson, & Seeto, 1983; Wimmer, Gruber, & Perner, 1984, 1985) draws heavily on the Piagetian framework (1932/1965). Piaget's focus was restricted, however, to mainly one aspect of children's judgments of lying, namely, the role of intentionality in children's definitions and evaluations of false statements. According to Piaget, children under six subscribed to an overinclusive definition of lying that encompassed swearing, naughty words, and every kind of false statement, including mistaken guesses. Between the ages of six and ten, children defined a lie as something that was not true and did not differentiate between intentional and unintentional false statements. By ten or eleven years, only intended false statements were defined as lies. For evaluations of lies, he proposed that younger children evaluated "lying as naughty because it is punished" (p. 161), not because it was intentionally deceptive.

The focus on intentionality by Piaget and other researchers has meant that certain aspects of children's judgments of lying have largely been ignored. One such aspect is the effect of the falsity of the statement on their judgments. To investigate this, here, children's moral judgments or false statements (lies) were compared to their judgments of true statements (truths). Thus, the first aim was to determine whether children could differentiate between lies and truthful statements and judge lies as more morally reprehensible than truthful statements. The second aim was to investigate the basis on which children made such judgments. What factors influenced their identifications and evaluations of these statements? Was it the falsity of the statement, the content of the statement, whether or not the statement was believed, or whether it was punished? The third aim was to investigate children's internal evaluative reactions, such as guilt or pride, associated with lying and truthfulness and the extent to which such reactions were affected by the factors listed previously.

The first aim was addressed by investigating whether children could discriminate between and differentially evaluate intentional false statements from intentional truthful ones. While this comparison is essentially theoretical, it is of practical importance too. Specifically, the legal system requires that children know the difference between a lie and a truth before they serve as witnesses. As well, parents regard teaching children to make this differentiation and to value truthfulness as crucial. Surprisingly, previous researchers have paid little attention to truthfulness (Peterson et al., 1983; Piaget, 1932/1965).

Lies and truthful statements used in this study were restricted to statements made in reaction to misdeeds. Piaget excluded this lie type from his research because he found that even the older children judged the seriousness of a lie in terms of the material consequences of the misdeed that preceded the lie. Yet, Peterson et al. (1983), using an innovative methodology, demonstrated that even young children were knowledgeable about this lie type. Children as young as five could identify lies involving misdeeds. It was exaggerations and mistaken guesses that proved more difficult for not only younger and older children but also for adults to identify. Other research suggests that children's knowledge about lying and truthfulness may emanate from lies told about misdeeds. In Stouthamer-Loeber's (1987) study, mothers reported that the most typical lies told by their four-year-olds were to conceal misdeeds. The present study, therefore, investigated children's understanding of lies and truthful statements specifically in reaction to misdeeds. Can children differentiate a lie from a truthful statement about a misdeed, and further, can they differentiate such statements from the misdeed itself. Will all statements about misdeeds be judged as lies, especially by young children, because they are about something naughty, as Piaget contended?

Belief and punishment are often associated with lies. Lies are either believed or not believed and are sometimes punished. These two factors may influence children's identification and evaluation of such statements. Although Piaget investigated belief and punishment associated with lies, his findings are problematic since these factors were confounded. For example, he showed that younger children who were at the moral realist level (six- to ten-year-olds) evaluated lies that were unlikely to be believed (e.g., exaggerations) as worse than ones that were likely to be believed. The reverse held for older children. Piaget thus inferred that for younger children the more a lie departed from reality the worse it was judged. It is possible however, that younger children judged lies they thought would not be believed more severely than older children not because they departed more from reality and were therefore not believed, but because they expected disbelief to lead to punishment. Consequently, this study sought to clarify the issue of belief, for children's appraisal of lies; children were asked to evaluate lies that were both explicitly believed and not believed.

Piaget (1932/1965) reported that younger children evaluated lies as naughty because "you get punished." When punishment was not forthcoming, lies were judged less naughty. In contrast, for older children, lies were judged as naughty independent of punishment. However, the scant data provided by Piaget make it difficult to verify his conclusions about the impact of punishment on children's judgments. Again, in Peterson et al.'s (1983) study, it is difficult to determine the impact of punishment on judgments as it was confounded with belief. In that study, the lie that was not believed was punished and the lie that was believed was not punished. There was no story in which a lie was not believed and punishment withheld. In this study the presence and absence of punishment were varied to establish whether young children judged statements that resulted in punishment as more reprehensible than statements not accompanied by punishment, independent of their belief.

Apart from the identification and moral evaluation of lies and truthful statements, the *personal value* ascribed by children to such statements has received little systematic investigation. According to Piaget, children under six evaluated lying as naughty because it was punished, and "if it were not punished no guilt would attach to it" (Piaget, 1932/1965, p. 161). Although he noted the importance of guilt for the internalization of moral principles, he did not elaborate these ideas. More recent research, however, has investigated children's development of personal standards for moral conduct. This research shows that as children mature they develop personal standards and self-evaluate their own conduct (Bandura, 1986, 1991). Children who have internalized such standards experience guilt and self-criticism when they know that they have done something wrong and experience pride and self-praise when they feel they have acted in a deserving manner (Grusec & Kuczynski, 1977; Perry, Perry, Bussey, English, & Arnold, 1980). However, no data have been reported concerning the internalization of personal standards associated with lying and truthfulness. A further goal of this study was therefore to assess children's internal evaluative reactions to lying and truthfulness and to investigate the extent to which these evaluative reactions were determined by the truth or falsity of a statement involving a misdeed, belief of the statement, or its punishment. Internal evaluative reactions were measured by children's positive evaluative reactions (feelings of pride, self-satisfaction) for truthfulness and negative evaluative reactions (guilt, self-censure) for lying. According to social cognitive theory (Bandura, 1986, 1991), while younger children may lie to avoid punishment for their misdeed, older children's lying and truth telling would primarily be guided by their anticipated evaluative reactions to their lying and truthfulness.

Method

Participants

Seventy-two White children enrolled in predominantly middle-class suburban schools served as participants. Twelve boys and 12 girls were randomly drawn from each of three grades: preschool (mean age = 4.9 years), grade 2 (mean age = 7.8 years), and grade 5 (mean age = 11.0 years).

Vignettes

Twelve vignettes were prepared. Each vignette had one of six different endings (vignette type): the vignette character said she or he did not commit the misdeed (lie) and was believed; the vignette character said she or he did not commit the misdeed (lie), was not believed, and was punished for committing the misdeed; the vignette character said she or he did not commit the misdeed (lie) and was not believed and not punished for committing the misdeed; the vignette character said she or he did commit the misdeed (truth) and was punished for committing the misdeed; the vignette character said she or he did commit the misdeed (truth) and was not punished for committing the misdeed; and, last, the character simply committed the misdeed. Truthful vignettes that resulted in disbelief were excluded since such vignettes lacked credibility when associated with misdeeds. Similarly, vignettes that involved a lie that was believed and punished were not included. Each subject heard each ending (vignette type) twice in different vignettes. Girls heard vignettes about a female protagonist and boys heard vignettes about a male protagonist.

Procedure

Each child was interviewed individually for approximately half an hour. The preschoolers were interviewed across two sessions, usually on consecutive days. The child was shown line drawings on 10×15 cm cards that depicted the main theme as the experimenter read each vignette. After each vignette, comprehension was assessed. Once comprehension was achieved, children were questioned about the vignettes, which were presented in one of six random orders. There were two orders for the definition question. In one, children were asked if the vignette character told a lie or the truth. In the other, this was reversed. Children were asked, "Did [name of speaker] lie to her [his] [mother, father, sibling, friend] or did she [he] tell her [him] the truth?" Further, for half the children, the *definition* question was asked first, that is, before the moral standards and evaluative reaction questions, and for the other half of the children it was asked last. The remaining questions were asked in the same fixed order for all vignette types. The questions for the *moral standards* measure specifically focused on the vignette character's statement. The experimenter said, "I want you to show me how good or bad

it was for [vignette character's name] to have said [restate lie/truth]?"
The child was shown a scale ranging from "very good" (three gold stars),
through "fairly good" (two gold stars), "a little bit good" (one gold star),
"a little bit bad" (one black spot), "fairly bad" (two black spots), to "very
bad" (three black spots).

Children rated four *internal evaluative reactions*. Ratings were on a
four-point scale ("not at all" to "very") comprising blue bars in ascend-
ing heights (0 cm, 6 cm, 12 cm, 18 cm) positioned in front of the child.
They were asked, "How would [the vignette character] feel about herself
[himself] for having said [state lie/truth]?" "Would [vignette character]
feel scared for having said [state lie/truth]?" "Would [vignette charac-
ter] feel pleased with herself [himself] for having said [state lie/truth]?"
"Would [vignette character] feel guilty [terrible inside] for having said
[state lie/truth]?" and "Would [vignette character] feel good for having
said [state lie/truth]?"

Results

Separate analyses were conducted on each of the three dependent measures: children's correct identification of lies and truthful statements
(*definition*), *moral standards*, and *internal evaluative reactions*. Preliminary
analyses included order and target of lie (adult vs. child) as factors.
However, as there were no order or target main effects or interactions
involving these factors for any of the dependent measures, they were
dropped from subsequent analyses.

Definition

A 2 (sex of subject) × 3 (grade: preschool, 2, 5) × 5 (vignette type)
repeated-measures analysis of variance was performed on children's
correct identification of lies and truthful statements. The only effect to
attain significance was grade, $F(2,66) = 26.77, p < .0001$. Preschoolers
($M = 71.3\%$) were less accurate at identifying lies and truthful statements than second graders ($M = 97.5\%$) and fifth graders ($M = 98.8\%$).
However, the preschoolers' performance was significantly greater than
chance, $t(23) = 4.27, p < .0005$. For all children, therefore, the falsity of
the statement rather than its belief, punishment, or that it involved a
misdeed was the major determinant of its definition.

Moral standards

A three-way repeated-measures analysis of variance (sex × age × vignette condition) was conducted on children's appraisal of the goodness/badness of the vignette character's statements and actions. The *F* ratios for the planned comparisons are presented in table 1 and the mean scores for each of the vignette conditions across the three age groups are presented in table 2. Planned comparisons of the vignette condition variable included: (*a*) truthful versus lie conditions, (*b*) misdeed only versus all lie conditions, (*c*) misdeed only versus all truthful conditions, (*d*) punishment versus no punishment for the misdeed, and (*e*) for lies only, believed versus not believed.

The first planned comparison tested if children's evaluative judgments of vignettes involving lies versus truthful statements differed. This contrast was significant, $F(1,66) = 194.10$, $p < .0005$, and it interacted with age, $F(2,66) = 17.82$, $p < .0005$. Lies were judged as being worse than truthful statements. Although this finding was significant for all the children, it was stronger for the older children than the preschoolers. Thus, even the preschoolers evaluated a statement on the basis of its falsity, since lies were rated more negatively than truthful statements.

The next planned comparisons tested if children's judgments of misdeeds differed from, first, their judgments of lies and, second, their judgments of truthful statements. The first contrast was significant, $F(1,66) = 13.01$, $p = .001$. Contrary to predictions from Piaget's theory (1932/1965), lies ($M = 5.39$) were evaluated significantly more negatively than misdeeds ($M = 5.11$) by all the children. The second contrast, between children's judgments of misdeeds and truthful statements, was also significant, $F(1,66) = 140.74$, $p < .0005$, as well as the interaction between this contrast and age, $F(2,66) = 17.30$, $p < .0005$. Although all children evaluated truthful statements more positively than misdeeds, this difference was not significant for the preschoolers.

The effect of punishment on children's evaluative judgments was investigated by comparing children's judgments of those vignettes that resulted in punishment with those vignettes in which punishment was absent. The punishment contrast was significant, $F(1,66) = 36.40$, $p < .0005$, as well as the interaction between punishment and age, $F(2,66) = 5.78$, $p = .005$. Preschoolers evaluated vignettes more negatively when punishment was present than when it was absent. The older

Table 1 Planned comparisons of standards, positive and negative evaluative reactions: F ratios

Effect	Standards	Evaluative reactions	
		Positive	Negative
Between subjects			
Grade (Gr)	1.33	2.77	2.22
Sex (S)	.91	.67	.12
Gr × S	2.60	.22	.05
Within subjects			
Type (Ty): Planned comparisons			
T vs. L	194.10****	43.67****	28.65****
L vs. M	13.01**	.03	15.08****
T vs. M	140.74****	34.08****	5.65
P vs. NP	36.40****	10.47**	30.18****
LB vs. LNB	.14	.13	3.25
Gr × Ty: Planned comparisons			
T vs. L	17.82****	10.42****	3.90
L vs. M	3.43	2.59	1.25
T vs. M	17.30****	6.21**	1.33
P vs. NP	5.78*	1.30	.58
LB vs. LNB	.23	.17	.95
S × yᵇ	.60	.22	.85
Gr × S × Ty	.44	1.31	.92

T = truth; L = lie; M = misdeed; P = punished; NP = not punished; LB = lie believed; LNB = lie not believed.

[a] For the planned comparisons, the significance level was adjusted using the Bonferroni method. Each comparison was only deemed significant if its probability exceeded .01. This method ensures an overall alpha level of .05.

[b] Only the averaged interactions effects were presented because none of the planned comparisons for the interactions involving sex were significant.

*$p < .01$; **$p < .005$; ***$p < .001$; ****$p < .0005$.

children, however, did not differentially evaluate the vignettes on the basis of the presence or absence of punishment.

The final analysis compared lies believed with those not believed. This contrast produced no significant effects. Thus, contrary to predictions

Table 2 Means of children's standards and evaluative reaction scores as a function of vignette type and grade

	Lie			Truth		Misdeed only
Grade	B	NB + P	NB + NP	P	NP	
Standards[a]						
Preschool	5.04	5.46	4.56	4.65	3.33	4.67
Second	5.63	5.50	5.50	2.90	2.15	5.54
Fifth	5.56	5.71	5.50	2.29	1.77	5.13
Positive evaluative reactions[b]						
Preschool	1.84	1.97	1.81	1.76	2.02	1.77
Second	1.17	1.20	1.22	1.98	2.45	1.41
Fifth	1.26	1.25	1.22	2.03	2.46	1.17
Negative evaluative reactions[c]						
Preschool	2.43	2.63	2.29	2.40	2.19	2.30
Second	2.73	3.03	2.84	2.30	1.75	2.43
Fifth	3.02	3.16	3.01	2.46	2.14	2.76

B = believed; NB = not believed; P = punished; NP = not punished.
[a] A higher mean indicates greater badness and a lower mean greater goodness (1 = very good to 6 = very bad).
[b] A higher mean indicates a greater positive reaction (on a four-point scale).
[c] A higher mean indicates a greater negative reaction (on a four-point scale).

from Piaget's (1932/1965) theory, neither the preschoolers nor the older children evaluated lies that were believed any differently from lies that were not believed.

Internal evaluative reactions

A 2 (sex of subject) × 3 (grade: preschool, 2, 5) × 6 (vignette type-within-subjects factor) MANOVA was performed on children's evaluative reactions (negative reactions and positive reactions) attributed to the vignette character. A positive evaluative reaction score was obtained by summing children's ratings on the pleased and goodness scales, since ratings on these scales were highly correlated. Similarly, a negative evaluative reaction score was obtained by summing children's ratings on the scared and guilty scales, since ratings on these scales were also highly correlated. The analysis yielded multivariate main effects for grade, $F(4,130) = 2.54$, $p < .05$, and vignette type, $F(10,658) = 16.63$, $p < .001$. These effects were qualified, however, by a significant multivariate interaction involving grade and vignette type, $F(20,658) =$ 3.19, $p < .001$. The univariate interactions for both positive reactions, $F(10,330) = 6.06$, $p < .0001$, and negative reactions, $F(10,330) = 2.32$, $p < .02$, were significant. To test the effects further, the planned comparisons computed for the standards measure were similarly computed for children's positive and negative evaluative reactions, separately. The F ratios for the planned comparisons are provided in table 1 and the mean scores for each of the vignette conditions across the three age groups, for both positive and negative evaluative reactions, are provided in table 2.

Children's *positive evaluative reactions* to the vignette character's statements and actions were subjected to a three-way analysis of variance (sex × age × vignette condition). The first planned comparison tested if children's positive evaluative reactions to vignettes involving lies and truthful statements differed. As for the standards measure, this contrast, $F(1,66) = 43.67$, $p < .0005$, and the interaction between this contrast and age, $F(2,66) = 10.42$, $p < .0005$ were significant. *Post hoc* tests revealed that second and fifth graders attributed greater pride to the character after truthful statements than after lies, whereas preschoolers did not.

Although the comparison between lies and misdeeds was significant for the moral standards measure, this comparison yielded no significant effects for the positive evaluative measure. Characters were rated as feeling little pride after both lies and misdeeds. In contrast, the comparison of vignettes involving truthful statements and misdeeds produced significant results, $F(1,66) = 34.08$, $p < .0005$, and this contrast interacted with age, $F(2,66) = 6.21$, $p = .003$. This interaction revealed that second and fifth graders, but not preschoolers, expected that the character would experience greater pride after truthful statements than after misdeeds.

The comparison between vignettes involving punishment with those in which it was absent was significant, $F(1,66) = 10.47$, $p = .002$. All the children rated the character as reacting more positively in vignettes in which punishment was absent than when it was present. The final planned comparison was of lies believed with those not believed. As for the standards measure, this analysis revealed no significant effects.

Similar analyses to those conducted on children's positive evaluative reactions were conducted for their *negative evaluative reaction* scores. Again, the first planned comparison was of vignettes involving lies versus truthful statements. This analysis was significant, $F(2,66) = 28.65$, $p < .0005$. All children expected the character to react with more displeasure after lies ($M = 2.79$) than truthful statements ($M = 2.20$).

The planned comparison between misdeeds and lies was significant, $F(2,66) = 15.08$, $p < .0005$. The character was rated as reacting with greater displeasure after lying ($M = 2.79$) than after simply committing the misdeed ($M = 2.50$). However, the comparison of misdeeds and truthful statements produced no significant results.

The planned comparison of vignettes involving punishment with those in which it was absent was significant, $F(2,66) = 30.18$, $p < .0005$. Negative evaluative reactions were greater after punishment ($M = 2.66$) than if punishment was absent ($M = 2.37$). The final comparison involving lies believed with those not believed produced no significant effects.

Discussion

These results showed that even preschoolers could differentiate between lies and truthful statements about misdeeds. Although the second and fifth graders were more accurate in their identification of both lies and truthful statements than preschoolers, the preschoolers' correct identifications were significantly above chance. For all children, correct identifications were independent of belief of the statement, punishment for the statement, or content of the statement (i.e., a misdeed).

Clear evidence of the development of moral standards associated with lying and truth telling was shown for all children. Children were more disapproving of lies than of truthfulness. Further, contrary to Piaget's findings, all children evaluated lies significantly more negatively than misdeeds alone. This suggests that even preschoolers' negative evaluation of lies was determined by the falsity of the statement rather than its content (i.e., a misdeed). Truthful statements were, however, not evaluated more favorably than misdeeds by preschoolers. Thus, while young children appreciated the naughtiness of lying, it was more difficult for them to appreciate the value of truthfulness about misdeeds.

Punishment affected the moral judgments of the preschoolers, but not of the older children. Preschoolers evaluated statements that led to punishment for the misdeed more negatively than statements that did not lead to punishment. This accords with both Piaget's (1932/1965) theory and Bandura's social cognitive theory (1986), in which observable physical consequences are predicted to be major determinants of preschoolers' judgments of lies and truthful statements. There was, however, no confirmation of Piaget's (1932/1965) finding that children of different ages evaluate lies believed versus those not believed differently. Belief or nonbelief of a lie did not affect the judgments of children from any of the grades. Thus the younger children in Piaget's studies may have judged lies such as exaggerations more harshly than older children not because of disbelief *per se* but because of the linkage of disbelief and punishment.

The internal evaluative reaction measure revealed that even the preschoolers evidenced rudimentary evaluative reactions to violations of moral standards. All children attributed greater self-censure to the character after lying than truthfulness, as well as greater self-censure after lying than simply after committing the misdeed. This finding parallels that found for moral standards and further calls into question Piaget's (1932/1965) assertion that children cannot differentially evaluate lies involving misdeeds from the misdeed itself. However, preschoolers' negative evaluative reactions to the vignette character's lies were not mirrored in their positive evaluative reactions for truths, as they were for the older children. Thus, for preschoolers, censure for lying and pride for truthfulness are not the inverse of each other.

This study has thus demonstrated two important developmental changes. First, children initially react with censure for lying and over time learn to react with feelings of pride for truthfulness, so that eventually children's reactions to lies and truthful statements are the inverse of each other. Second, there is a change from children's reliance on punishment as a basis for their moral judgments to a greater reliance on internal evaluative reactions. This greater reliance on internal rather than external factors, with increasing cognitive maturity and social experience, is consistent with the development of self-regulation posited by social cognitive theory (Bandura, 1986). In this theory, self-evaluative reactions are expected to promote congruence between moral standards and moral conduct. If socialization is successful, there is a transfer from external forms of control to more internal controls, that is, there is less reliance on external factors such as punishment. In this study, punishment did influence the preschoolers' but not the older children's moral judgments. Second and fifth graders relied more on their internal evaluative reactions than did the preschoolers. Further, the preschoolers expressed negative internal reactions to lying, but did not express positive reactions for truthfulness.

To the extent that lying and truthfulness are guided by self-evaluative reactions, it is speculated that young children may be more likely to avoid lying than they would actively seek to tell the truth, particularly if they expect punishment for truthfulness. Hence, for young children whose conduct is not regulated to the same extent as older children by internal evaluative reactions, particularly positive evaluative reactions, it would seem important that adults actively encourage and reward truthfulness. If children anticipate punishment for admitting to a misdeed, there is little incentive for them to tell the truth. Parents and other caregivers need to encourage children to accept responsibility for misdeeds and simultaneously feel proud of their truthfulness.

References

Bandura, A. (1986). *Social foundations of thought and action: A social cognitive theory.* Englewood Cliffs, NJ: Prentice-Hall.

Bandura, A. (1991). Social cognitive theory of moral thought and action. In W. M. Kurtines & J. L. Gewirtz (Eds.), *Handbook of moral behavior and development* (Vol. 1, pp. 45–103). Hillsdale, NJ: Erlbaum.

Bok, S. (1978). *Lying: Moral choices in public and private life.* New York: Pantheon.

Freud, S. (1964). An outline of psychoanalysis. In J. Strachey (Ed.), *The standard edition of the complete psychological works of Sigmund Freud* (Vol. 23). London: Hogarth. (Original work published 1940)

Grusec, J. E., & Kuczynski, L. (1977). Teaching children to punish themselves and effects on subsequent compliance. *Child Development, 48,* 1296–1300.

Perry, D. G., Perry, L. C., Bussey, K., English, D., & Arnold, G. (1980). Processes of attribution and children's self-punishment following misbehavior. *Child Development, 51,* 545–551.

Peterson, C. C., Peterson, J. L., & Seeto, D. (1983). Developmental changes in ideas about lying. *Child Development, 54,* 1529–1535.

Piaget, J. (1965). *The moral judgment of the child.* Harmondsworth: Penguin Books. (Original work published 1932)

Stouthamer-Loeber, M. (1987, April). *Mothers' perceptions of children's lying and its relationship to behavior problems.* Paper presented at the annual meeting of the Society for Research on Child Development, Baltimore.

Wimmer, H., Gruber, S., & Perner, J. (1984). Young children's conception of lying: Lexical realism – moral subjectivism. *Journal of Experimental Child Psychology, 37,* 1–30.

Wimmer, H., Gruber, S., & Perner, J. (1985). Young children's conception of lying: Moral intuition and the denotation and connotation of "to lie." *Developmental Psychology, 21,* 993–995.

NINETEEN

Cognitive Developmental Pathology

Introduction

An intriguing scene depicted in *Rain Man*, a movie about the relationship between an autistic adult (played by Dustin Hoffmann) and his younger brother (played by Tom Cruise), is the conversation between them after the autistic adult kissed his brother's girlfriend. When asked how he felt about the kiss, the autistic character replies: "Wet." This reply illustrates one of the puzzling characteristics of autism, that individuals suffering from this mental disorder often fail to appreciate and reciprocate social and emotional communications with others.

Since its identification in the 1940s, there has not been any shortage of theories to explain this disorder. One of the early, prevailing theories posited that an autistic child was the product of the mother's poor parenting skills and her lack of affection for the child. Subsequent research during the last two decades has failed to substantiate this theory; it has revealed instead that autism may be a cognitive disorder with a neurological basis. In her article, Uta Frith, a proponent of this theory, provides a clear and succinct argument about why autism is a cognitive disorder.

Further reading

Baron-Cohen, S. (1995). *Mindblindness: An essay on autism and theory of mind.* Cambridge, MA: MIT Press.

Bryson, S. E., Landry, R., & Wainwright, J. A. (1997). A componential view of executive dysfunction in autism: Review of recent evidence. In J. A. Burack & J. T. Enns (eds), *Attention, development, and psychopathology* (pp. 232–59). New York: Guilford Press.

Happé, F. (1994). *Autism: An introduction to psychological theory.* Cambridge, MA: Harvard University Press.

Cognitive Explanations of Autism
Uta Frith

Autism is a developmental disorder of the brain. It exists from birth and persists throughout life. The causes of the disorder are still unknown, but a strong genetic component as well as other organic causes have been implicated [for a recent comprehensive review see Bailey, Phillips & Rutter, 1996].

Autism was identified and labelled 50 years ago, by Kanner (1943), and independently, by Asperger (1944). Initially, these pioneers of child psychiatry considered a biological origin of autism. Unfortunately, theories about a psychogenic origin of the disorder held sway for a time, and this has been reflected in a variety of misunderstandings of the condition and in a variety of inappropriate treatments. These misunderstandings still linger on in the popular imagination, but films such as *Rain Man* have now promoted greater awareness and a broader image of autism.

For the rational design of treatment programmes, and indeed for the proper understanding of the disorder, it is essential to have a full account of the brain basis of autism and its manifestation in behaviour across all stages of development. We are still far removed from this desirable state of knowledge. However, cognitive explanations of autism have made considerable progress. In particular, the "theory of mind" account has vastly increased our understanding of many of the puzzling features of autism. It is this account that my brief review will focus on. By using the term "cognitive" I refer to a type of explanation that attempts to make links between brain and behaviour via mental processes. Mental processes and their dysfunction are what cognitive explanations are all about.

Diagnosis

The diagnosis of autism is based on behavioural criteria. The chief criteria are set out in ICD-10 (WHO, 1992) and in DSM-IV (APA, 1994) and include: abnormalities of social interaction, verbal and non-verbal communication, and a restricted repertoire of activities. Behaviour suggestive of these impairments can already be discerned in infancy, but the diagnosis is not usually made before the age of three years. A recent screening instrument, based on a cognitive account of autism, appears to be remarkably successful at 18 months (Baron-Cohen, Allen & Gillberg, 1992). Often the diagnosis is made much later, especially in cases with fluent language and without general intellectual delay, as in the variant of autism that is now labelled Asperger's syndrome. Asperger's syndrome is still a controversial diagnostic category showing much overlap with autism [see chapters in (Frith, 1991)].

The Autistic Spectrum

The notion of a whole spectrum of autistic disorders of different type and severity, not confined to "nuclear" cases, as originally described by Kanner (1943), derived support from an important epidemiological study (Wing & Gould, 1979). One of the major problems with behaviourally defined developmental disorders is how to identify and agree on the core features. During development, behaviour is extremely changeable. It varies not only with age and ability, but is modified by a multitude of environmental factors. This problem is compounded by the fact that many affected individuals show additional and possibly even unrelated problems, as well as secondary problems. Wing and Gould (1979) identified three core features, namely characteristic impairments in socialization, communication and imagination. These features form a triad, such that they co-occur in the same child and persist in development even though their outward manifestation is subject to change. The triad forms a common denominator throughout a spectrum of autistic disorders which includes also relatively mild variants.

Given the triad of impairments, the prevalence of autistic disorder, based on a number of studies in different countries, has been found to be 1 per 1000 births. There is a preponderance of males of about 3:1 and this ratio becomes even more extreme with higher levels of ability (Gillberg & Coleman, 1992). In the only population study available so far, the prevalence of Asperger's syndrome is estimated as between 3 and 7 per 1000 (Ehlers & Gillberg, 1993).

Mental retardation is one of the most strongly associated, but not defining features of autism: about three quarters of the autistic population have IQs in the retarded range. Regardless of overall IQ, the profile of intellectual abilities shows a characteristically spiky profile [reviewed in Happé, 1994]. Epilepsy is present in about one third of individuals with autism, and other neurological and neuropsychological signs are found in the vast majority of cases [for a review see Gillberg & Coleman, 1992].

A Cognitive Deficit in Understanding Other Minds

The three core behavioural impairments in socialization, communication and imagination presented a challenge to cognitive psychologists: the systematic occurrence of the features together suggested that they could all be due to one single faulty mental mechanism. If such a fault could be identified, then its basis in the brain might also be elucidated, and a much fuller understanding of the disorder would be gained (Frith, Morton & Leslie, 1991). The proposal of a specific problem in understanding minds (as opposed to understanding objects) was an answer to this challenge.

In normal development the understanding of mental states is not just a matter of learning, but crucially depends on a cognitive mechanism which is presumed to be innate. This is a very radical idea which Leslie (1987) proposed in order to explain the origin of pretend play in the young normal child. He argued that a particular cognitive (computationally expressed) mechanism exists whose purpose is to allow the infant to keep track separately of physical (real) and of mental (pretend) events. Without such a mechanism, pretence would be an absurdity instead of being the enjoyable activity that it is.

It was known that autistic children, compared to other handicapped children, showed extremely poor pretend play (Wing & Gould, 1979).

Hence the hypothesis was formulated that autistic children lacked Leslie's critical mechanism. The hypothesis that autistic children cannot keep track of mental states was originally tested by Baron-Cohen, Leslie & Frith (1985). It has since been confirmed in a large number of studies (Baron-Cohen, Tager-Flusberg & Cohen, 1993) and has become known under the catch phrase "theory of mind" deficit. The term "theory of mind" refers to an intuitive understanding of mental states as opposed to physical states, something that every normal individual seems to have. The original test was extremely simple and is worth examining here in some detail because it illustrates what is meant by "theory of mind".

The Sally–Ann Experiment

Two dolls, Sally and Ann, were used as props. Sally had a basket; Ann had a box. Sally put a marble into her basket, and covered it with a cloth. Sally then went out for a walk. While Sally was out (and by implication could not *know* what happened next), naughty Ann took the marble from the basket and hid it in her own box. Next, Sally came back from her walk and wanted to play with her marble. The critical question was: where would Sally look for her marble—where would she *think* it was?

Normally developing children of about four years can reliably answer this question, and so, perhaps surprisingly, can children who are mentally retarded due to Down's syndrome. They say that Sally will look for her marble in her basket (where she had herself put it). When asked, they can also indicate that Sally did not *know* what Ann had done (since she was out when Ann took out the marble).

By showing this degree of understanding young children demonstrate that they have *attributed a mental state*. They grasp that someone can have a *false belief* about a situation. The "false belief" is a mental state that is different from a physical state.

What good is it to the child to be able to attribute mental states? By considering mental states one can often explain and predict someone's behaviour and be prepared for subsequent events.

For instance, attributing a false belief to Sally allows one to predict that she will look for her marble in her basket—and that she will not find it there. In many situations it will be helpful to predict someone's behaviour, and in some situations one's life may depend on it.

The Sally–Ann task is about someone's false belief, but there are many other mental states that we attribute to ourselves and to each other. Understanding false belief normally goes together with understanding true belief, knowledge and ignorance. It also goes together with understanding intentions, desires and feelings. This is what is meant by having a "theory of mind".

Children with autism, even of a mental age well in excess of four years, find the simple Sally–Ann task a great puzzle, and they tend to get it wrong. They say that Sally will look for the marble in Ann's box (where it really is)—even though they remember correctly that Sally had put the marble into her own basket, and that she was not present when Ann transferred it to her own box. Despite watching and remembering the simple sequence of events, they cannot make sense of them by inferring that Sally must have a false belief.

The interpretation is that autistic children do not take into account what Sally thinks at all: they miss the important change in her mental state (her previously correct belief is now wrong). Thus they cannot predict Sally's behaviour. Clearly, they would get very confused in real life where they would find it odd that Sally looked for her marble in the wrong place. Their lack of understanding of false belief goes together with a lack of understanding of other mental states, including intentions and feelings. Hence the claim that autistic individuals do not have a "theory of mind".

What Does It Mean to Have No "Theory of Mind"?

Research to date suggests that we must assume that the majority of individuals with autism are mind-blind. But how does this help us understand the core features of autism?

Lack of theory of mind implies an inability to attribute mental states, such as know, believe, feel, to others and even to oneself. This is tantamount to not differentiating between the world of objects (with physical states) and the world of persons (with mental states). It is immediately plausible that an inability to attribute mental states must lead to a profound lack of insight into the nature of normal social interactions. This lack of insight would lead to strangely limited social relationships. It would mean, for example, being oblivious to what another person feels about something, and being ignorant of modes of deception. On the one hand, this would imply a lack of manipulative deviousness, on the other hand, a lack of empathy.

Mind-blindness would only impose a specific, but not a general limitation on sociability. Thus, not being able to appreciate other minds would not prevent a person with autism from showing genuine interest in social interactions, and an earnest desire to learn the complex "rules" of social etiquette (Frith, Happé & Siddons, 1994). While it would be possible to learn to recognize a number of basic emotions in other people, a whole variety of more complex emotions, such as embarrassment, guilt or pride, would be difficult to understand without some grasp of how mental states arise and change. Just such a difference in the understanding of emotions has been shown (Capps, Yirmiya & Sigman, 1992; Bormann-Kischkel, Vilsmeier & Baude, 1995).

How does the particular cognitive deficit proposed account for the other impairments in Wing and Gould's (1979) triad? Autistic children lack not only social insight, they also lack normal communication skills, and have particular problems with playful imagination. A common element in these impairments seems to be the lack of understanding that people can think thoughts that are interestingly different from reality and interestingly different from each other.

Lacking this understanding means, for example, not being able to take part in the normal to-and-fro of inconsequential small talk. Normal communication strongly depends on the ability to attribute mental states: A crucial aspect of verbal and non-verbal communication is to convey the intention to communicate (Sperber & Wilson, 1986). In other words, when we talk to each other we seem always to be aware that there is a meaning behind the message and a reason for the message to be sent. Both speaker and listener are in a cooperative venture together, and often use their mindreading abilities to the full. Happé (1993) showed that individuals with autism were impaired in typical communication tasks, and furthermore, that the degree of impairment related very closely to their impairment in Sally–Ann-type tasks. Frith and Happé (1994a, 1994b) suggested that an impairment in understanding the intention to communicate would have strong adverse effects on language acquisition. A delay in language learning and the accidental learning of inappropriate labels (idiosyncratic language) are characteristic features of autism and can be explained as consequences of the same cognitive deficit: not being able to conceive of mental states.

What of the third cord feature of the triad of impairments—impairments in imagination? According to Leslie (1987), a very early manifestation of the cognitive mechanism that underlies the understanding of mental states is pretend play. In order to understand pretence the young child needs to be able to keep separate real states of affairs from states of affairs that are being pretended about. Pretence can be seen as a playful attitude deliberately adopted towards an object. A banana may be used as a telephone—but this must not be confused with straightforward messages about the proper function of bananas and telephones! For an autistic child such confusion might be a real danger. Parents and teachers often state that a literal approach works best, and that there is a preference for sober documentaries and factual knowledge over fiction even in adulthood.

The Brain Basis of Theory of Mind

According to the theory of mind deficit hypothesis, the three core impairments of autism can all be explained by the three core impairments of autism can all be explained by the absence of one and the same cognitive mechanism. The question now arises: what abnormality in the brain causes this particular cognitive deficit? Fletcher et al. (1995) have carried out a PET scan study on normal volunteers while performing a story comprehension task which critically involved "theory of mind" ability. One story, for instance, involved the attribution of a white lie, another concerned a false belief similar to the Sally–Ann scenario. During this task a circumscribed brain area in left medial frontal cortex (Brodmann's area 8) was highly active. The control condition was a closely similar comprehension task which did not involve theory of mind. Here the comprehension was to do with physical rather than mental states. In this case this area was not activated.

In a preliminary analysis of a study with volunteers with Asperger's syndrome this same group of researchers found that Brodmann's area 8 (left medial frontal) was significantly less active than in the normal group. Such a result is suggestive of a localized and specific brain dysfunction. A dysfunction in this circumscribed part of the left medial frontal cortex might have a variety of causes. It is clear that more investigations are now warranted with the hope of pinpointing a critical brain area involved in the core deficits of autism. Guided by the hypothesis of a particular cognitive deficit, anatomical studies of the autistic brain can become more targeted.

Limitations of the Theory of Mind Deficit Account

Despite its success in explaining the triad of impairments the theory of mind deficit account has clear limitations. It does not address the reasons for the varying degree of severity of symptoms in autism. It does not address the question why mental retardation is so prevalent in autism. Even in relation to the specific features of social impairment in autism, much still needs to be explained. For instance, the hypothesis says little about the often reported poor emotional responsivity and about possible abnormalities at a very basic level (pre-theory of mind) of social interaction (Klin, Volkmar & Sparrow, 1992).

It is possible and indeed necessary to extend and modify the theory of mind deficit hypothesis in order to explore its limits. Modifications of the theory point to additional deficits in the ability to read facial clues to inner emotional states (Hobson, 1993), and in the ability to engage in joint attention and to appreciate demonstrative affect, e.g. praise (Kasari, Sigman, Baumgartner & Stipek, 1993). A deficit in the reading of eye gaze and subsequently in understanding the "language of the eyes" (Baron-Cohen, 1995) may be a critical subcomponent of theory of mind, which is faulty in autism.

One possible limitation of the theory is that in all studies of theory of mind abilities a proportion of individuals with autism succeed on critical tasks. In fact, on closer inspection, these successful individuals are not entirely "normal" in their theory of mind skills. First of all, they tend to be in their teens or older and have relatively high verbal IQs (Happé, 1994). No single child with autism has yet been found who demonstrated understanding of false belief at the right age, i.e., four to five years. Furthermore, the apparently successful individuals make the occasional telltale slip. In everyday life, their ability to mind-read seems to remain blunt and slow. Thus, it seems likely that they have achieved an understanding of mental states by a different and unusual route. For this reason, a delay in the acquisition of a theory of mind, as well as an apparently different quality in everyday mind-reading, can be said to apply to all cases of autism and Asperger's syndrome.

The main limitation of the mentalizing hypothesis is perhaps that it addresses only the triad of impairments. There are other features of autism, highly persistent and handicapping, which are increasingly recognized as in need of explanation. "Restriction of interests" and presence of "stereotyped" and "perseverative" behaviour are examples. Even less explained are the islets of ability and special talents which are present in a sizable proportion of autistic individuals, and more generally, the characteristically spiky profile of IQ test performance. Two cognitive theories currently tackle these unexplored features of autism.

Executive Function Impairments

These include abilities such as planning, impulse control and working memory, whose normal functioning is thought to depend on intact frontal lobes (Duncan, in press). Many of these abilities are as yet poorly explored in normal children and adults. Even though the theoretical basis of the abilities in question is not defined very precisely as yet, these tasks have aroused much interest. One reason is that they seem to provide a privileged diagnostic link from impaired test performance to brain dysfunction. Just how reliable and revealing this link is in the case of autism remains to be seen. However, evidence for poor performance on many "frontal" tasks in autism is increasing (Ozonoff, Pennington & Rogers, 1991; Hughes, Russell & Robbins, 1994). For instance, individuals with autism perform perseveratively on the Wisconsin card sorting test, and show poor planning on the Tower of London problem and on detour tasks where a prepotent response needs to be inhibited (Hughes et al., 1994).

Some of the puzzling features in everyday behaviour of individuals with autism, such as rigidity and perseveration, are also found in patients with frontal lobe damage. By analogy, this suggests the existence of frontal lobe impairment. On the other hand, it is striking that patients with frontal lobe lesions are not autistic. One possible explanation of this fact is that brain damage from birth and brain damage in later life present a very different picture, even if the same brain area is affected. A brain abnormality early in life would be expected to have wide-ranging effects on many aspects of development, while a later acquired lesion may have more specific consequences.

The theory of autism as a disorder manifested particularly in executive functions has much to be said in its favour. It does not replace the theory of mind deficit account, but has the potential to explain a number of features of autism that are not tackled by this account. In order for the theory to advance it will be important to explain exactly which components of executive functions are compromised.

Weak Central Coherence

A second cognitive theory which attempts to address unsolved features of autism, is the theory of weak central coherence. This theory takes as its starting point the spiky profile of performance on IQ tests. It is unusual in focusing on outstandingly good rather than on impaired abilities. Thus the theory proposes that underlying the performance peaks (marked by tests such as Block Design, Digit Span) is a cognitive processing style which favours segmental over holistic processing. This style is assumed to contribute to what has been labelled "weak central coherence" (Frith & Happé, 1994a, 1994b).

Frith (1989) reviewed earlier work on language, memory and perception in autism and concluded that autistic individuals were not strongly disadvantaged when processing meaningless and unconnected material compared to meaningful and connected information. In the normal case there tends to be a huge advantage in favour of meaningful material that can be integrated. For instance, meaningful sentences making up a story are much better recalled than jumbled sentences.

In the visuo-spatial domain Shah and Frith (1993) showed that the advantage of autistic individuals on the Block Design subtest of the Wechsler scales may be due to the spontaneous mental segmentation of the designs into units which are appropriate to the construction with the given individual blocks.

In a language task, Happé (in press) asked autistic people to read English homophones (e.g. "lead", related to leading vs lead, the metal), separately and in context. Weak central coherence would predict a relative independence from context, and therefore errors in the pronunciation of the homophones. This was indeed found. There is thus some evidence from verbal and non-verbal tasks for a distinctive cognitive style in autism.

The drive for coherence appears to be an organizing principle in normal human information processing. If this drive was weak in autism, then it might be possible to explain those puzzling aspects of autistic behaviour that relate to excessive attention to details.

How to Test Cognitive Theories of Autism

Both executive function and central coherence theories are currently being refined and empirically investigated. The benchmark, as established through the systematic testing of the theory of mind deficit account, is the "fine cut". Making a fine cut along a hidden seam implies that it is possible to make precise predictions of dissociations with a pair of otherwise extremely similar tasks. Performance should be good on one task, but poor on a closely matched comparison task—a task which only differs by one single critical component. For instance, without a theory of mind it is possible to understand seeing, but it is not possible to understand knowing. Two identical tasks which each explore the use of the concepts "seeing" and "knowing" can show a dissociation in an individual who does not have the ability to understand mental states.

Any new cognitive theory of autism has to be just strong enough to explain what it sets out to explain, but it should not be too strong. It would be too strong if it were in danger of predicting too global or too gross a handicap. A theory proposing a deficit that would render an individual backward on all conceivable tasks in unsatisfactory for the explanation of autism. Autistic people are not impaired across the board, and on some tasks they are not impaired at all.

One interesting problem for research that needs to be resolved is how the various core features of autism and the presumed underlying cognitive components relate to each other. In order to do this we need to know whether some of these features are also found in other disorders. This has not yet been systematically done.

In the case of executive function deficits it is clear that a variety of disorders with known frontal abnormalities would be expected to show similar problems. It is indeed a task for future research to show to what extent the "frontal" problems in autism are specific to autism. In the case of central coherence, the extent of individual differences in the normal population needs to be explored. It is possible that overlap of normal and abnormal groups will be found in terms of the distinctive cognitive style that appears to be oriented towards detail. Rigorous tests of any of the cognitive theories are necessary using a wide range of different clinical groups. Such tests remain to be done.

After the initial enthusiasm of the search for a single cognitive deficit that could best explain the core features of autism, research efforts have widened considerably. It seems unlikely that one single cognitive abnormality can be identified that would explain all the abnormalities present in autism. The existence of multiple deficits at the cognitive level is a realistic alternative and might help us understand why autism can exist in many different forms ranging from mild to severe. The explanation of autism at the cognitive level needs to be complemented by the explanation at the biological level. Cognitive theories are well suited to help in this endeavour and have already started to guide the search for the brain basis of autism.

References

American Psychiatric Association. 1994. *Diagnostic and statistical manual of mental disorders*, 4th edn (DSM-IV). Washington, DC: American Psychiatric Association.

Asperger, H. 1944. *Die autistischen Psychopathen im Kindesalter*.

Bailey, A. J., Phillips, W., & Rutter, M. 1996. Autism: Integrating clinical, genetic, neuropsychological, and neurobiological perspectives. *Journal of Child Psychology and Psychiatry, 37*, 89–126.

Baron-Cohen, S. 1995. *Mindblindness: An essay on autism and theory of mind.* Cambridge, MA: MIT Press.

Baron-Cohen, S., Allen, J., & Gillberg, C. 1992. Can autism be detected at 18 months? The needle, the haystack, and the CHAT. *British Journal of Psychiatry, 161*, 839–43.

Baron-Cohen, S., Leslie, A., & Frith, U. 1985. Does the autistic child have a "theory of mind"? *Cognition, 21*, 37–46.

Baron-Cohen, S., Tager-Flusberg, H., & Cohen, D. J., eds. 1993. *Understanding other minds: Perspectives from autism.* Oxford: Oxford University Press.

Bormann-Kischkel, C., Vilsmeier, M., & Baude, B. 1995. The development of emotional concepts in autism. *Journal of Child Psychology and Psychiatry, 36*, 1243–59.

Capps, L., Yirmiya, N., & Sigman, M. 1992. Understanding of simple and complex emotions in non-retarded children with autism. *Journal of Child Psychology and Psychiatry, 33*, 1169–82.

Duncan, J. In press. Attention, intelligence and the frontal lobes. In M. S. Gazzaniga, ed. *The cognitive neurosciences*. Cambridge, MA: MIT Press.

Ehlers, S., & Gillberg, C. 1993. The epidemiology of Asperger syndrome: A total population study. *Journal of Child Psychology and Psychiatry, 34,* 1327–50.

Fletcher, P. C., Happé, F., Frith, U., Baker, S. C., Dolan, R. J., Frackowiak, R. S. J., & Frith, C. D. 1995. Other minds in the brain: A functional imaging study of "theory of mind" in story comprehension. *Cognition, 57,* 109–28.

Frith, U. 1989. *Autism: Explaining the enigma*. Oxford: Blackwell.

Frith, U. 1991. Translation and annotation of *Autistic psychopathy in childhood*, by H. Asperger. In U. Frith, ed., *Autism and Asperger syndrome* (pp. 37–92). Cambridge: Cambridge University Press.

Frith, U., & Happé, F. 1994a. Autism: Beyond "theory of mind". *Cognition, 50,* 115–32.

Frith, U., & Happé, F. 1994b. Language and communication in the autistic disorders. *Philosophical Transactions of the Royal Society,* series B, *346,* 97–104.

Frith, U., Happé, F., & Siddons, F. 1994. Autism and theory of mind in everyday life. *Social Development, 3,* 108–24.

Frith, U., Morton, J., & Leslie, A. 1991. The cognitive basis of a biological disorder. *Trends in Neurosciences, 14,* 433–8.

Gillberg, C., & Coleman, M. 1992. *The biology of the autistic syndromes*, 2nd edn. London: MacKeith Press.

Happé, F. G. E. 1993. Communicative competence and theory of mind in autism: A test of Relevance theory. *Cognition, 48,* 101–19.

Happé, F. G. E. 1994. Wechsler IQ profile and theory of mind in autism: A research note. *Journal of Child Psychology and Psychiatry, 35,* 1461–71.

Happé, F. G. E. In press. Central coherence and theory of mind in autism: Reading homographs in context. *British Journal of Developmental Psychology.*

Hobson, P. 1993. *Autism*. Hove, Sussex: Erlbaum.

Hughes, C., Russell, J., & Robbins, T. W. 1994. Evidence for executive dysfunction in autism. *Neuropsychologia, 32,* 477–92.

Kanner, L. 1943. Autistic disturbances of affective contact. *Nervous Child, 2,* 217–50.

Kasari, C., Sigman, M. D., Baumgartner, P., & Stipek, D. J. 1993. Pride and mastery in children with autism. *Journal of Child Psychology and Psychiatry, 34,* 353–62.

Klin, A., Volkmar, F. R., & Sparrow, S. S. 1992. Autistic social dysfunction: Some limitations of the theory of mind hypothesis. *Journal of Child Psychology and Psychiatry, 33,* 861–76.

Leslie, A. M. 1987. Pretence and representation: The origins of "Theory of Mind". *Psychological Review, 94,* 412–26.

Ozonoff, S., Pennington, B. F., & Rogers, S. J. 1991. Executive function deficits in high-functioning autistic children: Relationship to theory of mind. *Journal of Child Psychology and Psychiatry, 32*, 1081–106.

Shah, A., & Frith, U. 1993. Why do autistic individuals show superior performance on the Block Design task? *Journal of Child Psychology and Psychiatry, 34*, 1351–64.

Sperber, D., & Wilson, D. 1986. *Relevance*. Oxford: Blackwell.

Wing, L., & Gould, J. 1979. Severe impairments of social interaction and associated abnormalities in children: Epidemiology and classification. *Journal of Autism and Developmental Disorders, 9*, 11–29.

World Health Organization. 1992. *The ICD-10 classification of mental and behavioural disorders*. Geneva: World Health Organization.

Index

accommodation 32, 40, 41, 42,
   43, 44
adaptation 32, 33, 34, 39, 41, 70,
   80
analogical reasoning 19
analogy 19, 47, 57, 165
appearance–reality distinction 7,
   16, 176, 180, 181, 184, 193
Asperger's syndrome 325, 330,
   331
assimilation 32, 39, 40–4
attention 2, 3, 107, 109, 114–15,
   152, 156, 331, 334
autism/autistic 5, 42, 151,
   323–35
auto-association 78, 84

belief psychology 153, 167, 168
biological constraints 15, 23
biology, concept of 241

causal understanding 11, 15, 285
cognitive capacity/capabilities 2, 4,
   11, 302
communication 170, 323, 325

concept formation 2
conceptual development 7, 53, 76
concrete and formal operation 21
concrete-operational period/stage
   13, 21, 32
concrete-operational skills 9
concrete-operational structure 16
connectionism 19, 23, 76, 86
connectionist model 19, 57, 64,
   70, 83, 85, 86, 220
connectionist modeling 63, 64, 70,
   71, 73, 87
conservation 32
conservation-of-liquid quantity
   problem 51
construction, definition of 35
content knowledge 14, 21
continuity/discontinuity issue 31
cortex 86, 114
covert (visual) attention 107, 108,
   109, 110, 114, 115

deception 10, 203
desire psychology 9, 153, 167,
   168

development change   234
developmental sequence   239
domain-general and domain-specific
    15, 16, 18, 20, 63, 71
domain specificity theorist/theory
    2, 16
domain-specific knowledge   14, 21
dynamic systems model   57, 76
dynamic systems theory/method   2,
    23, 92

egocentric/egocentrism   42, 44,
    178
emotion   3, 151, 166, 167, 329
encoding   19
epigenesis   33, 37, 45
epistemology/epistemological   3,
    33, 35, 37, 38, 39
equilibration   18, 19
equilibrium   19, 32, 41, 42, 43, 44
eyewitness   5, 201

false belief   16, 175, 176, 180, 181,
    183, 184, 186, 187, 189, 190,
    191, 193, 208
formal-operational period/stage   13,
    21, 32
formal operations task   13
frontal lobe   3, 330, 332

gender difference   241–3
gender role   3
generalization   11, 72, 215, 220,
    222, 223

habituation   122–4, 128, 129,
    131, 138, 165

imitation   10, 12, 42, 149, 153,
    215, 217, 232, 284, 332
infancy   11, 21, 32, 59, 65, 107,
    153, 325

infant perception/newborns'
    perception   11, 120–4, 127,
    129
information integration   10
information-processing capacity
    14, 18, 21, 22, 67, 69, 87
intention   151, 153, 154, 157,
    159, 160, 161, 162, 165, 167,
    168, 169, 170, 328
intermodal matching   9
intermodal perception   12

knowledge structure: *see also* origin
    of knowledge   1, 2, 5, 31

language development   2, 17, 18,
    53, 64, 213, 214, 215
lying   5, 307, 309, 310, 312,
    319–21

mathematical development   254,
    255, 261, 262
maturation   3, 14, 15, 37, 44, 76,
    91, 93, 115
memory   2, 5, 6, 7, 14, 72, 82, 83,
    95, 103, 149, 194, 201, 205
memory strategy   7, 22, 53, 55
mentalism   151
metacognition   21
metamemory   7, 201
microgenetic method   19, 49, 94,
    95
modeling   10, 57
morality   3
moral judgment   170, 310, 320,
    321
moral understanding   5, 307
motor development   91, 95

naïve theories: *see also* naïve theory
    of biology/physics/psychology
    268, 293

naïve theory of biology/naïve biology 16, 267, 284
naïve theory of physics/naïve physics 16, 267, 284
naïve theory of psychology/naïve psychology 16, 267, 284
neocortex 80
neo-Piagetian approach 15, 18
neo-Piagetian theorist 13, 14, 18
neural mechanism 19
neural network 67, 68, 70, 73, 75, 76, 85, 216, 223
neural plasticity 3
neural system 18, 80, 85
nonegocentric: see also egocentric 12
nonverbal 10, 11, 24, 153, 165
numerosity 12

object permanence, concept 12, 32, 35, 36, 66, 120
operation 37, 38
origin of knowledge 3, 38
overt (attention cue), 107

perceptual development 2, 119
perspective-taking 7, 179
Piagetian theory/Piagetian psychology 17, 20, 22, 31, 32
preoperational period/stage 32
pretence/pretend play 330
problem solving 54, 103, 256, 257, 260

reasoning process 14
reasoning system 267-9, 276, 277, 281, 282, 284

representation 1, 32, 42, 43, 63, 65-73, 75, 77-9, 84, 87, 137, 138, 140, 143
representational change 178, 180-7, 189, 190, 192-4
representational model of mind 151

saccade 110, 112, 113, 114, 115
schema, sensorimotor 31, 32, 34, 37, 41, 42, 43, 44, 46, 47, 66
scheme 40, 41, 42, 46
scientific reasoning 13, 52
sensorimotor period/stage 13
spatial concept 239, 249
spatial perception 244
speech perception 9, 223, 244
strategy choices 9, 19, 21, 52, 54, 55, 57, 58, 178, 204, 261, 262
symbolic function 229
symbolic game 42, 46
symbolic-processing model 57
symbolic rule system 72
symbolic schema 32
synaptogenesis 19, 60

theory of mind 7, 12, 52, 151, 152, 153, 165, 167, 175, 324, 327, 328, 330, 331
transitive inference 19

U-shaped curve/development 72, 291

verbal-nonverbal 10, 205, 325, 329, 333
visual perception 16, 128